DOS MADE EASY,
FOURTH EDITION

Herbert Schildt

Osborne **McGraw-Hill**

Berkeley New York St. Louis San Francisco
Auckland Bogotá Hamburg London Madrid
Mexico City Milan Montreal New Delhi Panama City
Paris São Paulo Singapore Sydney
Tokyo Toronto

Osborne **McGraw-Hill**
2600 Tenth Street
Berkeley, California 94710
U.S.A.

For information on translations or book distributors outside of the
U.S.A., please write to Osborne **McGraw-Hill** at the above address.

DOS Made Easy, Fourth Edition

    34567890 DOC 99876543

ISBN 0-07-881896-6

Acquisitions Editor
Scott Rogers

Technical Editor
Paul Sevigny

Project Editor
Wendy Rinaldi

Copy Editors
Judith Brown
Ann K. Spivack

Proofreader
Jeff Barash

Indexer
Richard Shrout

Computer Designer
Stefany Otis

Illustrator
Susie C. Kim

Cover Designer
Compass Marketing

CONTENTS

PREFACE

This book is for anyone who wants to learn how to use DOS. It assumes no prior experience with computers. If you have some previous experience running DOS, you will be able to advance quickly through the first few chapters, concentrating your efforts on the material with which you are not familiar. If you are completely new to DOS, and computers in general, then you will want to carefully read each chapter, working through each example.

DOS is a complex program with many commands and options. This book distills DOS into its most useful components and concentrates on getting you running DOS as quickly and easily as possible. After reading just the first three chapters you will be able to begin using your application programs. By the time you finish this book, you will be using DOS like a pro!

There are many versions of DOS in common use. This book covers all versions, including 3, 4, 5, and the latest version, 6. No matter what kind of computer you have, if it runs DOS, you can use this book.

You will begin with the basics, starting with what DOS is and what it does. Then you will learn the essential DOS commands. Understanding these few commands enables you to begin using the computer and your application programs. As you continue, you will learn to use the DOS editor, batch files, and configuration commands. Then, you'll learn the more advanced DOS commands that give you real power over your system.

If you are using DOS version 5 or later, you will also learn how to use the Shell, which is DOS's graphical user interface. The Shell can make running DOS both easier and quicker because it provides a visually based alternative to DOS's traditional interface.

Users of DOS 5 or later will also learn about DOS's error recovery system, which allows you to recover accidentally erased files or accidentally reformatted disks.

If you are using DOS 6, you will learn about its many new features. One of the most important is DOS 6's computer virus protection system. This system helps safeguard your computer from the harmful effects of computer viruses. Other DOS 6 features covered are its memory and disk management commands.

This book is tutorial in nature, with many hands-on examples and experiments. It is highly recommended that you have a computer available so that you can work along with the text. Although the examples are applicable to all versions of DOS, they reflect DOS version 6 because it is the most current version.

HS
February, 1993
Mahomet, IL

PART

1

DOS ESSENTIALS

CHAPTER

DOS
DOS
DOS
DOS
DOS
DOS
DOS
DOS

≈MADE EASY≈

1

COMPUTER BASICS

Before beginning your exploration of DOS, it is important to understand a few things about your computer, including what the individual pieces of the computer do and how they work together to form the complete system. Although you don't need to understand in detail how a computer works to use it, it does help to have some familiarity with its basic operation. In this chapter, IBM-style computers will be used for illustration, but the information is applicable to virtually all computers capable of running DOS.

The Parts of Your System

All microcomputers consist of at least the following three items:

✦ The system unit

✦ The keyboard

✦ The monitor (video display screen)

These represent the minimal amount of equipment needed to create a functional computer. They are illustrated in Figure 1-1. In addition to these, most computer installations include a printer. Another common device is a mouse, which is a pointing device. (In fact, most computers sold today include a mouse.) Many computer systems also have a modem, which is used to allow two computers to communicate over a telephone line. Your computer could contain other devices, such as a plotter.

The System Unit

The system unit is the heart of the computer and is composed of the following items:

✦ The central processing unit (CPU)

✦ Memory

✦ Disk drives

✦ Various adapters and options

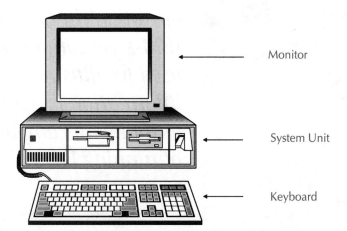

Monitor

System Unit

Keyboard

Basic elements
of a computer
Figure 1-1.

All other pieces of the computer plug into the system unit through connectors on the back. (If your computer is not set up and ready to run, refer to the installation guide provided with your system.)

1

The CPU

The central processing unit, or CPU, is the brain of the computer. It performs all the analytical, computational, and logical functions that occur inside the system. It operates by executing a program, which is a list of instructions. (We'll talk more about programs shortly.)

NOTE: There are several different types of CPUs. However, the kinds that can run DOS are all part of the 8086 family. This family of processors includes the 8086, 8088, 80286, 80386, and 80486. At this time, the 80486 is the most powerful processor generally available that can run DOS.

Memory

The memory of the computer stores information that will be processed by the CPU. The memory of your computer is made up of storage units called *bytes*. A byte represents the amount of memory required to store one character. Therefore, if someone says to you that your computer has about 640,000 bytes of memory, it means that it can store approximately 640,000 characters. Each byte is composed of 8 *bits*. A bit can be either on or off and it is the smallest unit of storage available within your computer.

You will often hear two terms associated with the memory of the computer: RAM and ROM. *RAM* stands for *random access memory*. This is the kind of memory your computer has the most of, and it is used to store and retrieve any type of information. The one fact you should remember about RAM is that anything stored in it is lost when the computer is turned off.

The other type of memory contained in your computer is called *ROM*, which stands for *read-only memory*. The contents of this sort of memory cannot be changed; they can only be read. ROM stores information that the computer needs when it is first turned on. (In a way, ROM in the computer is similar to instinct in an animal.) Unlike RAM, the contents of ROM are not lost when the computer is turned off.

Often you will see the letter *K* after a number when the amount of RAM in a computer is referred to. For example, most computers today come with at least 640K bytes of RAM. Loosely, K stands for 1000 and is the symbol used in the metric system to stand for *kilo*. Therefore, 640K is short for 640 kilobytes or 640,000 bytes. (Actually, when used with computers, K more precisely stands for 1024. But this distinction is not too significant, except for programmers.)

Another numeric prefix you will hear often in reference to computers is *mega*, which is short for (approximately) 1 million. For example, if a computer comes with 12 megabytes of RAM, it means that it can store approximately 12 million characters. (Again, for technical reasons, as mega is applied to computers, it does not mean exactly 1 million. But the difference is essentially irrelevant from a user's point of view.)

Disk Drives

A disk drive is used to read and write information to or from a diskette. (The diskette actually holds the information and the drive is the mechanism that reads or writes data to or from it. You will learn more about diskettes in the next section.) Data that is stored on a diskette is not lost when the computer is turned off. Since anything that is in the RAM of the computer is lost when the power is turned off, information that is important and that you wish to keep must be stored on a diskette.

All disk drives have two elements in common. First, they use a *read/write head* to read and write information to the diskette. This read/write head is similar to the play/record head on a cassette tape recorder. Second, all disk drives have a means of spinning the diskette. Because information is spread over the surface of the diskette, the diskette must turn in order to access all the information on it.

There are two basic types of disk drives: floppy and fixed. They are housed in the system unit. Most system units are configured one of these four ways:

✦ One floppy disk drive

1

◆ Two floppy disk drives

◆ One floppy and one fixed disk drive

◆ Two floppy disk drives and one fixed disk drive

These configurations are illustrated in Figure 1-2.

Although most personal computers are desktop units, sometimes the system unit is designed to stand on the floor, often away from the monitor and keyboard. The disk drives are mounted sideways in floor-standing system units, often referred to as *towers*. If you have one of these systems, it will still function with DOS as described in this book.

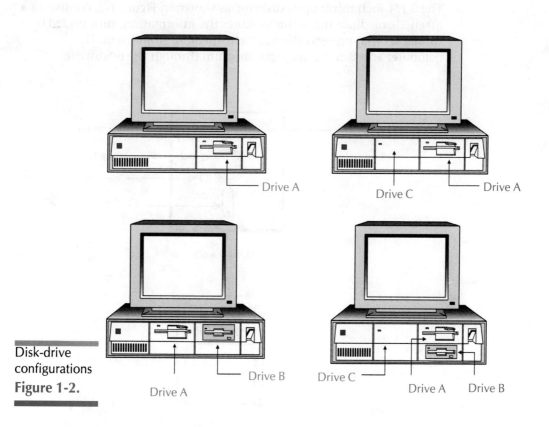

Disk-drive
configurations
Figure 1-2.

The drives in a system are labeled by letters, as shown in Figure 1-2. Generally, the fixed disk drive is drive C and the floppy drives are A and B.

The floppy disk drives use diskettes as their storage media. A *diskette* is a thin, flat, removable magnetic disk that stores information. There are two common types of floppy diskettes. The older one, but one that is still in wide use, is the 5 1/4-inch minifloppy. This is the type used by the original IBM PC. It is also used by XT, AT, and compatible computers. A newer type of floppy disk is the 3 1/2-inch microfloppy, which is used by IBM's PS/2 and PS/1 lines of computers as well as most other computers being made at the time of this writing. The elements of a diskette are shown in Figure 1-3.

Minifloppy Diskettes

The 5 1/4-inch minifloppy diskette, as shown in Figure 1-3, consists of a magnetic medium that actually stores the information, surrounded by a stiff jacket that protects the magnetic medium from harm. The computer accesses the magnetic medium through the read/write

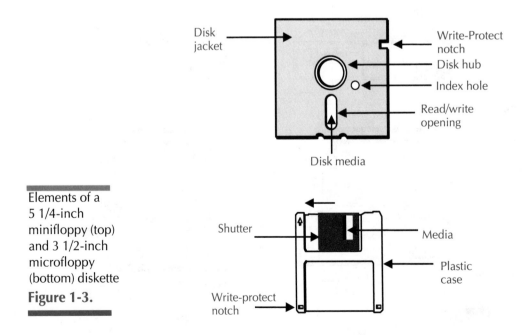

Elements of a 5 1/4-inch minifloppy (top) and 3 1/2-inch microfloppy (bottom) diskette

Figure 1-3.

1

opening. The *index hole* is used by the computer to properly align the diskette. Perhaps the single most important feature of the diskette is the *write-protect notch*. When the write-protect notch is left uncovered (as shown in the drawing), information can be both written to and read from the diskette. However, when this notch is covered using a *write-protect tab* (supplied along with the diskette), the computer can only read the information on the diskette, not write to the diskette. Covering the write-protect notch is a good way to prevent important information from being accidentally destroyed. Later in this book you will be instructed to cover the notch for this very reason.

Interestingly (and counter-intuitively), the smaller diskettes (3 1/2 inch) have greater storage capacities than the larger ones (5 1/4 inch)!

You insert a minifloppy diskette into a disk drive with the write-protect notch to the left and the read/write hole facing forward. Before the computer can use the diskette, the drive door must be closed or latched. The method of closing the drive door is shown in Figure 1-4. If your drive uses a different method of closing, ask a coworker for help inserting the diskette.

The diskette must be turning in order for the disk drive to read or write information from or to it. When you close the drive door, you are doing three things. First, you are telling the computer that there is a

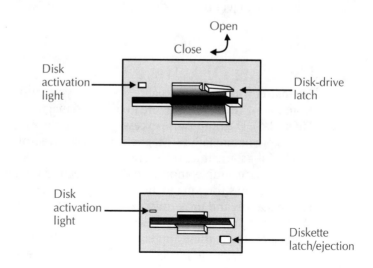

Closing the drive door

Figure 1-4.

diskette in the drive. Second, you are securing the diskette to the turntable that actually spins the diskette. Finally, you are enabling the read/write head of the drive to access the diskette.

Microfloppy Diskettes

The IBM PS/2 and PS/1 lines and virtually all other types of PC-compatible computers made today use microfloppy diskettes. In principle, these work the same way that minifloppy diskettes do except that they are smaller and provide more protection for the magnetic medium. As Figure 1-3 shows, a microfloppy diskette has a *shutter* that covers the read/write opening. This shutter is opened by the computer only when access to the diskette is required. This protects the magnetic medium from harm while the diskette is outside the computer and from dust while it is inside the computer.

The write-protect notch on a microfloppy diskette has a built-in slider that is used to cover the notch. The write-protect notch in a microfloppy diskette works opposite to the way it does in a minifloppy diskette. When the notch is open, the diskette is write protected; otherwise it is not.

The microfloppy disk drive does not use a latch. Instead, the diskette drops into place in the drive. To eject the diskette from the drive, press the diskette eject button on the front of the drive (see Figure 1-4).

Handling Diskettes

No matter what type of diskette you have, you must take care to protect it from harm. The basic rules are no dust, no magnets, and no folding (see Figure 1-5). Dust can cause excessive wear of the magnetic medium, which causes premature failure. Magnetic fields can destroy the data on the disk. Be careful—sometimes magnetic fields are produced by unsuspected sources. For example, motors in devices such as vacuum cleaners and floor waxers set up strong magnetic fields which can, given the right circumstances and proximity, erase a diskette. Never store your diskettes in the bottom drawer of your desk where they stand the greatest chance of being affected by these appliances. Finally, folding the diskette causes the magnetic medium to be destroyed where the diskette is creased.

1

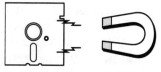

Do not place near magnetic devices.

Place in envelopes when not in use.

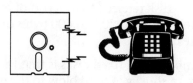

Keep away from the telephone.

Store in a safe location.

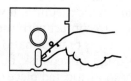

Do not touch disk medium.

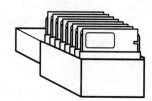

Always make a backup copy.

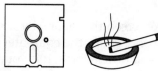

Do not smoke near diskettes.

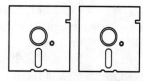

Keep room temperature 50°F to 100°F.

Protecting your diskettes
Figure 1-5.

Do not bend diskettes.

Fixed Disks

Many computers contain a special type of disk drive called a *fixed disk*. You will also see this referred to as a *hard disk*. A fixed disk is a high-speed, large-capacity disk drive. The disk cannot be removed from the disk drive; hence the term *fixed*.

A fixed disk can hold substantially more information than a minifloppy or microfloppy diskette. For example, minifloppy or microfloppy diskettes typically hold between 360,000 and 1,440,000 bytes of information, whereas fixed disks hold from 10,000,000 to over 300,000,000 bytes. As stated earlier, in computerese, 1 million is referred to by the prefix mega; hence, you will often hear the amount of storage available on a fixed disk referred to in terms of megabytes. For example, a disk drive that can hold 20,000,000 bytes of information will be called a 20-megabyte drive.

If you have a choice, always choose a color monitor. Most programs today are designed with color in mind and look significantly better in color.

An important fact to remember about fixed disks is that they do not like jolting vibrations or sharp shocks. A hard blow to the computer while it is accessing a fixed disk can damage the magnetic medium. The reason for this is that the read/write head of a fixed disk is positioned extremely close to the surface of the magnetic medium. If you jar it sharply, the head could actually come into contact with the medium and cause a scratch, which could cause a loss of information. You don't have to walk around on tiptoes when using a fixed disk, but you should treat a fixed disk as what it is: a highly sophisticated piece of equipment.

The Monitor

The monitor is the television-like screen that generally sits on top of the system unit. As you can probably guess, the computer uses the monitor to display information—in other words, it is your window into the computer. The monitor plugs into the back of the system unit. There are two basic types of monitors: black-and-white and color. For the most part, DOS doesn't care what type you have (although some things will look different on the two types of monitors).

The Keyboard

The keyboard allows you to communicate with the computer. There are two basic styles of keyboard commonly found with microcomputers: regular keyboards and extended keyboards. The regular keyboard was the first one developed by IBM for their PC/XT-style computers. Later, the IBM AT computer was developed, using the extended keyboard. The PS/2 and PS/1 computers also use extended keyboards. Both types are shown in Figure 1-6. For the most part, these keyboards are like that of a typewriter. However, there are a few special features that you should be aware of.

The 10 keys on the far left of the regular keyboard or 12 keys on the top row of the extended keyboard, labeled F1 through F10 (F1 through F12 for the extended keyboard), are called *function keys*. These, as well as other special keys, are usually gray instead of white. They have special meanings that depend upon what the computer is doing at any specific time.

Other special keys on the keyboard include the Esc (escape) key, which can be used to cancel certain operations. The Ctrl (control) and Alt (alternate) keys are used to generate special characters not readily available at the keyboard. The Caps Lock key operates the same way as it does on a typewriter; it forces all characters to be uppercase.

The numeric keypad has two separate purposes. The first is to allow the rapid entry of numbers; the other is to control the movements of the cursor on the screen. The Num Lock key determines whether the cursor control keys or the digit keys are active. By pressing the Num Lock key, you can toggle between the two uses of the number pad. The Prt Sc (or Print Screen) key causes what is currently on the computer screen to be

Regular

The two most common keyboard styles: Regular and Extended
Figure 1-6.

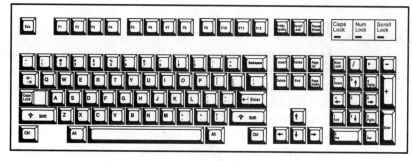

Extended

printed on the printer. The ⌴Break⌴ key is used to cancel certain computer operations. You will learn more about these and other special keys later, as you learn more about DOS.

Some laptop and notebook computers use special keyboards which often "compress" the features of a standard keyboard into a smaller space. If you are using a laptop or notebook computer, just remember that all the necessary keys to run DOS are still available. They just might be in different locations than they are on full-size keyboards.

TIP: Just because a key has a certain name does not mean that key will always perform the function described by its name. What a key actually does is largely determined by what a program running on the computer decides it will do! For example, just because a key is labeled ⌴Pause⌴ does not mean that pressing this key will always pause the computer.

The Mouse

A mouse is an alternate input device. Unlike the keyboard where you type in information, the mouse is a pointing device that is used to select various options. A mouse consists of a small, hand-held unit with one, two, or three buttons and a small ball on the bottom (A PC mouse generally has two buttons.) As you move the mouse across your desk, a small locator symbol, called the *mouse pointer,* moves across the screen. A typical mouse is shown in Figure 1-7.

Early versions of DOS did not support the mouse. However, modern versions of DOS have been designed to take advantage of it. Although you do not need a mouse to fully utilize DOS, it does make several tasks much easier.

The Printer

Most computer installations include a printer. As you might expect, the printer is used to create permanent output from the computer. It is possible that your computer will have more than one printer connected to it because different printers are used for different purposes. The most common printer is called a *dot matrix* printer. This sort of printer creates printouts quickly, but its print quality is not as good as that of a typewriter. Another type of printer is called either a *daisy wheel* or *letter-quality* printer. It creates high-quality output and is generally used in

A typical mouse
Figure 1-7.

word processing applications. Finally, you might have a *laser* printer attached to your computer. A laser printer is capable of producing typeset-quality output and is used when only the very best output quality will do. No matter what type of printer you have, if it is connected to the computer in the standard way, everything you learn in this book will be applicable to it.

The Modem

For a computer to communicate with another computer over telephone lines, you need a piece of hardware called a *modem*. There are two types of modems: internal and external. An internal modem is a special circuit card that plugs into the inside of the computer. All you will see is a telephone cord plugged into the back of the system unit. An external modem sits outside the system. DOS cannot directly communicate with a modem. If a modem is part of your computer, you will need a special communication program to run it.

Software

So far, we have discussed only the different pieces of *hardware* that make up a computer system. However, there is a saying in the computer business that "a computer without software is, at best, an expensive doorstop." *Software* consists of programs, and programs run your computer. Without programs, the computer hardware can do nothing because it doesn't know what to do. It is the software's job to make the computer do useful things. You will probably use several programs, including word processors, accounting packages, and spreadsheets.

Although you do not need to know how to program to fully utilize DOS, it is useful to understand what a program is and how a computer executes programs. A program consists of a sequence of instructions that the computer follows. When a program is run, all of its instructions are loaded into the memory of the computer. To begin execution, the CPU fetches the first instruction and performs the specified operation. Next, it gets the second instruction, performs that task; and then it gets the third instruction, and so on. The program ends when the last instruction is executed.

Computer programs are represented in *machine code,* which is read and executed by the computer. Aside from very experienced and knowledgeable programmers, people cannot read and understand machine code. Other terms for machine code which you might see are *object code* and *executable code.*

What Is DOS and What Does It Do?

First and foremost, DOS is a program; it is part of the software that your computer needs to function. But it is a very special program because it is the program that is in charge of the computer's hardware. With very few exceptions, any other program that runs on your computer does so with the help of DOS. Stated a different way, DOS is the program that manages the basic hardware components of the computer and allocates them to your programs as needed. DOS and programs like it are called *operating systems.* In fact, the name DOS is an acronym for *Disk Operating System.*

Although DOS controls other programs that run in the computer, DOS is under your control and exists primarily to give you a way to communicate your instructions to the computer. You give instructions to DOS via commands that it will recognize. For the most part, these commands consist of regular, English-like words. For example, here are a few actual DOS commands: ERASE, COPY, and PRINT.

There are two distinctly different ways that you can give a command to DOS. First, you can select a command from DOS's menu-driven interface, which is usually called the *DOS Shell* or just Sshell for short. The Shell presents you with lists of things that DOS can do (that is, a list of *commands*), and you simply select the operation desired. The second way to run DOS is to use the *command prompt.* From the command prompt you give DOS commands by typing the name of the command at the prompt. Early versions of DOS did not have a Shell and the command prompt was the only way to communicate with

1

DOS. Many users find the command prompt method preferable to the Shell because it is faster than selecting items from a menu. However, you can fully utilize DOS using either method, so the choice is yours.

The first part of this book teaches you how to run DOS using the traditional command prompt. The reason for this is twofold. First, the information applies to all versions of DOS. Second, once you have learned to use the command prompt, learning to use the Shell is extremely easy.

DOS Versions

Versions of DOS prior to 4 did not include a Shell. All versions beginning with 4 have one.

Like most things, DOS has changed over time. Since its creation, it has been improved and enhanced. Each time DOS was revised, a new version number was assigned to it. The first version of DOS was 1.00. The latest DOS version is 6.

In versions of software, the number preceding the decimal point is called the *major revision* number. This number is changed only when major alterations take place. The numbers to the right of the decimal point are called the *minor revision* numbers, and they indicate versions that differ only slightly from the previous one.

NOTE   For the most part this book will simply refer to DOS as "DOS," without any version number, except where a version-related difference may be important. In those cases, the specific version number that applies will also be included.

Summary

You should now be familiar with

+ The various parts of a computer system
+ The concept of programs and software
+ The function DOS serves in the computer
+ The way DOS version numbers are designed

In the next chapter you will learn to start the computer, make backup copies of your DOS diskettes, and run some simple DOS commands.

C H A P T E R

≋MADE EASY≋

RUNNING DOS

In this chapter you will learn how to start DOS running in your computer. You will also learn two useful DOS commands. For this, and the remaining chapters in this book, it will be best if you are seated at your computer so that you can try the examples.

NOTE: Part 1 of this book teaches you to run DOS using the command prompt. Depending upon what version of DOS you are using it is possible that when you turn on your computer the DOS Shell is automatically loaded. If this is the case, then you must first terminate the shell before proceeding with this book. To accomplish this, hold down the ⟨Alt⟩ key, press the ⟨F4⟩ key one time, and then release the ⟨Alt⟩ key. This causes the Shell to terminate, and the command prompt will be displayed. Later in this book the Shell will be explored in full detail.

Entering Information

Before beginning, it is important to understand how to enter information into the computer. As you will see shortly, there are many times when DOS will ask you a question. To answer the question, type in your response at the keyboard. But, for technical reasons, DOS does not have any idea of what you are typing until you *enter it* by striking the ⟨Enter⟩ key. In other words, until you press ⟨Enter⟩, DOS does not know what you have typed.

There is a very big advantage to this sort of approach to entering information into DOS: it allows you to correct mistakes. DOS always needs the information and commands you give it to be in a precise format, so misspellings and the like are not acceptable. If you see that you have made a typing error—or if you change your mind—you can correct it by using the ⟨Backspace⟩ key, as long as you have not yet pressed ⟨Enter⟩. The ⟨Backspace⟩ key is the gray key with the arrow pointing to the left (labeled Bk on some keyboards). Each time you press ⟨Backspace⟩ the cursor backs up one space, erasing what was previously there. Once you have erased the error, you simply begin typing again.

As far as DOS is concerned, uppercase and lowercase letters are the same. That is, any time you communicate with DOS, you can enter information without worrying about what case the letters are. However, keep in mind that many programs that run under DOS are case-sensitive and require either uppercase or lowercase. For now, you do not need to worry about it.

What If Things Look Different?

It is possible that the figures depicting DOS messages and screens in this book will differ slightly from what you see on your computer's screen. There are several possible reasons for this. First, there will be minor differences if you are running DOS from a floppy diskette rather than from a fixed disk. The figures in this book are generated on a computer that uses a fixed disk. (Computers with fixed disks are the most common.) Second, some messages and screens differ with different versions of DOS. The version used for this book is 6. Third, it is possible to customize DOS. If this has been done to your system, some screens and messages will differ. Most customizations do not affect the way that you control DOS or use it to help you run programs, but they may cause some things to look different.

As you read this chapter, if you find that your screen looks nothing like what is being shown in the book, you have two choices. First, if you have DOS 6, you can have DOS reinstalled on your computer so that it is running in its default configuration. (This may mean contacting the dealer that sold you the computer or requesting help from a coworker.) In this case, all the examples in the chapter will be the same as you see on the screen. Second, you can just ignore the differences and generalize what is presented here to what you see on your screen.

Loading DOS

Before you can use your computer, DOS must be loaded into its memory. For most systems, to load DOS, simply turn on the computer. If your computer has a fixed disk, DOS will be loaded automatically. Just make sure there is no diskette in drive A.

If your system does not have a fixed disk, you must insert a DOS startup diskette into drive A and then turn on the computer in order to load DOS. Such a startup diskette must be provided by either a coworker or the dealer that sold you the computer.

As DOS begins execution the screen clears and various messages are printed on the screen. Exactly what is displayed is dependent upon two things. First, each version of DOS displays something slightly different. For example, DOS version 6 displays the message "Starting MS-DOS...", but older versions do not. Second, what types of hardware initializations and/or self-checks are performed by your computer will affect what you see on your screen. For now, don't worry about most of what is displayed. Much of it will become clear after you learn more about DOS. However, there is an important exception, which is discussed next.

Entering the Date and Time

Depending upon how your system is configured you may be prompted to enter the current date and time when your computer first loads DOS. If this is the case, you will see the following prompt. Of course, the current date will be different. (If you are not prompted for the time and date, just skim this section.)

```
Current date is Wed 10-21-1993
Enter new date (mm-dd-yy): _
```

The cursor is positioned after the colon and is represented here with the underscore character. For the remainder of this book, the underscore will be used to indicate the cursor's position. The *cursor* is generally a small, blinking, underline character that indicates where the next character will be printed on the screen. It may be represented as a block in certain computers, but the concept is the same.

When DOS displays this prompt, it tells you what it thinks is the current date and prompts you for a new date in case the date is incorrect. If the current date is the correct date, you may simply press Enter. Otherwise, you should enter the correct date using numbers for each part in the (more or less) standard month-day-year format. For example, to enter the date February 28, 1994, you would type

2-28-94

You may also enter the date using slashes or periods to separate the parts. For example, 2/28/94 is also acceptable. For reasons that will become clear, it is important that DOS knows the correct date. Remember, if you make a typing error, use Backspace to correct it.

If you accidentally enter a date that DOS cannot understand or if the date you enter is invalid, DOS will print the following message and then reprompt you for the correct date:

```
Invalid date
```

NOTE: Most computers today are equipped with a battery-powered clock that maintains the time and date even when the system is turned off. For this reason, DOS will probably have the proper time and date and not prompt you for them. However, in older systems this option is not present, and DOS will always have the wrong time and date because, obviously, it has no way of knowing what time it is when the computer is not on. In this case, if you do not enter the correct information, the time and date that DOS generally uses is its default setting, which will always be wrong. Therefore, if you are prompted for the time and date, be sure to enter them correctly each time.

After you have entered the date you may see the following prompt:

```
Current time is 08:10:11.00
Enter new time: _
```

The time shown is the time that DOS thinks it is. (Remember, the time your system shows will be different.) The time is shown in the format:

hours:minutes:seconds.hundredths of seconds

When you set the clock you generally only enter the hour and minutes, —you do not enter seconds or hundredths of seconds. To specify a time in the afternoon, put a "p" after the time. For example, if the actual time is 2:30 in the afternoon, you would enter

2:30p

Alternately, you may also specify times after noon using the 24-hour system. In this system, 1:00 p.m. is specified as 13:00, 2:00 p.m. is 14:00, and so forth. Using this method, 2:30 p.m. is specified like this:

14:30

CAUTION: For versions of DOS prior to 4, you *must* enter the time using the 24-hour system.

The DOS Prompt

After DOS has been loaded and any startup messages have been displayed, you will see on the far left of your screen either C> or A>. If you have a fixed disk it will be C>. If you loaded DOS from a diskette, it will be A>. Either way, this is called the *DOS prompt*. Whenever the cursor is positioned immediately following the prompt it means that DOS is ready to accept a command.

If your system has been used by other people, there is a very good chance that the DOS prompt will look somewhat different. As you will see later in this book, it is possible to tell DOS exactly what style of prompt you want. So, if yours differs, don't worry about it.

Your First Command

By now you are probably eager to try something, so type **DIR** followed by Enter now. This causes the file directory to be displayed on the screen. You will learn about files and directories in the next chapter, but essentially, a *file* is a collection of related information. The *directory* is a list of the files contained on the disk. All files have names, so when you tell DOS to display the directory, it responds by printing the list of file names. In many ways, files and the directory are analogous to file folders inside a file cabinet.

The first part of the list scrolls off the top of the screen because, generally, there are more files on the disk than there are lines on the monitor. Don't worry about this—it's completely normal and is exactly what is supposed to happen. Later you will learn ways to control how information is displayed. Your screen will look similar to that in Figure 2-1. (Don't worry if file names and dates differ.)

Notice that once the directory has been listed, DOS returns the prompt to the screen. Whenever DOS finishes a command, it redisplays the prompt. This lets you know that it has completed the task. When DOS is accessing a disk, the small red *drive-active* light comes on. Never

2

```
            INTERLNK  EXE     17133 10-15-92    6:00a
            MSBACKUP  RST        96 01-21-93    4:57p
            CONFIG    UMB       601 01-17-93    2:20p
            MSBACKUP  INI        43 11-25-92    3:31p
            SYSTEM    UMB      1589 11-20-92    2:23p
            MSAV      INI       248 01-20-93   10:17a
            DEFAULT   SET      4250 01-21-93    1:33p
            DEFAULT   SLT       784 01-21-93   10:51a
            CC21127A  FUL      2752 11-27-92    2:59p
            DEFAULT   CAT        66 01-21-93   10:52a
            CC21127B  FUL      2752 11-27-92    3:41p
            INTERSVR  EXE     37266 10-15-92    6:00a
            QBASIC    INI       132 01-13-93    4:52p
            CC30121A  FUL      1856 01-21-93   10:51a
            MOVE      EXE     17091 10-15-92    6:00a
            MSCDEX    EXE     25377 10-15-92    6:00a
            MSBACKUP  LOG     40651 02-03-93   11:02a
            MOUSE     INI        28 12-19-92    2:10p
            RAMDRIVE  SYS      5873 10-15-92    6:00a
            SMARTDRV  EXE     42073 10-15-92    6:00a
            COMMAND   COM     52841 01-28-93    6:00a
                  176 file(s)     5620367 bytes
                                  1433600 bytes free

            C:\>
```

A disk directory

Figure 2-1.

remove a diskette from the drive when this light is on; you might destroy some of the information on it.

The directory listing includes the following items from left to right: the name of the file, the size of the file (in bytes), and the date and time the file was created. We will explore the meaning of these items thoroughly in the next chapter.

Besides listing the directory, the DIR command does two other things. First, it counts the number of files on the disk. (If you are using DOS version 5 or greater, the number of bytes of storage used by those files is also displayed.) Second, it tells you the amount of free space on the disk. The storage capacity of different types of disks varies greatly, and you should consult your owner's manual for specific information.

One final point: as stated earlier, DOS does not care whether you enter commands in uppercase or lowercase. This book uses uppercase so that it is easy to distinguish a command, but in actual practice you will probably use lowercase most of the time.

Backing Up Your DOS Master Diskettes

If your system is new and you are in charge of it, the most important first step you can take is to back up the diskettes that contain DOS. You will want to do this whether you run DOS from your fixed disk or from a floppy. Also, even if DOS was loaded on your computer when you purchased it, you will still want copies of your DOS diskettes. Here is why. If you are running DOS from a floppy, that diskette could be destroyed or lost. If one of these events occurs you will need to make a new set of DOS diskettes. If you use a fixed disk, your fixed disk could break. When repaired, you might need to reinstall DOS on it. Also, a computer virus could destroy the contents of your fixed disk. In either case, the problem that destroyed your fixed disk could also damage your DOS master diskettes when you try to reinstall DOS. For this reason, you never want to take a chance on destroying your only copy of DOS. You should always reinstall DOS using backup copies.

 CAUTION: In rare cases, a computer hardware error will be so insidious that it can override many of the protections built into your computer. For example, even though a diskette is write-protected, a severe enough error could render this protection ineffective. Because of this possibility, you should never insert your master copy of a DOS diskette into a computer that is broken or performing erratically.

If the backup has already been made by someone else, you should still read this section just so you will know how to do it should the need arise.

In general, never work with the original DOS master diskettes but always with the backup. It is best to keep the DOS masters in a safe place so that they are not accidentally destroyed.

The exact backup procedure varies between systems with two disk drives and those with either one disk drive or a disk drive and a fixed disk. The following sections cover both configurations. Read the section that is appropriate for the configuration of your computer.

NOTE: To back up your DOS diskettes, you need as many blank diskettes as there are DOS diskettes. Have them ready before beginning.

2

Backup with Two Disk Drives

The following procedure assumes that you have two disk drives of the same type and storage capacity in your system. If the drives differ, follow the instructions for a single-drive system.

To begin the backup procedure, type the command **DISKCOPY A: B:** and press ⌷Enter⌷. Just before you press ⌷Enter⌷, the line should look similar to this:

```
C>DISKCOPY A: B:
```

DISKCOPY is the DOS command that copies the contents of one diskette to another. After pressing ⌷Enter⌷, you will see the following:

```
Insert SOURCE diskette in drive A:

Insert TARGET diskette in drive B:

Press any key when ready ...
```

Put the first DOS diskette in drive A, and put a blank diskette in drive B. After that, strike any key. Now, DOS copies the contents of the DOS diskette onto the blank diskette.

DISKCOPY displays some information about what it is doing, but don't worry about it now. Later, you will be able to understand what it means. The copy process takes a few minutes on most computers so be prepared for this.

After the copy is complete you will see the message:

```
Copy another diskette (Y/N)?
```

If you have more DOS diskettes to copy, type **Y** and the copy process will repeat. Each time you repeat the process, copy another DOS diskette until you have copied them all. When you are finished, type **N**. As you will see, there are many DOS commands that require yes/no responses. The (Y/N)? tells you this.

Backup with One Disk Drive

To begin the backup process in a system with only one floppy disk drive, type the following at the prompt: **DISKCOPY A: A:** and press [Enter]. Prior to pressing [Enter], the prompt line should look similar to this:

```
C>DISKCOPY A: A:
```

DISKCOPY is the DOS command that copies the contents of one diskette to another. After pressing [Enter], you will see the following:

```
Insert SOURCE diskette in drive A:

Press any key when ready ...
```

If the first DOS diskette is not already in drive A, put it there now and close the drive door. After that, strike any key. DOS will first read the contents of the DOS diskette into the memory of the computer. Once this has been done, you will see this message:

```
Insert TARGET diskette in drive A:

Press any key when ready ...
```

At this time, remove the DOS diskette from the computer and put the blank diskette into drive A and press a key. DOS then copies the information it read from the DOS diskette onto the blank one. Depending upon the configuration of your computer, you may need to swap the diskettes one or more times for each disk you have to copy.

DISKCOPY displays some information about what it is doing, but don't worry about it now. Later, you will be able to understand what it means. The copy process using only one drive can take a few minutes, so be patient.

After the copy is complete you will see the message:

2

```
Copy another diskette (Y/N)?
```

If you have more DOS diskettes to copy, type **Y** and the copy process will repeat. Each time you repeat the process, copy another DOS diskette until you have copied them all. When you are finished, type **N**. As you will see, there are many DOS commands that require yes/no responses. The (Y/N)? tells you this.

What to Do If Something Goes Wrong

Once in a while an error occurs when you are copying a diskette and you will see some sort of error message. Generally, this is caused by a faulty target diskette. The first thing you should do is to try the entire process again. Sometimes things will straighten themselves out. If this doesn't work, try a new target diskette. If this still doesn't work, you should seek advice from a coworker or the supplier of your computer.

TIP: Since you are just learning DOS, don't be afraid to ask for help if things don't seem right. You might be overlooking a small but important detail. Often a few words from a co worker can save you hours of frustration.

Labeling Copies of the DOS Diskettes

Any diskette that contains information should have a stick-on label. The label should include the following items:

✦ A brief description of what is on the diskette

✦ The copy number

✦ The date

✦ Your name

The reason for the description is obvious: you must have some way to remember what is contained in the diskette. It is a good idea to describe each backup diskette in the same way as the original. For example, if the original diskette is called "DOS Startup," then the backup should also be called "DOS Startup." Since you might want to have several backup copies, a copy number is a good idea. You can indicate this by writing "copy: 1" for the first copy, for example. Indicate the date the diskette was first put in service. This way you can keep diskettes with similar descriptions separate. Finally, it is a good idea to put your name on it. In large offices, diskettes have a way of getting lost in the shuffle. Your name helps to ensure that it will find its way back to you. A good layout for a label is shown in Figure 2-2.

Be sure to prepare the label *before* you put it on the diskette. Once the label is on, you should only use a felt-tipped pen to make changes or corrections to it. Using a ball-point pen or pencil may result in the loss of data by damaging the magnetic surface.

Another Command

One of the simplest commands in DOS is the VER command, which displays the version number of DOS that you are using. To see how it works, type it now. You will see a message similar to this:

```
MS-DOS Version 6.00
```

Of course, your version number may differ. Since some commands and options are available only with specific versions of DOS, make note of the version number at this time.

Restarting DOS

It is not necessary to actually turn your computer off and then on again to cause DOS to be loaded. Pressing Ctrl , Alt , and Del at the same time causes the computer to reload DOS and begin running it. Try doing this now. If you load DOS from a floppy disk, be sure the proper diskette is in drive A.

Suggested
format for a
diskette label
Figure 2-2.

DOS Operating Diskette
Copy: 1
Date: 2/28/94
Return to: Herb Schildt

NOTE: Restarting DOS in the manner just described is virtually the same as turning the computer off and then on again. Anything that the computer was doing is completely lost.

You are probably wondering why you would want to restart DOS. There are two possible reasons. First, causing DOS to be reloaded also causes the computer to stop whatever it is doing. Therefore, if the computer begins to do something you think it shouldn't, you can always stop this by reloading DOS. In a sense, pressing Ctrl, Alt, and Del is an emergency stop signal. For now, since you don't know much about DOS yet, if you think that you have accidentally done something that you shouldn't have, just reload DOS.

The second reason you may need to reload DOS is because a program has crashed and DOS is unable to display its prompt. Fortunately, because of the high quality of software available today, program crashes are rare. However, they still occur. Contrary to popular belief, computer programmers are not perfect and can make mistakes. A mistake in a computer program is called a *bug*. Some bugs are simply annoyances while others are so bad that they can actually cause the computer to stop running. This is called a *crash*. Because the computer has stopped, DOS cannot run, which means you must restart the computer by reloading DOS. You shouldn't have to do this very often.

Turning Off the Computer

When you are ready to turn the computer off remember to do one thing first: remove all diskettes from the drives. When power is cut, there is a fraction of a second when the electricity stored in the power supply of the computer "bleeds" out. During this time of decreasing power, the electronics in the computer are in an unstable state. Although unlikely, it is possible that the disk drive could write random information onto your diskette. This could destroy valuable data. Most computers today have safeguards built in to prevent this, but no safeguard is 100 percent effective.

Summary

At this point you should know how to

✦ Start the computer and load DOS

✦ List the directory

✦ Back up the DOS diskettes

✦ Use the VER command

✦ Reload DOS

✦ Safely turn off the computer

In the next chapter you will learn more about DOS files and directories.

CHAPTER

3

DOS BASICS

Before you can go much further in your study of DOS, it is important to understand some specifics about how DOS operates and some additional DOS-related terms. In this chapter, you will learn about file names, file types, and error messages. You will also learn about DOS's internal and external commands and how DOS actually stores information on a disk.

What Is a File?

A file is a collection of related information stored on either a diskette or the fixed disk. (For the rest of this discussion, the word *disk* will refer to both a floppy disk and the fixed disk.) The magnetic media of a disk is essentially the same as recording tape used in an audio tape recorder. The process of placing information onto the disk is actually very similar to making a tape recording. Reading the information from a disk is similar to playing a tape recording.

A disk can hold several files. In a sense, a disk is like a file cabinet and the disk files are like paper files in the file cabinet. As stated, a file is a collection of related information. For example, the same disk might contain a letter, a mailing list, and a general ledger. Because they are in separate files, there is no chance that they will become "mixed up." You can visualize the way files are stored on a disk by looking at Figure 3-1. (As you will see later in the chapter, it is a little more complicated than this.)

Information is stored on a disk in much the same way that it is stored in memory: byte by byte. (Remember, a byte is roughly the same as a

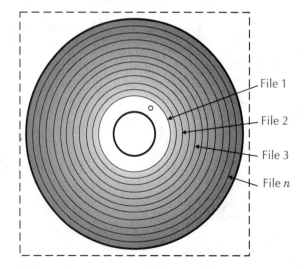

A simplified
view of files
stored on a disk
Figure 3-1.

character.) For example, a file might contain the sentence "This is a test." The individual characters that make up that sentence are stored on the disk.

The single most important thing that you can understand about disk files is that they are concrete, physical entities. They are as real as paper files. Anything you can do with a paper file can be done to a disk file. This includes copying it, changing it, adding to it, changing its name, and, unfortunately, losing it. If you can keep this in mind you will have no trouble running DOS or using the computer in general.

3

File Names

Each file on a disk must have a unique name to identify it. A file name may consist of two parts. The first part, traditionally called the *filename,* is essentially what you will think of as the name of the file. It may be between one and eight characters long. The second part of the file's name is called the *extension,* and it is optional. The extension exists to help create groups of similar files or to distinguish two files with the same filename from one another. The extension may be up to three characters long. In a way, the filename is like a person's first name and the extension is like a person's last name.

List the directory at this time. (At the DOS prompt, enter **DIR** followed by Enter.) See how each name has two parts? For example, one file name you might see is "SORT EXE". The filename is "SORT" and the extension is "EXE". Although the directory listing uses one or more spaces to separate the filename from its extension, when you specify a file's name you must place a period between the two parts of the name. For example, to tell DOS about the file "SORT EXE", you type **SORT.EXE**. There can be no spaces in the name.

NOTE: Although most files have names that attempt to reflect their contents, technically, a file's name has nothing to do with what the file contains. For example, a file called PAYROLL could actually contain inventory information.

In general, most file names are made up of letters of the alphabet and the digits 0 through 9. The only characters that cannot be used in a filename are

. " / \ [ ] : | < > + = ; ,

Also, control characters are not allowed. (A control character is generated by holding down the [Ctrl] key and pressing another key. You will learn more about these characters later.)

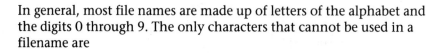

The Directory

The directory of a disk is a little like the table of contents of a book: it tells what is on the disk. The directory contains the names of the files, each file's length, and the time and date of creation. These are shown in Figure 3-2.

The length of the file is shown in bytes. For example, a file to hold the sentence "Hi there." will be nine bytes long. (As far as the computer is concerned, the space and the period are also characters, so they have to be counted.) A file's time and date indicate either when the file was first created or the last time it was altered.

Versions of DOS before 5 did not assign serial numbers to diskettes. If you are using an old version, the serial number will be missing.

When you list the directory you will probably notice the three lines of information it begins with. If you list the directory of a diskette in the A drive, it will look something like this:

```
Volume in drive A has no label
Volume Serial Number is 3665-17FB
Directory of A:\
```

Don't worry about trying to make sense of this now. Later you will understand what it means.

All files listed in the directory must have unique names. Two files with the same filename and extension are not allowed.

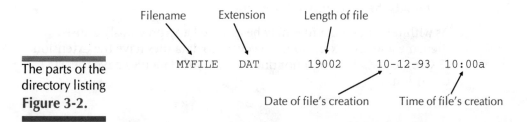

The parts of the
directory listing
Figure 3-2.

3

File Types

There are three types of files that can be stored on a disk:

✦ Text

✦ Data

✦ Program

Text Files

A *text file* contains information that you can read. It consists solely of
characters that can be displayed on the screen. A common way text files
are created is by word processors. In most cases, text files are created
and maintained by you. (You will see how later in this book.)

Text files may have any previously unused filename and any extension.
However, no text files should have the extension .EXE or .COM because
these extensions are reserved for program files.

Data Files

A *data file* contains information that a program, not a person, can read.
Most of the information in a data file cannot be displayed on the
monitor because it is in a form only the computer can understand. The
special internal representation used by the computer for data is
sometimes referred to as *binary* data.

Data files are created and maintained by programs. For example, an inventory management program will create and maintain a data file that holds the inventory information.

As with text files, data files may be assigned any previously unused filename and any extension. However, no data files have the extension .EXE or .COM. Although not universal, many data files have the .DAT extension.

Program Files

Program files contain programs that the computer can execute. All program files have one of the following extensions:

✦ COM

✦ EXE

Although there is a technical difference between program files with the .COM and .EXE extensions, for your purposes they are both simply program files and are functionally the same. Program files are created by programmers.

Many of the programs you will use fall into the category called *application programs*. As the name implies, an application program is a program that applies itself to a specific task for which it was designed. For example, a general ledger is an application program in the area of accounting. In essence, an application program is used to solve a specific problem or to perform a specific task.

Reserved Extensions

DOS reserves a few file extensions for special purposes. As you saw, .EXE and .COM are used for program files. The .SYS extension is used to indicate files that only DOS uses. A file extension of .BAT indicates a *batch file,* which contains a sequence of commands for DOS to perform. (You will learn how to create batch files in Chapter 8.) The extension .CPI is reserved by DOS for hardware-specific information. The extension .PIF is used when running Windows (an optional, graphics-based operating system that overlays DOS). The extension .BAS is used to indicate BASIC program files. Other extensions reserved by DOS are .HLP, .INF, .OVL, and .INI. It is best not to use any of the reserved extensions in the file names that you create.

Opening and Closing Files

When you take a paper file from a file cabinet you open the file folder to examine or alter the contents of the file. When you are done, you close the file folder and replace the file in the cabinet. The act of opening and closing a file is paralleled by DOS. Before a file can be used, it must be opened. When the file is through being accessed, it is closed. When a file is open, its contents may be examined or changed. When it is closed, nothing can happen to the file. Whether a file is open or closed will become important as you begin to use DOS to run application programs.

The EOF Marker

All files have a beginning and an end. This seems intuitive and simple enough. But for the computer, knowing where the file stops is not a trivial matter. DOS uses two different methods to determine the end of a file. The first is the *end-of-file* marker—*EOF*, for short. The EOF marker is a special character (a control-Z to be exact), which signals the end of a file. The EOF marker works very well on text files because it is not a printing character. However, on data and program files, the EOF marker is not effective because actual data or program statements might look like an EOF marker, thus making DOS think that the file is shorter than it is. In these situations, DOS uses the length of the file to determine where the end of the file is located.

Changing the Current Drive

When you type the DIR command, you get a directory listing of the drive that corresponds to the letter in the prompt. This drive is called the *current drive*. (Sometimes, for historical reasons, it is also called the *logged-in drive*.) You can switch to another drive by typing its drive letter followed by a colon and pressing (Enter). For example, to switch to the A drive you would enter **A:**. To try this, first put a DOS diskette into drive A and then enter **A:**. You will see something like this:

```
C>A:
A>_
```

As you can see, the DOS prompt has been changed to reflect the switch to a new drive.

NOTE: If you have a floppy-only system, try changing to drive B by entering **B:**.

Next, try the DIR command. DOS automatically uses the new drive. In general, all DOS operations occur on the current drive. (It is possible to override this, as you will see later.)

To switch back to the C drive, follow the same format as shown above, substituting the proper drive designation. Switch back to the C drive now. (Or, if you are using a floppy-only system, switch back to drive A.)

Internal and External Commands

DOS commands are divided into two major groups: internal and external. An *internal* command is a command that is contained in the part of DOS that stays loaded in the memory of your computer. Both DIR and VER are examples of internal commands. When you enter an internal command DOS responds almost instantly. The DOS internal commands are those that you are most likely to need frequently as you use the computer.

The second type of DOS command is called *external*. An external command is not loaded into memory with the rest of DOS; rather, it remains on disk. The reason for this is to conserve the computer's memory. There is a fairly large number of little-used commands that are part of DOS. Instead of taking memory away from your application programs, DOS leaves these on disk until they are needed. This means, however, that each time you use an external command it must be available on the current drive. Because external commands are loaded by DOS as needed, there is a slight delay before DOS responds when you use one. After an external command has executed, it is no longer kept in memory; it must be reloaded each time that it is used.

DOS's internal and external commands are listed in Table 3-1. (If you have a version of DOS earlier than 6, you may not have all the external commands shown.)

To see an example of an external command in action, enter **CHKDSK** at the DOS prompt. CHKDSK is short for "check disk." It is the external command used to check the validity of the disk as well as to report the total space, number of files, and amount of free space on the disk;

3

Internal Commands			
BREAK	DATE	MKDIR (MD)	TIME
CHCP	DEL (ERASE)	PATH	TYPE
CHDIR (CD)	DIR	PROMPT	VER
CLS	ERASE (DEL)	RENAME (REN)	VERIFY
COPY	EXIT	RMDIR (RD)	VOL
CTTY	LOADHIGH(LH	SET	

External Commands			
APPEND	DOSKEY	JOIN	PRINT
ASSIGN	DOSSHELL	KEYB	QBASIC
ATTRIB	EDIT	LABEL	RECOVER
BACKUP	EDLIN	LOADFIX	REPLACE
CHKDSK	EMM386	MEM	RESTORE
COMMAND	EXE2BIN	MEMMAKER	SETVER
COMP	EXPAND	MIRROR	SHARE
DBLSPACE	FASTOPEN	MODE	SORT
DEBUG	FC	MORE	SUBST
DEFRAG	FDISK	MOVE	SYS
DELTREE	FIND	MSAV	TREE
DISKCOMP	FORMAT	MSBACKUP	UNDELETE
DISKCOPY	GRAFTABL	MSD	UNFORMAT
DOS	GRAPHICS	NLSFUNC	VSAFE
FASTHELP	HELP	POWER	XCOPY

DOS's Internal and External Commands
Table 3-1.

information about the format of the disk; and the total and free amounts of RAM in the computer. CHKDSK will display something like this:

```
362496 bytes total disk space
 45056 bytes in 3 hidden files
293912 bytes in 39 user files
 22528 bytes available on disk

  1024 bytes in each allocation unit
   354 total allocation units on disk
    25 available allocation units on disk

655360 bytes total memory
604416 bytes free
```

Don't worry about what all this information means now. Later in this book, the CHKDSK command will be discussed in detail.

NOTE: If you are wondering about the "hidden files" in the CHKDSK output, they are some special files used only by DOS. They do not show up in the directory listing, but they are still on the disk.

You should have noticed a slight delay before the CHKDSK command was executed. This delay was caused by the time it took to load CHKDSK into memory so it could be executed. (You probably noticed that the drive-active light came on after you entered the command, indicating that the command was being loaded.) In general, all external commands have to be loaded and, therefore, have a slight delay before they begin execution.

As you will see in the next chapter, it is easy to copy files between diskettes, so if you know that you will need one or more of DOS's external commands, it is possible to copy only those needed to another diskette so that you can have easy access to them.

Of Tracks and Sectors: A Closer Look at How DOS Stores Files

3

The first part of this chapter provided a simplified explanation of the way DOS stores files on a disk. This section describes this process in detail. Although the exact method used by DOS to store a file is not important as far as using DOS goes, it will be helpful if you understand the concept so that you can interpret certain DOS error messages. Also, many books, user manuals, and magazine articles will assume you have a loose but basic understanding of the way DOS files are stored.

Information is recorded on a disk in concentric circles called *tracks*. When the disk drive loads a program you can sometimes hear the read/write head move between tracks. Each track consists of a number of *sectors*. (The exact number varies and is not important.) Each sector can hold a fixed number of bytes (characters) and is the smallest accessible unit of storage on the disk. The size of a sector depends upon the storage capacity of the disk. The most common sector size in use today holds 512 bytes. When DOS records a file on a disk it does not necessarily use sectors and tracks that are adjacent to each other. That is, for technical reasons, DOS may scatter a file throughout the disk's surface. (This is why even a small amount of physical damage to a disk can destroy several files.) Sectors and tracks are depicted in Figure 3-3.

It may seem strange, but a file can be completely empty and, thus, be zero bytes long!

As mentioned in the preceding paragraph, the smallest accessible unit of disk storage is the sector. This does not mean, however, that the smallest file is one sector long. On the contrary, you can actually have files of any length. However, even if a file is only three bytes long, the full sector will be allocated to it even if the rest of the space is not used. (For this reason, several small files can sometimes fill up a disk faster than a few large ones.)

As you can guess, when a file longer than one sector is stored on a disk there must be some way for DOS to know which sector goes with which file. The way DOS accomplishes this is by storing the location of the sectors associated with each file in a special part of the directory called the *file allocation table* (FAT).

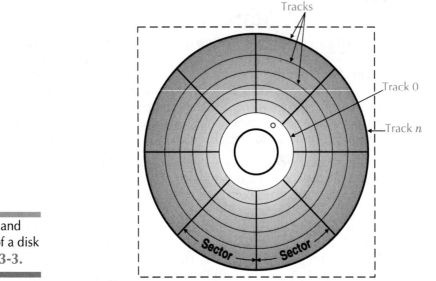

Sectors and
tracks of a disk
Figure 3-3.

NOTE: Because the FAT tells DOS where files are located on a disk, if the FAT is destroyed, the information on the disk is effectively lost. This is another reason why a small amount of damage to a disk can render it unusable.

The exact position of the tracks and sectors on a disk is determined when it is *formatted.* When you made a backup of the DOS master disk, the copy procedure automatically formatted the disk prior to placing information on it. All disks must be formatted before being used. (The DOS command to format a diskette will be discussed a little farther on in this book.) When a disk is not formatted, DOS and the computer have no way of knowing where to put information on the disk.

 ## A DOS Error Message

Whenever DOS encounters a situation in which it cannot perform its job it displays an error message describing the problem. Since error messages are, unfortunately, fairly common, now is a good time to introduce them. Let's begin with an example, by generating an error message now. First, if necessary, insert a DOS diskette into drive A and then switch to drive A by entering **A:**. Next, open A's drive door and then attempt to list the directory by entering **DIR**. Since the drive door is open, DOS cannot access the drive. In a few seconds you will see the following message:

```
Not ready reading drive A
Abort, Retry, Fail?
```

NOTE: If you are using a version of DOS prior to 3.30, the error message will read "Abort, Retry, Ignore?". For the sake of this discussion, "Ignore" and "Fail" mean the same thing.

Let's examine what this message means.

First, DOS is telling you that it cannot access (read) the diskette in drive A. This is, of course, because the drive door is open. However, DOS cannot know the exact cause of the problem, it just knows that the drive is "not ready" to be used. There are several conditions that could cause this error other than the drive door being open. For example, a faulty or unformatted diskette could cause the error message to be displayed.

"Abort, Retry, Fail?" means abort the command, retry the command, or ignore the error.

DOS gives you three ways to respond to this error. You may abort the command, retry the command, or ignore the error. Let's look at these now.

To abort the DIR command you can type **A**. This causes DOS to stop trying to read the diskette. You should use Abort when there is no way to remedy the condition causing the error.

You can tell DOS to retry the command. The reason for this option is that it lets you correct the condition causing the error. For example, close the drive door and then type **R**. The disk directory will be displayed. Use Retry when you can eliminate the error.

The Fail option has limited applications. (Remember, prior to version 3.30, the term "Ignore" is substituted for "Fail"; however, its effect is the same.) It tells DOS to ignore the immediate error and continue on with the command. Generally, once one error has occurred, more will follow. Frankly, this option is generally used only by programmers because, to be used successfully, it requires significant knowledge about how the computer and DOS function.

If you have not done so, close the drive door and type **R** for Retry. Also, switch back to drive C by typing **C:**.

Other DOS Error Messages

In the previous section you saw an example of a DOS error and its associated message. In reality there are several occurrences other than a drive door being open that can cause DOS to issue an error message. As you continue to use DOS it is very likely that you will see one or more of these error messages. It is important to respond correctly when presented with an error, so let's take a look at some of the most common errors. (Other error messages will be discussed as the need arises.) Many errors are followed by the prompt that you saw in the previous example:

```
Abort, Retry, Fail?
```

An Ignore option may also appear, which effectively means the same thing as Fail. (The slight difference between Fail and Ignore is meaningful only to programmers.)

The most common error messages are discussed next. Depending upon your specific version of DOS, some of the messages may be worded slightly differently.

Bad Command or File Name

This is easily the most common error message you will see. It is DOS's way of telling you that it does not understand what you are asking it to do. This message requests no response—you simply reenter the command properly. Generally this message is the result of misspelling a command. For example, if you type **DUR** instead of **DIR**, you will see this message.

Non-System Disk or Disk Error

This message will occur if you try to load DOS from a diskette that does not contain it. You should insert the DOS diskette and strike any key.

You will also see this message if, when you turn the computer on or restart it by pressing Ctrl-Alt-Del, there is a diskette in drive A that does not contain a copy of DOS. This is common on systems that load DOS from the fixed disk. It is easy to accidentally leave a work disk in drive A. The next time you turn on the computer, it will attempt to load DOS from that diskette. To correct the trouble, simply remove the diskette from drive A and then restart the computer.

General Failure

This error message is displayed when you attempt to access a diskette that either has not been formatted, is damaged, or is not intended for use by DOS or in a DOS-compatible computer. To remedy the problem either abort the operation or insert a correct diskette and try again.

Insufficient Disk Space

As you know, a disk only has a finite amount of space on it. When you run out of space you will see this message. The solution is to either start using a new disk or to remove files from the existing disk. (You will see how to remove files in the next chapter.)

Invalid Drive Specification

This message occurs if you try to specify a drive that does not exist. For example, if you type **Z:** in an attempt to reach the (nonexistent) Z drive, you will see this message. Simply retry with the proper drive letter.

Non-DOS Disk

This message is caused by a damaged diskette. Usually, it means that the diskette directory is completely or partially destroyed. Either abort or retry with a different diskette.

Sector Not Found

This error message is displayed when a sector that is part of a file cannot be found. This can happen for various reasons, including a damaged file allocation table. Generally, all you can do is try a different diskette. If this error occurs on a fixed disk, you will have to use a new copy of the file.

Seek Error

This message means that the disk drive was unable to find a track. This has three main causes: First, the disk drive is out of alignment, which requires a professional technician to repair. Second, the diskette could be improperly inserted in the drive. Try inserting it again. Finally, the disk could be physically damaged. In this case, replace it.

 ## Summary

You should now understand

+ What a file is
+ How file names are constructed
+ The purpose of the directory
+ The difference between text, data, and program files
+ How to change the current drive
+ The difference between internal and external commands
+ The meaning of track and sector
+ How to interpret various DOS error messages

Now that the DOS basics are behind you, the next chapter teaches you several new and useful DOS commands including copying files, printing the screen, and erasing a file.

CHAPTER

4

THE ESSENTIAL DOS COMMANDS

This chapter presents the core commands that you need to operate the computer and begin using application programs. At first reading, you may think that there is a lot to remember, but if you work through the examples, you will be surprised at how easy it is to keep everything straight. Although these commands just scratch the surface of DOS, they will get you started.

This, and subsequent chapters, will present a number of examples, many of which include listings of the DOS directory. Since many versions of DOS exist, it is possible that you will have some files not included in the examples or, if you have an early version of DOS, you may be missing a few files. Don't worry about this.

NOTE: From this point on the examples are written from the perspective of a system that has a fixed disk as drive C. This is by far the most common configuration in use today. If your system has only floppy disks or is configured in some other way, simply adjust the examples to fit your system.

Changing to the DOS Subdirectory

To follow along with the examples, you need to have access to the DOS external commands and files. Typically, when your system starts, you automatically have access to these files. However, as you read this chapter and try the examples, if you don't have access to these files, follow the procedure described here.

Generally, the DOS files are stored in a special part of your fixed disk called *DOS*. Your fixed disk is organized into sections called *subdirectories*. The DOS files are generally stored in the *DOS subdirectory*. We will study subdirectories in detail in Chapter 6, but loosely, a subdirectory is a portion of your disk that contains related files. If the DOS files are not available, you will have to switch to the DOS directory. To do this, execute the following sequence of commands. (Don't worry about what they mean now; they will be explained in a later chapter.)

```
C>CD \
C>CD DOS
```

If, for some reason, after issuing these commands you still do not have access to the DOS files, ask a coworker (or the person that sold you the computer) for help. Frankly, access to the DOS files is essential. You cannot use your computer for most meaningful tasks without them.

A Closer Look at DIR

You learned the simplest form of the DIR command in Chapter 2. However, as you will soon see, DIR is much more flexible. We will take a look at two DIR options in this section.

Two DIR Options

DIR is the most commonly used DOS command.

Many DOS commands allow one or more *options* that alter slightly the meaning or effect of the command. Generally speaking, a DOS command option begins with a / (a slash) followed by the specific option. The / signals DOS that an option follows. The DIR command allows several options. The two most common are examined here.

The first DIR option is /P, which tells DOS to pause the directory listing when the screen is full. You might remember that when you listed the directory in Chapter 2, a number of file names scrolled off the top of the screen. The /P option will prevent this. At each pause, you will see the message:

```
Press any key to continue. . .
```

This means that when you are ready for more of the directory, press any key and another screen of the listing will be shown.

TIP: Older versions of DOS display the message "Strike a key when ready." Both messages mean the same thing.

To execute the DIR command with the pause option, your command line should look like this:

```
C>DIR /P
```

The first screen shown will look similar to the one in Figure 4-1.

4

```
Volume in drive C is CDISK
Volume Serial Number is 1A42-5599
Directory of C:\DOS

.              <DIR>       11-16-89    9:56a
..             <DIR>       11-16-89    9:56a
EGA      SYS      4885 01-28-93    6:00a
FORMAT   COM     22717 01-28-93    6:00a
NLSFUNC  EXE      7036 01-28-93    6:00a
COUNTRY  SYS     17066 01-28-93    6:00a
EGA      CPI     58870 01-28-93    6:00a
HIMEM    SYS     14160 01-28-93    6:00a
KEYB     COM     14983 01-28-93    6:00a
KEYBOARD SYS     34694 01-28-93    6:00a
ANSI     SYS      9065 01-28-93    6:00a
ATTRIB   EXE     11165 01-28-93    6:00a
CHOICE   COM      1754 01-28-93    6:00a
CHKDSK   EXE     12908 01-28-93    6:00a
EDIT     COM       413 01-28-93    6:00a
DBLSPACE BIN     51246 01-28-93    6:00a
EDLIN    EXE     12642 04-09-91    5:00a
DEBUG    EXE     15715 01-28-93    6:00a
DOSSWAP  EXE     18756 01-28-93    6:00a
Press any key to continue . . .
```

Directory
listing using
the pause
(/P) option
Figure 4-1.

There are many times when all you want is a list of the files on a disk, and you are not interested in all the other information that DIR displays. This can be accomplished by using the /W option, which causes DOS to display only the file names in the directory. The file names are displayed in five columns across the screen, allowing many more file names than usual to be displayed at one time. To use this option, your command line should look like this:

```
C>DIR /W
```

The outcome of this command is shown in Figure 4-2.

```
CHKSTATE.SYS  MEMMAKER.HLP  MEMMAKER.INF  MONOUMB.386   UNDELETE.EXE

DBLWIN.HLP    MSTOOLS.DLL   VSAFE.COM     MSAV.EXE      DBLSPACE.EXE

MSAVIRUS.LST  MSAV.HLP      DOSSHELL.INI  MSAVHELP.OVL  DBLSPACE.HLP

DBLSPACE.INF  DBLSPACE.SYS  DOSSHELL.HLP  EMM386.EXE    TEST.TXT

SIZER.EXE     MOUSE.SYS     MEMMAKER.EXE  DELTREE.EXE   INTERLNK.EXE

MSBACKUP.RST  CONFIG.UMB    MSBACKUP.INI  SYSTEM.UMB    MSAV.INI

DEFAULT.SET   DEFAULT.SLT   CC21127A.FUL  DEFAULT.CAT   CC21127B.FUL

INTERSVR.EXE  QBASIC.INI    CC30121A.FUL  MOVE.EXE      MSCDEX.EXE

MSBACKUP.LOG  MOUSE.INI     RAMDRIVE.SYS  SMARTDRV.EXE  COMMAND.COM

       160 file(s)    4839429 bytes
                      6668288 bytes free
```

A wide
directory listing
Figure 4-2.

4

TIP: You can remember the /W option as "wide listing." You can remember the /P as "pause."

Looking for Specific Files

Until now, you have been using DIR to list the entire contents of the directory. However, you can use DIR to look for a specific file by specifying its name after DIR. You can use this method to quickly determine whether a file is in the directory or not. For example, try this by entering

DIR DISKCOPY.COM

DOS will display the following (or something similar):

```
Volume in drive C is CDISK
Volume Serial Number is 1968-89D7
Directory of C:\DOS
```

```
DISKCOPY COM    11879 01-28-93   6:00a
        1 File(s)    11879 bytes
                     1353728 bytes free
```

As you can see, DOS displays information only about the file you request, not the entire directory. (At this time pay no attention to the volume message that precedes the filename. You will learn about it later in the book.)

NOTE: If DISKCOPY.COM is not found, you need to switch to the DOS subdirectory, as described at the beginning of this chapter.

If you specify a file that is not in the directory, you will see this message:

```
File not found
```

To see an example of this, enter this command:

    DIR GARBAGE

If you think that the file you requested is really in the directory, you may have made a typing error. If, after a second try, DOS still reports it as nonexistent, try listing the entire directory; you may have forgotten its name.

Wildcards in File Names

Wildcard characters are like wildcards in poker; they can stand for any type of character.

Up to this point, you have learned how to list either the entire directory or a specific file. However, DOS allows you to list groups of related files. You can also list a file without knowing its full name. To accomplish these things requires special *wildcard* characters. Let's see how, starting with an example.

Assume that you want to list the names of all the files on a disk that share the .EXE extension. To do this, enter the following, exactly as shown:

    DIR *.EXE

This causes DOS to display all files with an .EXE extension. The output will be similar to that shown in Figure 4-3.

When used in a file name that is part of a DOS command, the asterisk (*) is a special character that tells DOS to match any sequence of characters. Specifically, it means that any character can occupy the position of the * and all character positions after it. Note that the filename and extension are separate, so the * only applies to the part of the name in which it is used.

You can use the * to find files whose names have one or more initial characters in common by specifying those characters followed by the *. For example, enter this command:

DIR S*.EXE

DOS will display all files that begin with S and have the .EXE extension. This is because the letter *S* is specified, but after that any sequence of characters may follow. You will see that the command displays files such as SHARE.EXE. SORT.EXE, and SUBST.EXE. (Depending upon your version of DOS, other files will also be displayed.)

```
SETVER   EXE     12015 02-02-93   10:44a
SORT     EXE      6922 01-28-93    6:00a
FASTOPEN EXE     12034 01-28-93    6:00a
PRINT    EXE     15640 01-28-93    6:00a
POWER    EXE      8052 01-28-93    6:00a
REPLACE  EXE     20226 01-28-93    6:00a
SHARE    EXE     10912 01-28-93    6:00a
SUBST    EXE     18478 01-28-93    6:00a
MSBACKUP EXE      5506 01-28-93    6:00a
UNDELETE EXE     26420 01-28-93    6:00a
MSAV     EXE    172185 01-28-93    6:00a
DBLSPACE EXE    273458 01-28-93    6:00a
EMM386   EXE    115294 01-28-93    6:00a
SIZER    EXE      6625 01-28-93    6:00a
MEMMAKER EXE    118577 10-15-92    6:00a
DELTREE  EXE      9603 10-15-92    6:00a
INTERLNK EXE     17133 10-15-92    6:00a
INTERSVR EXE     37266 10-15-92    6:00a
MOVE     EXE     17091 10-15-92    6:00a
MSCDEX   EXE     25377 10-15-92    6:00a
SMARTDRV EXE     42073 10-15-92    6:00a
          47 file(s)    1991714 bytes
                        6668288 bytes free
```

Outcome of
the DIR *.EXE
command

Figure 4-3.

It is not possible to use the * to find files that have different characters at the beginning of their filenames but have common endings. That is, this command,

DIR *ST.EXE

will *not* find all files with filenames that end in ST. Instead, it will display all files that have the extension .EXE. This is because the * matches any and all characters from its position in the name to the end.

You can use the * in the extension field of a file name. For example, the following command reports all files that begin with S and have any extension.

DIR S*.*

Try some examples on your own at this time.

TIP: There is no reason to use more than one * in either part of a file name. For example, the command DIR SH**.EXE is not wrong; it is simply redundant.

The second wildcard character is the ?, which will match any one character in its position. That is, unlike the *, it only matches a single character—not a sequence of characters. For example, this command will find all files that end with DISK:

DIR ?DISK.*

To this command DOS responds with FDISK.COM (and possibly others).

As another example, assume that these files are on your disk:

TEST1A.DAT
TEST2A.DAT
TEST3A.DAT
TEST1B.DAT
TEST2B.DAT

If you enter this command,

DIR TEST?A.DAT

the files TEST1A.DAT, TEST2A.DAT, and TEST3A.DAT will be displayed.

In practice, no one would use DIR ????????.??? because DIR *.* is much easier!

Now try some examples of the ? wildcard. To fully understand the effect of the * and ?, keep in mind that the following commands are equivalent as far as DOS is concerned.

DIR
DIR *.*
DIR ????????.???

All three list the entire contents of the directory.

As you will see later in this book, the wildcard characters prove very useful in commands other than DIR because they allow you to easily handle related groups of files.

Another Way to Stop the Display

A control character is entered by holding down the [Ctrl] key and then pressing another key.

The /P option to the DIR command provides a convenient way to stop the display of the directory, but there is another way which you will probably use more frequently. If you press [Ctrl]-[S], the display will stop until you hit another key (or [Ctrl]-[S] again). The [Ctrl]-[S] key acts as a *toggle* that can be remembered as "stop/start." To try the [Ctrl]-[S] command, list the directory, freezing it at various points.

DOS also lets you stop the display by pressing the [Pause] key. If you stop the display by pressing [Pause], you must restart it by pressing a different key—[Pause] does not serve as a toggle the way the [Ctrl]-[S] key does. (Note, some PC-compatible computers may behave slightly differently in regard to how these keys are interpreted.)

TIP: For the original PCs, there is no [Pause] key. Instead, you can stop the display by pressing [Ctrl]-[S] or [Ctrl]-[Num Lock]. If you use [Ctrl]-[Num Lock], you must restart the display by pressing another key.

Not all application programs that run under DOS recognize the Ctrl-S or the Ctrl-Num Lock keys. Therefore, it may not always be possible to stop the display of some programs.

Drive Specifiers

In Chapter 3 you learned how to change the current drive by entering the name of the drive you wanted to switch to followed by a colon. The combination of the drive name and the colon is called a *drive specifier*. Beyond the specific use of changing the current drive, a drive specifier is used to tell DOS what drive to use for a variety of commands. To see how a drive specifier works, let's begin with a simple example. Insert a DOS diskette in drive A, but keep C the current drive. Next, enter the following:

DIR A:

This causes the directory of the A drive to be displayed. In general, when a drive specifier follows DIR, the directory of that drive is displayed. The reason for this is that DOS uses the drive specifier to determine which drive is the focus of the DIR command.

As a second example, try this command:

DIR A:DISKCOPY.COM

Again, drive A, not drive C, is searched for the file DISKCOPY.COM. This is because the drive specifier told DOS to look on the A drive for the file.

Although DOS treats all drive specifiers the same, you can think of them as performing two slightly different tasks. First, they tell DOS what drive to use to perform a specific command. This is the case with the DIR A: command. The A: tells DOS to list the directory of the A drive. Second, you can think of the drive specifier as a prefix to a file's name, as in the second example given above. It is the way of telling DOS which drive contains the file. Consider: if you have the file SORT.EXE on both the C and A drives, then the file that is on C is referred to as C:SORT.EXE and the one on A as A:SORT.EXE. In a sense, the drive specifier lets DOS keep files with similar names on different drives separate.

If an external command is on a disk that is not the current drive, you can still execute it simply by placing a drive specifier before the command name. For example, if you are currently using the A drive and CHKDSK is on the disk in drive C, then you would type

   C:CHKDSK

This will cause DOS to look for the external command on the C drive rather than the currently active A drive.

You will see more uses for drive specifiers as you advance in your understanding and use of DOS.

Clearing the Screen

It's time to take a little break and look at one of DOS's simplest commands: CLS. This command clears the monitor's screen. Try this now. As you can see, the screen is cleared and the DOS prompt is redisplayed in the upper-left corner of the screen.

The CLS command is useful for three reasons. First, you may have sensitive information on the screen which you do not want everyone to see. When you are done with the information, executing the CLS command is an easy way to wipe it off the screen. Second, occasionally an application program will leave the screen in a "messy" condition. Clearing the screen is a good way to remedy this situation. Finally, if you are not going to be using the computer for a while, it is advisable to clear the screen in order to save the phosphors in the picture tube from undue wear. (The phosphors in a picture tube slowly burn out as they are used.)

TIP: Another way to save the phosphors of your monitor is to purchase a *screen saver* program. Typically, screen savers display a moving image on the screen that lets you know the computer is still "alive" while saving the phosphors at the same time.

Printing the Screen

This section assumes that you have a printer attached to your computer. If this is not the case, skip ahead to the next section. If you do not know how to attach the printer to the computer, refer to the installation guide that came with your computer, ask the person who sold you the computer, or ask a coworker.

It is sometimes very useful to have a printed record of what is displayed on the screen. DOS lets you do this through the use of the PRINT SCREEN command. Unlike most other DOS commands, you do not need to type a special command word—you simply press the `Prt Sc` key. (To reach `Prt Sc` may require the use of the `Shift` key.) To try this, do a directory listing. Once the DOS prompt is displayed, press `Prt Sc`. As you can see, the information that is on the screen is printed at the printer.

If you wish to keep a paper record of everything that transpires during a session at the computer you can do this by pressing `Ctrl`-`Prt Sc`. This is done by holding down the `Ctrl` key while pressing `Prt Sc`. Now, whatever is displayed on the screen will also be printed by the printer. To stop the continuous printing, type `Ctrl`-`Prt Sc` a second time. The `Ctrl`-`Prt Sc` acts as a toggle: pressed once, it activates the continuous print facility; pressed again, it deactivates it. Try this now.

TIP: Another way to activate the continuous printing of the screen is to press `Ctrl`-`P`. Pressing it a second time deactivates the printing function.

At this point, you can only print screens that contain text. You will need to learn more about DOS before you can print screens that contain graphics images.

Formatting Diskettes

Before you can use a diskette to store information it must be formatted. The formatting process prepares the diskette by setting up the tracks and sectors that DOS uses to store information and creating the disk's directory. The simplest form of the FORMAT command is

FORMAT *drive-specifier*

where *drive-specifier* determines which drive will be used to format the diskette. Note that FORMAT is an external command which must be loaded from disk. This means that you must have FORMAT on the disk that you are using. (It will be in the DOS subdirectory of your fixed disk.)

The FORMAT command requires care in its use. The reason for this is that the formatting process destroys any data that may already exist on a diskette. If you are preparing a new diskette for use, then of course, there is no data to destroy. However, if you accidentally format a diskette that contains data, that data might be lost forever. Later in this book you will learn that in some situations (and with some versions of DOS) it is possible to unformat a disk. However, this procedure is not always effective and cannot always be used. Therefore, it is best to assume that formatting a disk destroys any preexisting contents.

4

C**AUTION:** Don't format your fixed disk! Generally, the fixed disk is formatted for you and will not need to be formatted again. Doing so will destroy all files on the disk.

You will need a blank diskette in order to perform the examples in the rest of this chapter, so let's format one now. Enter

    FORMAT A:

You will then see this message:

```
Insert new diskette for drive A:
and strike ENTER when ready . . .
```

If you have a diskette in drive A, remove it and insert the blank diskette. Once the blank diskette is in the drive, press Enter. The drive will then start up and the formatting process will begin.

When the formatting process is finished, this message and prompt will be displayed:

```
Format complete.
Volume label (11 characters, ENTER for none)?
```

Versions of DOS before 4 do not display the volume label prompt.

A *volume label* is essentially a name for a disk. We will discuss volume labels later in the book, so for now, simply press [Enter]. Next, you will see something similar to this:

```
1457664 bytes total disk space
1457664 bytes available on disk

    512 bytes in each allocation unit.
   2847 allocation units available on disk.

Volume Serial Number is 112D-1701

Format another (Y/N)?_
```

Since you only need one diskette for the examples, answer the prompt with **N**.

Keep in mind that the message you see may differ from that shown. First, there are several different types of floppy drives in use in PC-compatible computers. These drives have different storage capacities. So, if the number of bytes of total or available disk space differ, do not worry about it. Another way the message may differ is if part of the floppy diskette was bad and could not be formatted. Although this is not common, you are sure to encounter it at some point. If this happens, the number of bytes of total disk space will differ from available disk space, and you will see another line that tells you the exact number of unusable bytes. In this case, it is usually best to discard the diskette and try a new one. Often a diskette that has bad sections deteriorates quickly over time.

The other parts of the FORMAT message tell you the size of each allocation unit and the number of allocation units on the disk. An *allocation unit* is a group of sectors. These numbers change with the size and type of diskette being formatted. These messages will only be displayed if you have version 5 or later of DOS.

Finally, if you are using DOS 5 or later, your diskette will be given a unique serial number. At this time, DOS does not use the serial number, but it may do so in the future.

In Chapter 9 you will learn about several FORMAT options that let you control exactly how a diskette is formatted.

An Introduction to the COPY Command

COPY is one of the most important DOS commands because it lets you make a copy of a file. The COPY command is very powerful, and we will look only at its most common use here.

The basic form of the COPY command is

COPY *source-filename destination-filename*

You might remember it more easily as:

COPY *from to*

4

In the COPY command, the destination file is also referred to as the target file.

However you think of it, the result is that the COPY command copies the contents of the first file to the second. It is possible to use the COPY command to make multiple copies of a file (but with different names, of course) on the same disk, or to copy the file to another disk. For example, the following command copies the file SORT.EXE to SORT2.EXE on the same disk.

COPY SORT.EXE SORT2.EXE

Try this now. As the COPY command begins execution, the disk drive will start up and the drive-active light will be lit. After the DOS prompt returns, give the following command:

DIR SORT*.EXE

DOS will respond with the files SORT.EXE and SORT2.EXE. Notice that the lengths and dates of the two files are the same. In fact, the only thing that differs between them is the filename—the contents of the files are exactly the same. When you make copies of an audio tape, each copy gets progressively lower in quality, but a copy of a disk file is *exactly the same as the original*. In fact, the millionth copy is still exactly the same as the original, so you need have no fear of a file degenerating through the copy process. (It is possible, of course, to have a computer failure which could cause the copy process not to work, but this is fairly rare and DOS will report it so that you can try again.)

Probably the most common use of the COPY command is to copy a file to another disk for backup purposes. In general you will always want at least two (three to four are much better) copies of important files in case one should be destroyed. Assuming you have at least two drives in your computer, to copy a file to another disk is an easy process. The COPY command allows you to specify the disk drive of both source and destination files by using their drive specifiers. For example, to copy SORT.EXE from the fixed disk to a floppy diskette, you would give the following command. (This command assumes that drive C is the current drive.)

    COPY SORT.EXE A:SORT.EXE

Here is another example. This command causes a file called SORT.EXE to be copied from the A drive to the B drive. (This command assumes that SORT.EXE is on the diskette in drive A.)

    COPY A:SORT.EXE B:SORT.EXE

TIP: If you only have one disk drive and you want to copy a file from one diskette to another, use the form of the COPY command just shown. COPY will prompt you to swap diskettes in and out of the A drive.

Frankly, the command shown to copy SORT.EXE to drive A is seldom used in practice because a shorter form exists. When the destination file is going to have the same name as the source file, only the destination drive specifier need be used—there is no need to specify the file name again. For example, this will also copy SORT.EXE to drive A:

    COPY SORT.EXE A:

In fact, the only time you need to specify a file name for the destination is when it will not be the same as the source file.

Using Wildcards with COPY

It is very common to want to copy several files from one disk to another. Although you could copy each file separately, often you can use the wildcard characters to copy several at once. To see how this works, let's begin with an example. First, if it is not already there, put the diskette that you just formatted into the A drive. Next, enter the following command:

COPY *.EXE A:

This tells DOS to copy all files with the .EXE extension to the A drive. (If you don't have sufficient room on A for all the files, don't worry; this is only an example.) During the copy process DOS prints the name of each file copied on the screen. A directory listing of the target diskette shows only files that have the .EXE extension. (Try this now.)

4

One of the first things you should notice about the command just given is that the destination file name is missing—only the drive specifier is present. As stated earlier, when you do not specify a destination file name, DOS assumes that you want the destination file to have the same name as the source file. This same principle applies to wildcard copies—each file copied to the destination disk will have the same name as it did on the source disk. It would have been perfectly valid to have given the command as COPY *.EXE A:*.EXE, but you will seldom see anyone do this because it is redundant.

TIP: You can use the ? and * wildcard characters with the COPY command in the same way you use them with the DIR command. In fact, if you are unsure as to exactly what files will be copied using a wildcard filename, first enter DIR using the same wildcard name and see what DOS reports.

If you wish to copy all the files listed in the directory of one disk to another, use the wildcard ***.***. For example, to copy the contents of the diskette in drive A to the diskette in drive B, use the following command:

COPY A:*.* B:

Although this may seem obvious, it must be stated: you cannot copy a file onto itself. That is, a command like this is invalid:

COPY TEST TEST

As a final point, if you try to copy a file that does not exist, DOS will display this message:

```
File not found
```

You should now be able to copy files between disks without any trouble. If you do not feel confident, try a number of examples before continuing. Later in this book you will learn that the COPY command has several more features and options which make it one of the most powerful DOS commands.

Creating a Short Text File

Before you can go much further in your study of DOS, you will need to have available a short text file. The method used here to create a text file is not the way you will normally create text files, but it will work for now, and it's easy. Enter the following command:

COPY CON: TEST

This is a special form of the COPY command that causes whatever you type at the keyboard to be written to the file called TEST. (Don't worry too much about this now; it is just a way to create a text file. You will learn more about COPY later in the book.) Next, enter the following lines:

This is a sample
text file.

Be sure to press Enter after the period. Now, hold down the Ctrl key and strike Z. This generates a control-Z, which tells DOS to stop the copy process. After Ctrl-Z, press the Enter key. Your screen should look like this:

```
C>COPY CON: TEST
This is a sample
text file.
^Z
        1 file(s) copied
C>
```

If you enter the command DIR TEST, you will see that TEST is in the directory and that it is 30 bytes long.

The TYPE Command

Now that you have created a text file, you can use DOS's TYPE command to display its contents on the screen. For example, try this command now:

TYPE TEST

This will display the two lines you just entered in your text file.

In general, you can use the TYPE command to list the contents of any text file on the screen. (Actually, TYPE can list any sort of file, but only text files will display meaningful information.) The sample file that you used is very short; longer text files will quickly scroll off the screen unless you stop them. You can freeze the display by using the same control keys you used for stopping the DIR command: either [Ctrl]-[S] or [Pause].

An important point to remember is that DOS has no way of knowing which files are text files. That is, as far as DOS is concerned, a file is a file, and text, data, and program files all look pretty much alike to it. It is your responsibility to remember what files are what.

Although we won't be using TYPE again for a while, you will find that in actual practice it is one of the more usual DOS commands because it lets you easily examine a file to see what's in it.

Printing a Text File on the Printer

This section assumes that you have a printer attached to your system and, further, that it is attached in the standard fashion. If this is not the case, you should still read this section, but do not try the examples. If you have a specialized printer, contact either a coworker or other knowledgeable person to find out how to print files on it.

PRINT can only print text files, not data or program files.

If you wish to make a hard copy of a text file you may do so by using the PRINT command. PRINT is an external command, so you will need to have the DOS external commands available on the current drive. The simplest form of PRINT is

PRINT *filename*

where *filename* is the name of the text file to be printed. For example, enter this command now:

PRINT TEST

Here, TEST is the file you just created. When the PRINT command begins you will see this message:

```
Name of list device [PRN]:_
```

The DOS PRINT command allows some flexibility in how a printer is hooked to your system. However, if your computer is connected in the standard way you should simply press ⟨Enter⟩. (If your computer is configured in a nonstandard way, ask a coworker how to respond to this prompt.) You will then see these messages:

```
Resident part of PRINT installed

   C:\TEST is currently being printed
```

The first message tells you that the proper part of the PRINT command that communicates with your printer is now loaded into memory. If you execute the PRINT command again, you will not see the initial prompt because DOS will remember what to do. (If the computer has been turned off, then you will, of course, have to respond to the initial prompt again.) The second message informs you that the file TEST is being printed.

You can use a drive specifier in the file name to print a file that is not on the current disk. For example, the following command prints the file TEST that is found on the B drive:

PRINT B:TEST

Although the TEST file is very short, you should notice that the DOS prompt returns before the printing has finished. The PRINT command is one of the few DOS commands that runs in *background mode*. This means that you can print a file while using the computer to do something else. This is a very convenient feature. A background task is a very simple form of *multitasking*, which essentially means that the computer is doing two (or more) things at the same time.

Cancelling a Printout

You may wish to stop the printing of a file. For example, in the middle of a long printout you may decide that you really don't need it. To cancel the PRINT command, enter

PRINT /T

The /T is an option to the PRINT command that stands for "terminate."

Printing More Than One File

It is possible to give PRINT a list of files to print. You can do this two ways. First, you can execute the PRINT command repeatedly, giving it one file at a time, or you can specify a list of files from the beginning. To see how this works, copy the file TEST into these files: TEST1, TEST2, TEST3. Now, execute this PRINT command:

PRINT TEST TEST1 TEST2 TEST3

PRINT will respond as follows:

```
C:\DOS\TEST is currently being printed
C:\DOS\TEST1 is in queue
C:\DOS\TEST2 is in queue
C:\DOS\TEST3 is in queue
```

PRINT creates a *queue,* or list, of the files you want printed and then proceeds to print them one at a time in the order they are given. Using the default setting, you may queue up to ten files.

If you decide, for example, that you need to print a file called TEST4 while the other files are still being printed, you can add it to the print queue by entering

PRINT TEST4

This will cause TEST4 to be added to the list of files to be printed.

TIP: You can see the status of the print queue by entering PRINT by itself.

Removing Files from the Print Queue

Suppose that you have just specified a list of files to be printed, and you decide that one of the files doesn't need to be printed after all. You can remove a specific file from the queue using the /C PRINT option. To remove a file from the queue use this general form:

PRINT *filename*/C

For example, to remove TEST2 from the print queue, enter

PRINT TEST2/C

When removing a file, be sure to use its full name. For example, if the file is called SAMPLE.WP, then you must enter

PRINT SAMPLE.WP/C

Also, if you used a drive specifier with the file name when it was added to the queue, you must use the same drive specifier to remove it from the queue.

If you wish to cancel all files, the easiest way is to use the /T option, which terminates the PRINT command and removes all files from the queue.

Experiment with PRINT at this time.

 ## Removing a File from a Disk

Often, you will only need a file for a short period of time, or you might put a disk to a different use and need to remove those files that no longer relate to the new use. Either way, it is a simple matter to remove a file from a disk by using the ERASE command. DOS allows a second name for ERASE called DEL, but this book will continue to use

4

ERASE—you can use whichever form you like. The general form of the ERASE command is

ERASE *filename*

where *filename* is the name of the file to be erased. It may include wildcards.

To see how this works, first execute this command:

COPY TEST TEST2

(TEST is the name of the file created in the previous section. If you have not created it, do so now; then execute COPY.) This, of course, causes DOS to make a copy of TEST called TEST2. You can verify that the copy was actually made by using the DIR command.

To erase TEST2 enter

ERASE TEST2

Verify that TEST2 is no longer present by entering

DIR TEST2

DOS will respond with,

```
File not found
```

which means that the file no longer exists on the disk.

You can erase all files in the current directory with the following command. Do *NOT* try this command!

ERASE *.*

DOS will prompt you with the message:

```
Are you sure (Y/N)?
```

If you, in fact, want to erase all the files in the current directory type **Y**; otherwise type **N**.

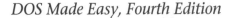

NOTE: It is important to remember that when you erase a file, you should consider it permanently and irreversibly gone. While it is possible in some circumstances to recover an erased file, several events can prevent successful recovery. Also, and very importantly, erased file recovery was not added to DOS until version 5. Therefore, if you have a version of DOS that predates version 5, you may not be able to restore an erased file under any circumstances. Later in this book, how, when, and *if* an accidentally erased file can be recovered is discussed. But for now, it is best to be very careful about the files that you erase.

Changing a File's Name

You can change the name of a file with the RENAME command. DOS allows a short form of this command called REN. This book will continue to use RENAME to avoid confusion. The general form of the command is

RENAME *old-name new-name*

You can use RENAME to alter any part of the file's name, including the extension.

As a first example, try the following command. (This assumes that you have the file TEST on the current disk.)

RENAME TEST RALPH

Once the DOS prompt returns, execute the DIR command. You will see that the file TEST is no longer in the directory, but the one called RALPH is. By using the TYPE command to look at the contents of RALPH, you can be assured that the contents of the file are the same; only the name has changed.

Since RALPH is a pretty silly name for a file, use RENAME to change it to SAMPLE.TXT by entering this command:

RENAME RALPH SAMPLE.TXT

You can use drive specifiers with the RENAME command. For example, this changes the name of the file TEST to OLDTEST on the B drive:

RENAME B:TEST B:OLDTEST

If you try to rename a file to a file name that already exists, or if you try to rename a file that does not exist, DOS will respond with the message:

```
Duplicate file name or file not found
```

Cancelling a Command

Sometimes you will enter a command, change your mind, and want to cancel the command. Many, but not all, DOS commands can be cancelled by pressing the [Ctrl]-[C] or [Ctrl]-[Break] key. For many purposes [Ctrl]-[C] and [Ctrl]-[Break] are equivalent, but in some situations [Ctrl]-[Break] is a little "stronger." For this reason, it is a good idea to get used to using it. To try cancelling a command, execute DIR and then press [Ctrl]-[Break] before the directory listing has finished. As soon as you press the [Ctrl]-[Break] key, the screen will display a ^C (short for cancel) and the DOS prompt will return. Try this now.

As stated, not all DOS commands can be cancelled in this way. For example, because the PRINT command runs as a background task, you must use the the /T option to stop it. Also, most commands cannot be cancelled "midstream," so to speak. That is, most DOS commands have a point of no return. After this point, it is not possible to stop the command from proceeding. For example, once the RENAME command has begun to actually change a file's name, it cannot be cancelled until it is done. In more technical language, most DOS commands have a *critical section* that, once entered, cannot be aborted because doing so would corrupt the structure of the disk. You don't need to worry about destroying anything by trying to cancel a command, because DOS will not let you cancel at an inappropriate time.

Summary

In this chapter you learned

✦ How to more fully utilize DIR

✦ About wildcard file names

✦ How to freeze the display

✦ How drive specifiers work

✦ About clearing and printing the screen

✦ How to format a diskette

✦ How to copy files

✦ About displaying and printing files

✦ How to erase files and cancel commands

In the next chapter you will learn more DOS commands.

PART

2

USING DOS

C H A P T E R

≈MADE EASY≈

5
MORE USEFUL DOS COMMANDS

This chapter presents some more useful DOS commands. Also, some of the commands introduced in the preceding chapters will be examined more closely. The chapter begins by explaining how you can receive a synopsis of any DOS command.

NOTE: Make sure that the DOS subdirectory is current. If necessary, switch to it using the procedure described at the start of Chapter 4.

Obtaining Online Help

If you are using version 5 of DOS or later, then you can receive online help about any DOS command. (In this context, *online* means that your computer can give you information.) To obtain a synopsis of any DOS command, enter the name of the command followed by the /? option. Doing this will cause a brief description of the command and its options to be displayed, but the command will not execute. For example, to receive help on CHKDSK, enter this command:

CHKDSK /?

While the information displayed is no substitute for a good working knowledge of the command, it can help jog your memory when trying to remember a specific option or usage. As you proceed in your learning about DOS, you may find the help information useful.

NOTE: Beginning with DOS 6, a more extensive online help system is provided. This system is discussed later in this book.

Checking the Diskette Using CHKDSK

Whether it is a floppy diskette or the fixed disk drive, the state of the magnetic medium that holds your information is of crucial importance. Aside from obvious physical damage, it is impossible to determine if the information on a diskette is valid simply by looking at. To help verify that the magnetic information on the disk is correct requires the use of a computer and the special command CHKDSK. CHKDSK gives you a status report on your disk. CHKDSK is an external command, so you will need to have a copy of it on the disk that is in the current drive. To execute the simplest form of this command simply enter **CHKDSK** at the DOS prompt and press Enter. For example, your command line should look like this:

```
C>CHKDSK
```

This command produces output similar to that shown in Figure 5-1.

Hidden files are not normally visible in a directory listing.

As you can see, the CHKDSK command reports the number of bytes of total disk space, the number of bytes used by DOS's hidden files, the number of bytes used by the disk directory structure, the number of bytes in user (accessible) files, and the amount of storage still available on the diskette. The hidden files are special files that do not show up in the directory listing. (DOS uses some hidden files and so do some application programs.) Hidden files are not meant to be directly used by you. The term *user files* essentially means those files which you can see and manipulate. If there are parts of the disk that were marked as damaged and unusable when the disk was formatted, then the number of bytes lost to this damage will also be reported.

CHKDSK reports the size (in bytes) of each allocation unit, the number of allocation units on a disk, and the number of unused units. (This information is only reported when using newer versions of DOS.) As you may recall from the previous chapter, an allocation unit is simply a

5

```
Volume CDISK        created 11-19-1992 9:04a
Volume Serial Number is 1993-712A

33454080 bytes total disk space
   86016 bytes in 5 hidden files
  116736 bytes in 46 directories
31287296 bytes in 1305 user files
 1964032 bytes available on disk

    2048 bytes in each allocation unit
   16335 total allocation units on disk
     959 available allocation units on disk

  655360 total bytes memory
  605344 bytes free
```

Sample output from the CHKDSK command
Figure 5-1.

An allocation unit is a group of sectors and is also called a cluster.

group of sectors that are all in one track. (An allocation unit is also called a *cluster*.) DOS allocates space on the disk for a file one allocation unit at a time.

CHKDSK also reports both the total system memory and the amount of free memory. The difference between the total free memory and the total system memory is the amount of memory used by DOS and any other programs that may be resident in memory. CHKDSK will also report the disk volume label, if defined, and the serial number, if present.

Disk Errors

Ignoring actual physical damage, a disk may become partially unusable for two reasons. First, an application program could have a bug in it that causes that part of the disk to become "detached" from the directory. Second, a system fault or unplanned power loss may cause the links between the sectors that hold a file to contain incorrect values. In most cases, these types of errors can be detected and corrected by CHKDSK—although information may be lost. In CHKDSK's default mode shown earlier, errors will be detected, but not corrected. In order to make CHKDSK correct errors, you need to use the /F (fix) option after the CHKDSK command. For example, the following command will cause any error detected to be fixed (if possible).

    CHKDSK /F

One of the most common errors you will encounter is reported with this message:

```
X lost allocation units found in Y chains.
Convert lost chains to files (Y/N)?
```

X is the number of lost allocation units and *Y* is the number of chains. You should recall from Chapter 3 that DOS organizes files into sectors. As stated earlier, an allocation unit is a group of sectors that are all in one track. A *chain* is a group of allocation units. If an allocation unit becomes disassociated from the directory, then it is said to be lost because DOS no longer knows what file it belongs to. What CHKDSK does with this space is up to you. If you answer Yes to the question, then new files composed of the lost allocation units will be created. They will be called by file names of this form: FILE*num*.CHK, where *num* is the number of the file. The files will be numbered 0 through 9999. In theory, you can examine these files to determine if they contain useful information; if they do not, erase them. In practice, however, these files seldom contain information that is usable and, even if they do, in most cases you won't know it simply by looking at the file. For these reasons, you should generally answer No to the prompt. CHKDSK will then free the space for future use.

NOTE: DOS versions prior to 5 called allocation units clusters. Therefore, for early versions of DOS, the term *cluster* will be substituted for *allocation unit* in the preceding CHKDSK message.

5

It is a good idea to run CHKDSK frequently to make sure that the disk is in good working condition. Once a day is normally sufficient unless you have reason to suspect that an error has occurred. Remember, CHKDSK can clean up certain types of disk errors, but it can do nothing to help a disk that has been physically damaged.

Backing Up a Diskette

Just as you made a backup copy of the DOS master diskette in Chapter 2, you can make backup copies of any diskette using DISKCOPY. The general form of DISKCOPY is

DISKCOPY *source-drive destination-drive*

For example, to copy the contents of the diskette in A to the one in B enter

DISKCOPY A: B:

If the destination diskette is not formatted, DISKCOPY will format it prior to copying the source diskette. The formatting process does increase the time it takes to copy a diskette, however, so it is an advantage to have a number of formatted diskettes on hand.

If you have only one floppy drive, use this form of the DISKCOPY command:

DISKCOPY A: A:

When using only one drive, DISKCOPY will prompt you to swap diskettes as necessary.

DISKCOPY may not be used to copy to or from the fixed disk or to copy the fixed disk.

As has been stated earlier in this book, there are several different types of diskettes and disk drives in use, all of which have different storage capacities. The general rule for applying DISKCOPY is that the source and destination disks must have the same storage capacity and be of the same size. If this is not the case, DOS will issue an error message. Generally, you need not worry when you are simply backing up diskettes which were created on the system that is performing the backup.

It is important to understand that DISKCOPY creates an exact copy of the source diskette. That is, sector by sector, the source diskette and the destination diskette will be exactly the same. On the other hand, executing a COPY *.* command will copy all the user files, but the resulting destination diskette, although containing the same files, will not be an exact duplicate of the original. Most of the time this difference does not matter, but later in this book you will see that there are some special situations which will cause one method of copying the contents of a diskette more desirable than the other. For now, however, when you want to copy an entire diskette you should use DISKCOPY.

Although a number of things can go wrong during the disk copying process, fortunately they seldom do. However, if an error does occur, your course of action is determined by the nature of the error. If DISKCOPY reports an error *reading* the source diskette, you should abort DISKCOPY and try a different diskette, if a duplicate is available. If a duplicate diskette is not available, try removing the source diskette from the drive and reinserting it. Sometimes, a diskette is simply misaligned in the drive. As a last resort, tell DOS to ignore the error and continue. This may lead to the loss of data, however. If DISKCOPY reports an error *formatting* or *writing* the destination diskette, start over again with a new target diskette.

TIP: DISKCOPY has the /1 option that causes it to copy only side one of a diskette even if the diskette is double-sided. Using both sides of a diskette effectively doubles the storage capacity. Virtually all disk drives in service today are double-sided, but the original drives issued when the first IBM PCs came out were single-sided. You will use the /1 option only when you need to copy an old type of diskette to one of the more common double-sided variety.

5

If you purchase a program, there is a possibility that the diskette it comes on will be copy-protected. Copy protection was commonly done to prevent the unauthorized duplication of programs. However, it has fallen out of general use because it is such an annoyance to the honest user. Keep in mind that, generally, you cannot use DISKCOPY to copy a copy-protected diskette.

Although DISKCOPY seldom fails to copy a diskette correctly, you can add an extra measure of assurance by specifying the /V option. This option verifies the copy against the original during the copy process. Verifying slows DISKCOPY and, except for the most important diskettes, is seldom used.

When to Back Up Diskettes

Although you are new to DOS, it is never too early to learn about the importance of backing up diskettes. When you made the backup of the DOS system master in Chapter 2, it was to protect the original from harm. This concept can be generalized. Whenever you have valuable data on a diskette, you should make one (or more) copies in case the original diskette is lost, destroyed, or accidentally erased.

Most computer professionals, such as programmers, systems analysts, and maintenance personnel, recommend a system of rotating backups. In this method, you create one master diskette and two backup diskettes: a primary backup and a secondary backup. At the end of each work period in which the master diskette is altered, it is copied to the primary backup diskette. Periodically—weekly, for example, the master

The best way to protect data is to establish and adhere to a rigid backup procedure.

diskette is copied to the secondary backup diskette. Finally, occasionally—such as monthly—the secondary diskette is "retired" and put in a safe place. A new secondary backup diskette is then created. In this way you reduce the chances of losing important information. Later in this book, we will look at backup and protection of diskettes in greater detail.

Comparing Two Files

From time to time you may find yourself in the position of being unsure whether two files on different diskettes but with the same name are, indeed, the same file. For example, imagine that you have an inventory program that creates and maintains a file called INV.DAT. If you have two copies of this file, how do you know that they both contain the same information? Another situation that can arise is when you suspect that two files with different names may actually be the same file. How can this be determined? Finally, sometimes you will want to be sure that a file has, indeed, been accurately copied. How can you be sure that the destination file is 100 percent the same as the source file? These are not trivial questions because your data is only as good as your confidence in it. Although you can use the TYPE or PRINT command to visually compare text files, other types of files do not lend themselves to this sort of manual inspection. (Also, visual inspection is not a reliable way of comparing large files.) One way to be sure that two files are the same is to use the COMP file comparison command. COMP is an external command.

COMP may not be included if you are using DOS version 6. If this is the case, refer to the FC command in Chapter 17.

So that you can work along with the examples, execute the following command:

    COPY TEST TEST2

Remember, TEST is the text file created in the previous chapter. (If you did not create it, do so now.)

There are two ways to execute COMP; one is to simply enter **COMP**. You will then be prompted for the two files to compare. For a first example, let's compare the files TEST and TEST2. The first prompt is

```
Name of first file to compare:
```

Respond with **TEST**. Next you will see the prompt:

```
Name of second file to compare:
```

Respond with **TEST2**. Next, you will be prompted for an option. At this time no option is needed, so simply press ⌷Enter⌷. COMP will then compare the files. Since the files are the same, they will compare as such and you will see this message and prompt:

```
Comparing TEST and TEST2...
Files compare OK

Compare more files (Y/N)?_
```

At this point answer No. As you would expect, since the two files are identical, COMP finds them to be the same. It reports this by printing the message "Files compare OK." Shortly, you will see what happens when the files differ.

Tɪᴘ: There is no special significance to which file is specified first and which is second. The outcome of the comparison will be the same.

For older versions of DOS, the messages prompting for the files to compare will refer to the first file as the "primary file" and the second file as the "2nd file." It doesn't matter which file is which.

Using the Command Line

A much easier way to invoke the COMP command is to place the two files to be compared on the command line after the COMP command. For example, to compare TEST and TEST2, your command line would look like this:

```
C>COMP TEST TEST2
```

5

This form of the command does not prompt you for the file names; it simply performs the comparison.

Keep in mind one thing: when you use the command line form of the command, the files you are comparing must be on disks that are already mounted in the drives because the comparison operation begins immediately. If you must switch diskettes, for example, use the other form of COMP which prompts you for the file names. This will give you a chance to insert the proper diskettes.

A Comparison with Differences

To see a comparison of two files that differ, enter this command:

    COMP TEST SORT.EXE

You will see the message "Files are different sizes," and no comparison will take place. The COMP command will not compare files that have different sizes because it assumes (rightly) that different-sized files cannot be the same.

In order to see what happens when two files of the same length differ, we will need to create a new file that is the same length as the TEST file, but different in content. To do this, enter the following:

    COPY CON: TEST3
    This is a simple
    test file.
    ^Z

If you remember, TEST holds the sentence "This is a sample text file.", so TEST3 will differ from TEST with the *i* in "simple" and the *s* in "test." Now, try this command:

    COMP TEST TEST3

You will see the following output:

```
Compare error at OFFSET B
File 1 = 61
File 2 = 69
Compare error at OFFSET 14
File 1 = 78
File 2 = 73
```

This rather odd-looking output is telling you that the two files differ in bytes number 11 and 20. Although hard to believe, it further reports that TEST has an *a* where TEST3 has an *i* and an *x* where TEST3 has an *s*. For rather murky reasons, the COMP command reports the position and contents of bytes that differ in hexadecimal. *Hexadecimal* is a number system based on 16—a number that computers like. Our common-usage number system is based on 10. The hexadecimal digits are the standard digits 0 through 9 plus the letters *A* through *F*, which correspond to 10 through 15. Therefore, the number 10 in hexadecimal is 16 in decimal. The number 1A in hexadecimal is 26 in decimal. The message "Compare error at OFFSET B" means that there was a difference between the two files at character number 11. COMP reports the characters at the point of difference using the computer's internal code to represent the character set. For example, the 61 is the code for the letter *a* (97 in decimal) and 69 (105 in decimal) is the code for the letter *i*. Frankly, unless you intend to become a programmer, it isn't worth worrying about hexadecimal or the character codes at all. What is really important is that the two files differ—it doesn't generally matter how they differ.

Although the COMP command uses the term *error* when the two files differ, this is really not a proper usage of the word. Remember, just because two files are not the same does not mean that one is in error—it just means that they are different. It is certainly possible that the files differ because of an error, but it is not the only, nor most likely, reason.

Comparing Files on Separate Diskettes

It is very easy to compare a file on one disk to one on another disk. Just use drive specifiers before the file names. For example, to compare the file TEST on the fixed disk to the file TEST on a floppy disk in drive A, you would use this command:

COMP C:TEST A:TEST

However, because both file names are the same except for the drive specifier, you can shorten this command to

COMP C:TEST A:

Of course, if the files are called by different names, you must fully specify both.

Some COMP Options

As you just saw, by default COMP displays any differences between two files in hexadecimal. However, if you use the /D option, the differences will be displayed in decimal. Although decimal is an improvement over hexadecimal, COMP can still behave more rationally. If you specify the /A option, then any differences are shown using the actual letters—not numbers. However, you should only use the /A option on text files.

You can have COMP tell you the line number of each line that contains a discrepancy by using the /L option. This option can be used only on text files.

By default, COMP considers upper- and lowercase letters to be different. However, by using the /C option, COMP will ignore case differences. That is, an uppercase *C* and a lowercase *c* will match. This option can be used only on text files.

Finally, you can have COMP compare only the first part of two files by using the /N option, which has this general form:

COMP *file1 file2* /N:*num*

Here, *num* is the number of lines to compare. This option only makes sense on text files.

The COMP options can be used on the command line, or they can be entered when COMP prompts for options when no files are specified on the command line.

Remember, COMP may not be included if you are using DOS 6.

A COPY Option

It is possible to have COPY automatically verify that the file it has just copied is exactly the same as the original without having to actually use the COMP command. Although it is quite rare, occasionally a file copy will not be successful. This can happen for several reasons. By far the most common is a transient power loss or fluctuation which causes the disk drive to temporarily write incorrect data. To guard against this sort of trouble, you can tell COPY to verify the destination file against the original file as the copy process proceeds. This will cause COPY to take longer, but on very important files this extra time is worth it.

To tell COPY to verify the destination file you use the /V option. This option follows the rest of the command. For example, to copy with verification the file SORT.EXE to the A drive, your command line will look like this:

```
C>COPY SORT.EXE A: /V
```

Comparing Diskettes

In some situations it may be easier to compare an entire diskette rather than individual files. For example, if you back up your data diskettes using DISKCOPY, then to determine if the files on a backup diskette are up-to-date with the original you must compare all files on the diskette. This can be tedious if there are several files. To solve this problem, DOS provides the DISKCOMP command, which compares two diskettes for equality.

By far the easiest way to compare two diskettes is if you have two disk drives, in which case you enter this form of the DISKCOMP command:

DISKCOMP A: B:

You will then be prompted to insert the two diskettes you wish to compare into the drives.

If you only have one floppy drive, use this form of the command:

DISKCOMP A: A:

You will then be prompted to insert the first diskette into drive A. As DISKCOMP runs, it will prompt you to swap diskettes.

If the two diskettes are identical, DISKCOMP will display the message "Compare OK." If there are differences, DISKCOMP reports the side and track in which the difference occurs. Frankly, knowing the side and track is not too meaningful (except occasionally to programmers). Generally, all you want to know is whether the diskettes are the same or not, so you can ignore the side and track information.

Just as two files of different sizes cannot be compared using COMP, two diskettes of different capacity cannot be compared using DISKCOMP. As has been mentioned, there are several different types of disk drives in current use. The smallest capacity diskette holds about 160,000 bytes while the larger ones hold a megabyte or more. Generally, diskettes formatted and used on the same computer will be of the same size, so this is not often a problem when comparing diskettes. However, be prepared for this trouble when trying to compare diskettes created on different computers.

NOTE: It is important to keep in mind that it is not possible to compare the fixed disk. Even if you have two fixed disks in your system, they cannot be compared.

One particularly good use for DISKCOMP is to verify that a DISKCOPY successfully copied the contents of an important diskette. Although DISKCOPY contains its own error checking, if the data on a backup diskette is extremely important, executing DISKCOMP using the original diskette and the copy is a very good idea—if for nothing else than peace of mind.

DATE and TIME

As you are probably aware, your computer contains a clock that keeps track of the time and date while it is on, and most computers today also maintain the time even when the computer is turned off. However, depending upon your computer, you might need to reset the time and date each time you turn on the computer. Also, for one reason or another, the date or the time of the system may not be correct and you may need to reset them. For example, you or a coworker may have

altered the time or date. Or, a program malfunction may have changed
the time or date of the system. To solve these problems, DOS provides
the TIME and DATE commands, which set the time or date,
respectively. To execute either command, simply enter its name.

NOTE: As mentioned in Chapter 2, if your computer automatically
prompts you for the date and time when you turn it on, it uses the
DATE and TIME commands to accomplish this.

5

The DATE command first displays the current system date and then
prompts you for a new date. You can just press Enter if you do not wish
to change the date after all. Otherwise, enter the correct date using
digits in the format shown when the date is displayed. If you live in the
U.S., enter the date using the format month-day-year. If you live in
another country, enter the date using the form common to your
country. Separate the parts of the date using the dash.

You can also specify the new date on the command line after the DATE
command. If you do this, you will not be prompted for the date. For
example, this command sets the date to January 1, 1994:

        DATE 01-01-94

To set the time, enter **TIME**. The TIME command displays the current
system time and then prompts you for a new time. If you wish to leave
the time unchanged, simply press Enter. DOS displays the time using
the normal 12-hour clock, with *a* for a.m. and *p* for p.m. Versions of
DOS beginning with 5 allow you to enter the time using either a
24-hour or 12-hour method. When using the 12-hour method, for
times after 12 noon, enter **p** or **pm** on the end of the time you enter.
For example, enter 2:45 in the afternoon as **2:45p**. Without the *p* or
pm, DOS assumes that the time you enter is a.m. If you use the 24-hour
approach, then hours after 12 noon range from 13 to 24. This means,
for example, that you enter **9** for 9:00 a.m., **13** for 1:00 p.m., **14** for
2:00 p.m., and so on.

REMEMBER: Older versions of DOS require that you enter the time using a 24-hour clock.

To enter the correct time, separate the hours, minutes, and seconds using a colon. (Technically, both the seconds and minutes are optional.) When you have entered the correct time, press Enter.

TIP: To obtain the current time or date, use the TIME or DATE command, but don't reset the time or date.

DOS Editing Keys

Up to this point, when you made a mistake while typing a command you used the Backspace key to back up to the error and then retyped the rest of the line. Also, if you wished to reexecute a command, you retyped it. In this section you will learn how to use some special keys that will make the entry of DOS commands a little easier. These special keys are called *editing keys* because they allow you to edit (make changes to) what you type on the command line.

Fundamental to using the editing keys is the concept of the input buffer. The *input buffer* is a small region of memory that is used by DOS to hold the commands that you enter from the keyboard. The important thing to understand is that the input buffer will contain the last command that you typed until you enter a new one. This fact lets you reuse, alter, or fix the immediately preceding command through the use of the DOS editing keys. The DOS editing keys and a synopsis of their functions are shown in Table 5-1. Let's look at each in turn.

NOTE: For the remainder of this section, disregard the "Bad command or file name" error message. Some of the examples will send DOS unknown commands. This will hurt nothing, but it will cause an error message to be displayed.

Key	Function
F1	Redisplays one character from the input buffer each time it is pressed
F2	Redisplays all characters up to, but not including, a specified character in the input buffer
F3	Redisplays all characters in the input buffer
F4	Deletes all characters up to, but not including, a specified character from the input buffer
F5	Reedits the line you just typed
Del	Deletes a character from the input buffer
Esc	Cancels the current line just typed prior to pressing Enter
Ins	Inserts the next character typed at the current location in the input buffer

DOS Editing Keys
Table 5-1.

5

The F1 Key

At the DOS prompt, enter the following sequence of characters:
123456789. Be sure to press Enter. Doing this loads the DOS input
buffer with "123456789". Once the DOS prompt returns, press the F1
key three times. Your command line will look like this:

```
C>123
```

As is obvious from the example, the F1 key redisplays one character at
a time from the input buffer. Continue to press the F1 key until the 9
appears. At this point pressing F1 again has no effect because you have
reached the end of the buffer. (DOS does not store the Enter key in the
buffer.) Press Enter now.

The F2 Key

The F2 key redisplays all characters in the input buffer up to the
character that you specify. To use the F2 command, you first press F2

and then the character. For example, if you press F2 followed by a 6, the command line will look like this:

```
C>12345
```

Try this now. DOS has redisplayed all characters up to the 6. At this time press F1 until the 9 is redisplayed and then press Enter.

The F3 Key

Probably the most useful editing key is F3 because it redisplays the entire input buffer. This is especially nice because it lets you reexecute the previous command without retyping it. Press F3 at this time. The command line will look like this:

```
C>123456789
```

Do not press Enter.

The Esc Key

At this point, the cursor should be immediately following the 9 on the command line. Press Esc now. As you can see, DOS prints a \ (backslash) and positions the cursor directly under the 1. The command line will look like this:

```
C>123456789\
  —
```

The Esc key cancels whatever is on the command line. DOS uses the \ to indicate this cancellation. The DOS prompt is not redisplayed, but the cursor is placed directly under the location it occupied when the prompt was present.

After cancelling a command with Esc you may still use all the editing keys to redisplay or change the previous command. For example, type F3 followed by Enter at this time.

The [Del] Key

If you wish to delete a character from the input buffer use the [Del] key. Each time you press it, a character will be deleted. You will not see the characters you delete, so use this key with caution. By way of example, press [Del] three times and then press the [F3] key. The command line will look like this:

```
C>456789
```

If you press [Esc] prior to pressing [Enter] you can cancel the effects of the [Del] key. Press [Esc] followed by [F3] and [Enter] now.

5

Using [F4] to Delete Several Characters

If you wish to delete several characters the [F4] key is for you. It is somewhat similar to the [F2] key in that you first press [F4] and then a character. DOS will then delete all characters from the current position up to but not including the character you typed. For example, press [F4], then [4], and then [F3]. The command line will look like this:

```
C>456789
```

Keep in mind that nothing is displayed when you use the [F4] command, so it is easy to forget what you have deleted. Use [F4] with caution.

The [Ins] Key

At the DOS prompt enter this line: **This a test.** Assume, for the sake of example, that you wished to enter "This is a test." You can correct the command by first using [F1] to position the cursor after the space that follows "This", pressing [Ins], typing "is ", and then pressing [F3]. When you press the [Ins] key, DOS lets you insert any number of characters at that point without overwriting what is already in the buffer. You should try some examples of this process.

The F5 Key

All the other editing keys let you manipulate the command that is already in the input buffer. Let's suppose, however, that you began typing a new command and made a mistake. By pressing the F5 key, you will cause DOS to load the input buffer with what you just typed—giving you a chance to correct it—without executing it.

Some More DIR Options

Before concluding this chapter, let's take another look at the DIR command. For versions of DOS beginning with 5, DIR has several options that greatly increase its power. First, DIR can sort the directory listing several different ways. Second, it can display only those files that meet a set of attributes that you specify. Third, you can have greater control over how DIR displays files on the screen. These options are examined here.

Sorting the Directory Using DIR

By default, when you issue the DIR command, the directory is displayed in the order in which the files occur on the disk. However, using the /O option, you can have DIR sort the directory a number of different ways. The /O option takes this general form:

/O:*order*

The value of *order* determines how the /O command sorts the directory. The values of *order* are shown here:

Order	Sort By
C	Compression ratio (requires DOS 6)
–C	Reverse order by compression ratio (requires DOS 6)
D	Date and time
–D	Reverse order by date and time
E	Extension

Order	Sort By
–E	Reverse order by extension
G	Display directories before files
–G	Display directories after files
N	Filename
–N	Reverse order by filename
S	Size
–S	Reverse order by size

5

For example, this command displays the directory sorted by name in reverse order:

DIR /O:–N

This example first displays all files and then any subdirectories:

DIR /O:–G

You should try various combinations of the /O option at this time. Keep in mind that all /O options are mutually exclusive. (That is, you can only use one /O option at a time.)

REMEMBER: The C option applies only to DOS version 6.

If you want to see files that have only certain attributes, use the /A option. It takes this general form:

/A:*attr*

Here, *attr* must be any combination of the following.

Attr	Files Listed
A	Files with archive attribute on
–A	Files with archive attribute off
D	Directories only
–D	Files only
H	Hidden files
–H	Non-hidden files
R	Read-only files
–R	Non-read-only files
S	System
–S	Non-system

This command displays all system files:

DIR /A:S

This command displays all read-only files that are also hidden:

DIR /A:RH

REMEMBER: Typically, hidden files are files that don't show in a directory listing. However, using the /H option, you can see the hidden files. (Hidden files are often special files used by DOS and not intended to be used by you. So, it is best to leave them alone.)

Changing the Way DIR Displays Files

DIR has two options that affect the way files are displayed on the screen. First, you can cause only the file names and extensions to be displayed without any further information, by specifying the /B option. Using this option, file names are displayed with a period separating the filename and the extension. You might find this option useful as you become more experienced with DOS.

You can display DIR's output in lowercase using /L.

TIP: you can use the /B and /L option together to produce a list of files that is in lowercase and that has a period separating the filename and the extension.

Summary

In this chapter you learned

◆ How to receive help information about a DOS command

◆ How to check a disk using CHKDSK

◆ How to back up a diskette

◆ How to compare files and diskettes

◆ How to verify files when they are copied

◆ About the TIME and DATE commands

◆ About the DOS editing keys

◆ About several options to DIR

In the next chapter you will learn more about DOS's directory structure and subdirectories.

5

CHAPTER

6

SUBDIRECTORIES

For the first five chapters of this book the directory of a disk has been largely taken for granted. However, the directory structure is very important because it governs how files are organized. Up to this point, you have only had a partial view of how the DOS directory works. We have talked about the directory in the singular, as if each disk could only have one directory. In actuality, a disk may contain several directories, where each directory contains a group of related files. In this chapter you will learn how to create, utilize, and maintain directories.

In order to follow along with the examples, format a fresh diskette now.

Root and Subdirectories

DOS organizes a disk's directory into a system. This system consists of a *root* directory and possibly one or more *subdirectories*. Combined, they organize the files on your disk.

The root directory exists on all disks.

The root directory is the only directory that is guaranteed to be found on a disk. The root directory is created by the formatting process. The root directory is the default directory if no other directories are specified. You will see how to specify other directories later in this chapter.

It is possible to define subdirectories to the root directory. A *subdirectory* is more or less a directory within a directory. You can think of the root directory as enclosing the subdirectory. A subdirectory usually holds a group of related files. The exact nature of the relationship is purely subjective. For example, a subdirectory could hold all of a certain employee's files—no matter how divergent in purpose and use those files are. Another subdirectory might hold wage information for all the employees of a company. The point is that DOS doesn't know—or care—how the files are related; it simply treats a subdirectory as a group.

It is possible, indeed common, for a subdirectory to have its own subdirectories. In fact, assuming there is sufficient disk space, any directory can contain a subdirectory.

You can think of the root directory as being a filing cabinet with each drawer labeled and used for its own specific purpose. The drawers can be thought of as subdirectories. Each drawer (subdirectory) is enclosed by the cabinet (root). Within each drawer, the files can be further organized by topic. This is analogous to a subdirectory within a subdirectory.

It is important to understand that a subdirectory is simply a term used to describe a relationship between two directories. The directory that encloses a subdirectory is called the *parent directory*. The only directory that does not have a parent is the root. Throughout this chapter and the rest of the book, unless specific clarification is required, the term *directory* will refer to any type of directory—root or subdirectory.

NOTE: If you had to switch to the DOS directory, as described in Chapter 4, to have access to the DOS external commands, then you have already been using a subdirectory. Versions of DOS beginning with 4, automatically store their external commands in the DOS subdirectory.

Directories Are Tree Structured

The disk directory structure used by DOS is called *tree structured* because, when drawn in a diagram on paper, the root and subdirectories resemble the root system of a tree. For example, the directory structure of a disk that is used by a small hypothetical insurance office may look like that shown (conceptually) in Figure 6-1.

In Figure 6-1, the root directory contains three subdirectories: Word Processing, Accounting, and Games. In turn, Word Proccessing contains two subdirectories of its own: Form Letters and Temporary Letters. The Accounting subdirectory contains three subdirectories: A/R, A/P, and G/L. The Games subdirectory has no further subdirectories.

6

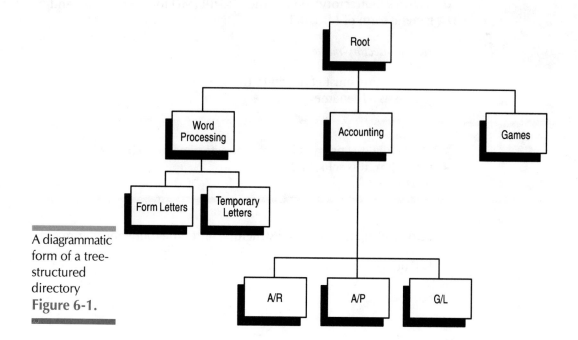

A diagrammatic form of a tree-structured directory
Figure 6-1.

The way that DOS structures directories is sometimes referred to as hierarchical.

The theory and rationale behind tree-structured directories is that related groups of files can be treated as units of increasing specialization. For example, from the root, the directory for word processing is created because word processing is a logically separate task from accounting and games. However, within word processing, there are two main types of documents: reusable form letters and disposable one-time correspondence. As you move down the tree from the root, each directory becomes more specialized in what it contains.

Creating Subdirectories

Before going much further in our discussion of subdirectories it is important to create actual examples that you can work with. It is strongly recommended that you be at your computer and work along with the examples in order to gain the fullest understanding. Place a newly formatted diskette in drive A and switch to drive A at this time.

In this section, you will create a disk directory structure that implements the conceptual version shown in Figure 6-1.

To create a subdirectory you use the MKDIR (MD for short) command. The general form of MKDIR is

MKDIR *directory-name*

A directory name must conform to the same conventions and restrictions as a filename.

TIP: While it is permissible for a directory name to be given an extension, it is seldom done.

To begin creating the directory structure, enter the following command:

MKDIR WP

Here, WP is short for word processing, which is too long to be a directory name. Once the prompt returns, enter **DIR** You will see that the only entry looks like this:

```
WP        <DIR>      11-12-93    2:58p
```

(Of course, your date and time will be different.) The <DIR> signifies that WP is a directory rather than a file. Keep in mind that you are still in the root directory.

Before moving on, create the other two directories that branch off the root. Enter these two commands:

MKDIR ACCOUNTS
MKDIR GAMES

Here, ACCOUNTS is short for accounting. You might want to list the directory again, just to see the effect of these commands.

Changing Directories

Now that you have created three subdirectories it is time to see how to activate one. The CHDIR (CD for short) command is used to change the current directory. Just as you can change the current drive, you can change the current directory. For example, to make the WP directory current, enter

CD WP

Try this now. (When a short form of a command exists, this book generally uses the long form to avoid confusion. However, since CD is used almost universally over CHDIR, it will also be the form used in this book.)

Once the prompt returns, list the directory. You will see the following display:

```
Directory of A:\WP

.        <DIR>      11-12-93    2:58p
..       <DIR>      11-12-93    2:58p
```

6

Let's take a close look at this. One of the first things you should notice is that the directory name is shown in the line that reads "Directory of A:\WP". If you recall, when you list the root directory, only the backslash is displayed. In DOS, the backslash is used to represent the root directory, which has no name. The combination \WP specifies a *path* to the WP directory. That is, begin at the root and then go to WP. You will learn more about paths a little later.

The two directory entries are represented in DOS shorthand. The single period is shorthand for the current directory and the two periods represent the parent directory—which in this case is the root directory. For example, if you enter

DIR ..

the root directory will be displayed. Typing

DIR .

lists the current subdirectory. Remember, to list the current directory (subdirectory or root) you can simply enter **DIR**. The period is redundant.

REMEMBER: The .. represents the parent directory and the . represents the current directory.

Creating Subdirectories Inside a Subdirectory

You create a subdirectory inside a subdirectory in exactly the same way that you created a subdirectory from the root. Let's create the two subdirectories to WP at this time. Enter the following commands and then list the directory.

MKDIR FORMLET
MKDIR TEMP

In our imaginary insurance office, FORMLET will be used to store form letters while TEMP will hold correspondence that will only be in the system a short period of time. A directory listing will now look like this.

```
Directory of A:\WP

.           <DIR>      11-12-93   2:58p
..          <DIR>      11-12-93   2:58p
FORMLET     <DIR>      11-12-93   3:20p
TEMP        <DIR>      11-12-93   3:21p
```

(Again, the date and time will differ.)

Switch to the FORMLET directory by entering

CD FORMLET

As you can see, you switch to a subdirectory of a subdirectory exactly like you switch to a subdirectory off the root.

Next, list the directory. The directory line will now look like this:

```
Directory of A:\WP\FORMLET
```

As you might guess, \WP\FORMLET specifies the path to the FORMLET directory. It is interpreted like this: Start at the root and go to the WP directory; from the WP directory go to the FORMLET directory. This path is shown in Figure 6-2.

Before continuing, you will need to create a short text file in the FORMLET directory. To do this, execute COPY as shown here. (In the next chapter you will learn how to use DOS's text editor, which will make the creation of text files easier.)

```
COPY CON: SAMPLE
```

Next, enter the following lines, followed by Ctrl-Z to terminate the input process.

The summer soldier,
The sunshine patriot

^Z

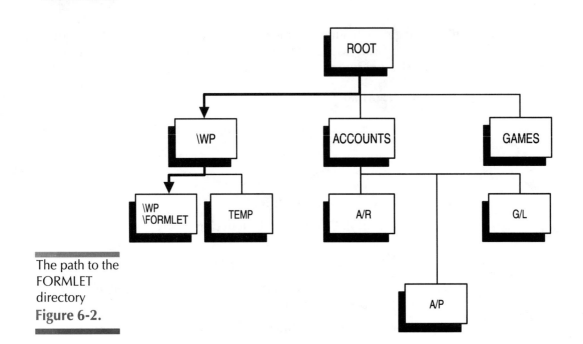

The path to the
FORMLET
directory
Figure 6-2.

Returning to the Parent Directory

There are two ways to move from a subdirectory to its parent. The first, and by far the most common, is to issue this command:

CD ..

Since the two periods are shorthand for the parent directory's name, this works no matter what the parent directory is called.

The second way to return to the parent directory is to explicitly specify its name. For example, to go from the FORMLET directory to the WP directory you can enter

CD \WP

The backslash is necessary for reasons that will soon become clear.

TIP: The most common way to return to the parent directory is to use CD ...

Returning to the Root Directory

No matter how deep you are in subdirectories, you can always return to the root directory by entering this command:

    CD \

Because the backslash is DOS's name for the root directory, this causes DOS to make the root directory active.

Of course, you may always return to the root directory by entering repeated CD .. commands until the root is reached.

6

Creating More Directories

If you haven't yet done so, return to the root directory at this time. Next, switch to the ACCOUNTS directory and enter these commands:

    MKDIR AR
    MKDIR AP
    MKDIR GL

The disk directory structure is now complete and is like that shown in Figure 6-1.

Paths and Path Names

Each directory has a unique path from the root to itself. For example, the path to the GL directory, beginning at the root, is first to ACCOUNTS and then to GL. In the language of DOS, you specify a path by using a *path name*. The path name for the GL directory is \ACCOUNTS\GL. By using the complete path name it is possible to access any file in any directory no matter what directory is currently active. For example, to display the SAMPLE file that you created in the FORMLET subdirectory of WP, enter this command:

TYPE \WP\FORMLET\SAMPLE

A path contains the route to a file.

The first backslash is DOS's name for the root. The backslash that precedes the file name SAMPLE is necessary and acts as a separator between the path name and the file name. In general, you use backslashes to separate directory and file names. There can be no spaces in the path name.

As another example, try this command:

DIR \WP\TEMP

You will see the directory of the TEMP directory displayed.

The general form of a path name is

*dir-name**dir-name*...*dir-name*

where *dir-name* is an appropriate directory name. For example, if TEMP under WP had a subdirectory called HARRY, then the HARRY directory could be listed using this command:

DIR \WP\TEMP\HARRY

You may precede a path name with a drive specifier if needed. For example, to list a directory called SPRDSHT on the B drive you would enter

DIR B:\SPRDSHT

DOS restricts the length of a path name to 63 characters.

TIP: Even though the examples in this book use uppercase, a path name can be in either upper- or lowercase.

Moving Between Directories

In DOS, there is often more than one way to accomplish the same thing. This is true of moving between directories. The one way that will always work no matter what directory is currently active is to use the

CD command followed by the complete path name of the directory to which you wish to go. For example, return to the root directory by entering **CD **, then move to the WP directory by entering **CD WP**. Now, to move from the WP directory to the AR subdirectory of ACCOUNTS, you can use this command:

    CD \ACCOUNTS\AR

To go back to the WP directory, enter

    CD \WP

Go to the WP directory now.

If you type an invalid path or misspell a directory name, DOS will respond with the message "Invalid directory". In this case, enter the command again, correcting the error.

6

To move from the WP directory to its TEMP subdirectory you can *not* use this command:

    CD \TEMP   (This is an incorrect command.)

(If you try this command, DOS will respond with the message "Invalid directory".) The reason that this will not work is because the backslash preceding TEMP tells DOS to start at the root and then move to the TEMP directory. However, TEMP is not a subdirectory of the root, it is a subdirectory of WP. Hence, to move from WP to TEMP you must use one of these commands:

    CD TEMP
    CD \WP\TEMP

The first version is essentially shorthand for the second. Because the WP directory is active and TEMP is a subdirectory of WP, you can simply use CD TEMP because DOS already knows the rest of the path. The second form works, of course, because the entire path is explicitly stated. In general, any time you move from a parent directory to a subdirectory, you only have to specify the subdirectory's name. However, the reverse is not true. To move from a subdirectory back to the parent you must use either the CD .. command or a complete path name.

REMEMBER: If you have any doubts about what to type to move from one directory to another, simply specify the target directory's full path name. This will always work.

Displaying the Current Directory Name

In addition to allowing you to change directories, the CD command will also display the current directory and path if it is executed with no arguments. To try this, simply enter **CD** at this time. If you ever have any doubts about being in the proper directory, this is the way to find out.

For example, switch to the TEMP subdirectory of WP and enter **CD**, your display will look like this:

```
A:\WP\TEMP
```

Removing a Directory

To remove a directory you must use the RMDIR (RD for short) command.

The general form of the RMDIR command is

RMDIR *directory-name*

where *directory-name* specifies a valid path to the directory you wish to remove.

Directories cannot be removed using ERASE. There are two restrictions to removing directories. First, the directory must be empty. It can contain no files or other subdirectories. That is, when you list the directory the only thing that can be present is

. <DIR>
.. <DIR>

Directories cannot be removed using ERASE.

Second, it may not be the current directory. That is, you cannot remove a directory that you are currently using.

Switch to the ACCOUNTS directory at this time. Since the GL directory is empty, remove it now by entering

RMDIR \ACCOUNTS\GL

If you list the directory you will see that GL is no longer shown.

Before continuing, recreate the GL directory.

If you try to remove the current directory, a non-existent directory, or one that contains files or subdirectories, you will see this message:

```
Invalid path, not directory,
or directory not empty
```

REMEMBER: You can only remove a directory that is empty and that is not current.

Copying Files Between Directories

6

The only trick to copying a file from one directory to another is to fully specify the path names. For example, switch to the AR directory of ACCOUNTS and try this command:

COPY \WP\FORMLET\SAMPLE \ACCOUNTS\AR

If you list the AR directory you will see that the SAMPLE file has been copied into it.

Technically, if the destination directory is the current directory, then the destination need not be specified. That is, if AR is the current directory, then this form of the COPY command will also copy the file SAMPLE:

COPY \WP\FORMLET\SAMPLE

To copy a file from a subdirectory to the root directory, use the backslash as the destination path. For example, this copies the file SAMPLE to the root. (Assuming that the AR directory is current.)

COPY SAMPLE \

Earlier in this book, you were told that no two files on the same diskette could have the same name. Although this statement is still true, it needs to be elaborated upon in light of subdirectories. Put more fully, no two files on the same diskette and sharing the same path name can have the same name. That is, within any directory no two file names can be the same. However, files in other directories can have similar names. DOS keeps things straight because it always associates a path name with a file name.

CAUTION: When copying files between directories, if you have any doubt in your mind about how to specify the target directory, simply specify the full path name.

Displaying a Disk's Directory Structure

As your directory structures become more complex, sometimes it is helpful to refresh your memory as to the exact nature of their organization. DOS provides two commands to display the directory structure of a disk. The first is TREE which shows all directories and subdirectories. The second is CHKDSK when used with the /V option. Let's look at both of these now.

Before proceeding, return to the root directory of drive A by entering **CD ** at this time.

TREE

The TREE command displays the names of all directories on the specified disk. The general form of TREE is

> TREE *drive-specifier*

TREE can help you remember the directory organization of a disk.

The *drive-specifier* is unnecessary if you want the structure of the disk in the current drive. TREE is an external command which means that you must have it on your work disk.

To see how TREE works, copy the file TREE.COM into the root directory of your work disk and enter **TREE** at this time. (Make sure that the A drive is active.) You will see output similar to that shown in Figure 6-3.

```
              Directory PATH listing
          Volume Serial Number is 3765-11FA


         A:\.
         ├──WP
         │    ├── Formlet
         │    └── Temp
         │
         ├──Accounts
         │    ├── AR
         │    ├── AP
         │    └── GL
         │
         └──Games
```

Output from
the TREE
command
Figure 6-3.

6

If you also wish to see the files in each directory, use the /F option. For
example, this lists both the directory structure and files in each directory:

TREE /F

The output from this form of the command is shown in Figure 6-4.

By adding a drive specifier to the path name, you can use TREE to
display the directory structure of a disk in a different drive.

NOTE: If you are using an early version of DOS (prior to 4) then the
output shown in Figures 6-3 and 6-4 will appear substantially different.
However, the informational content will be the same. In early versions of
DOS, TREE does not display the directory structure in a graphical manner.

Using CHKDSK to Display the Directory Structure

You can use CHKDSK to display a list of the directories and files on a
disk by specifying the /V option. (Remember that CHKDSK is an
external command.) The output is not in the same form—or as easy to
read—as that created by TREE, but it does have the advantage of

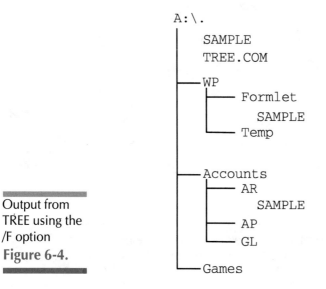

```
           Directory PATH listing
       Volume Serial Number is 3765-11FA


A:\.
    |
    |    SAMPLE
    |    TREE.COM
    |
    |--WP
    |    |--- Formlet
    |    |       SAMPLE
    |    |--- Temp
    |
    |
    |--Accounts
    |    |--- AR
    |    |       SAMPLE
    |    |--- AP
    |    |--- GL
    |
    |--Games
```

checking the disk and providing other useful information. To use CHKDSK to display the directories and files, use the following form. Remember to copy CHKDSK.EXE (or CHKDSK.COM, if you have an early version of DOS) to your work disk first.

CHKDSK /V

The output generated by this command is shown in Figure 6-5.

NOTE: If you are using a version of DOS prior to 4, then CHKDSK /V will display the same information as shown in Figure 6-5, but it will look a little different.

```
Volume Serial Number is 3765-11FA
Directory A:\
Directory A:\WP
Directory A:\WP\FORMLET
A:\WP\FORMLET\SAMPLE
Directory A:\WP\TEMP
Directory A:\ACCOUNTS
Directory A:\ACCOUNTS\AR
A:\ACCOUNTS\AR\SAMPLE
Directory A:\ACCOUNTS\AP
Directory A:\ACCOUNTS\GL
Directory A:\GAMES
A:\SAMPLE
A:\TREE.COM

     730112 bytes total disk space
       8192 bytes in 8 directories
      10240 bytes in 4 user files
     711680 bytes available on disk

       1024 bytes in each allocation unit
        713 total allocation units on disk
        695 available allocation units on disk

     655360 total bytes memory
     628320 bytes free
```

6

The output
displayed by
CHKDSK using
the /V option
Figure 6-5.

Removing an Entire Directory Tree

As you know, before you can remove a directory using RMDIR, it must
be empty. This means that it cannot contain either files or
subdirectories. Thus, if you want to remove an extensive subdirectory
system, you must manually remove each subdirectory, starting from the
bottom, up—erasing all files and removing directories as you go. In the
case of complex directory trees, this process can be very tedious and
time consuming. However, if you have DOS 6 then you can remove an
entire directory system with a single command. In the language of
DOS, a directory system is referred to as a *tree*. The command that will
remove an entire tree is called DELTREE and it has this general form:

DELTREE *directory*

A directory tree is a system of related subdirectories.

Here, *directory* is the name of the top level directory of the directory tree that you want to delete.

The DELTREE command automatically erases all files in the entire directory tree and then deletes all of the directories.

For example, assuming the directory structure shown in Figure 6-1, which you created on your work disk, the following command removes all word processing files and directories:

DELTREE A:\WP

Before DELTREE actually removes the directory tree, you will be asked to confirm the deletion. If you don't want this confirmation, specify the /Y option. This option must go immediately after DELTREE, before the directory to be deleted. For example, this deletes the tree associated with /WP and does not ask before doing so:

DELTREE /Y A:\WP

CAUTION: Use DELTREE with care. If you misunderstand what it is deleting, you might erase several important files by accident.

Directory Capacity

The root directory of a disk has a fixed number of entries that it can hold. An entry is either a file or subdirectory name. This number varies, depending upon the capacity of the disk. Table 6-1 shows the number of entries for the most common diskette formats. The root directory of the fixed disk can hold 512 entries.

Unlike the root directory, a subdirectory can hold as many entries as available disk space allows. The reason for this is that DOS will simply continue to allocate space on the disk to hold the entries. As a general rule, however, it is not advisable to have extremely large directories because they are difficult to manage. Once you have more than about 100 to 200 entries, it is time to think about creating a new subdirectory and moving some of the files to it.

Diskette Capacity in Bytes	Maximum Directory Entries
160/180K	64
320/360K	112
720K	112
1,200K	224
1,440K	224

The Directory Capacity of Various Diskettes Table 6-1.

Searching Subdirectories Using DIR

If you have DOS version 5 or later then you can use another option to DIR to search for files in the current directory plus all of its subdirectories. The option to search all subdirectories is /S. For example, this command causes DIR to display all files in the current directory and all subdirectories:

   DIR *.* /S

An especially good use of the /S option is to look for a specific file when you can't remember what directory it is in. For example, to search for the file INV.DAT in the current directory as well as any subdirectories, use this command:

   DIR INV.DAT /S

If DIR finds the file, then it also displays the directory in which it was found. As you become more experienced with DOS, you will find that the /S option to DIR is useful for a number of different purposes.

Managing Your Directories

Although we will look more closely at the topic of directory management later in this book, a few pointers will be given now. First and foremost, subdirectories should be used to hold logically related groups of files. Files can be related to each other in a number of different ways. For example, if a computer is shared by a number of different people, then creating a subdirectory for each individual is probably a good idea. Even though all the files in a user's subdirectory

6

may be quite different in purpose from one another, they are all related because they belong to that user. However, if a computer is being used by one person for several separate tasks, as in the insurance company example used in this chapter, then the subdirectories are best organized by functional areas. Generally, the way the computer is used will dictate how the directories should be designed.

It is important to mention one fact. Each subdirectory uses disk space. Creating an unnecessarily large number of subdirectories will waste disk space. Also, subdirectories that are "deeply nested" and require long path names will slow DOS's access time to any files they contain. You must balance these factors against the advantages that subdirectories have to offer.

Summary

In this chapter you learned

✦ That DOS uses a tree-structured system of directories

✦ The difference between the root and subdirectories

✦ How to create and remove subdirectories

✦ How to move between directories

✦ What a path name is

✦ How to display the directory structure of a disk using TREE or CHKDSK

✦ How to remove an entire directory tree

✦ How many directory entries the various types of disks can hold

✦ How to search subdirectories for files using the /S option to DIR

In the next chapter you will learn how to use EDIT, the DOS text editor.

CHAPTER

7

USING THE DOS EDITOR

Until now, you have created new files by using a special form of the COPY command. However, as you advance in your study of DOS it will be necessary to create and modify several short text files, and the COPY command is completely inadequate for this task. Also, there will almost certainly be times when you will want to create a text file, such as a memo, and print it on the printer. To handle both these needs, DOS includes a text editor.

A *text editor* is a special program that lets you manage text files. If you have used a word processor, you can think of a text editor as a very limited word processor. Typically, word processors are designed to handle special formats, type fonts, and the like. A text editor simply allows you to maintain a text file; it provides no special features.

The DOS editor, called EDIT, contains about 35 commands and is quite powerful. However, you will not have to learn all the commands at once. The most important commands deal with inserting, deleting, and moving text. Others include searching and replacing text. Once you have mastered these basic areas, you will be able to easily learn the rest of the editor commands and put them to use as you need them.

NOTE: Early versions of DOS provided a text editor called EDLIN. Beginning with DOS 5.00, the editor was upgraded to EDIT, and it is this editor that is discussed here. If you are using an older version of DOS, refer to your user manual for an explanation of EDLIN.

Editor Commands

Before beginning, it is important to explain how you give commands to EDIT. EDIT allows many operations to be selected from menus within the editor. (A *menu* is a list of options in a program, from which you can select one.) In addition, special keystrokes are supported, which are shortcuts to menu selections. However, not all editor options may be selected using the menus. Some can only be activated using special keystrokes. Many of the shortcut and keystroke commands are control-key combinations. Also, many editor commands may be entered using the mouse. If you have a mouse, you will want to have it available for use.

EDIT Is Window-based

EDIT is a window-based application. Since most modern applications use windows to support user input, menu selection, and the setting of options, windows are probably not new to you. However, if they are, the following brief description provides the necessary overview.

A *window* is a region of the screen that is dedicated to some purpose that relates to the program you are currently using. In most applications, windows come and go as needed. For example, when you are using EDIT and you need to find a piece of text, the search window will be displayed, which prompts you for the text you wish to find. Once you have entered the text, the window disappears. Windows in EDIT are virtually intuitive to use and you will have no trouble adjusting to them.

Frankly, the windows inside the DOS editor are so easy to use that we won't spend much time on them here. Later in this book, the DOS Shell is discussed. The Shell makes extensive use of windows, and a thorough discussion of them is presented there.

Invoking EDIT and Entering Text

EDIT is an external command. To execute EDIT, use this general form,

EDIT *filename*

Generally, you will execute EDIT using a file name.

where *filename* is the name of the text file you wish to edit. If the file does not exist, it will be created for you. Otherwise, an already existing file will be loaded. If you do not specify a file name, you will edit an untitled file, but when you try to save it, you will be prompted for a file name.

To begin, execute EDIT as shown here:

EDIT MYTEXT.TXT

Your screen will look like that shown in Figure 7-1. This is the *editor window*.

The top line of the editor window contains the editor's *menu bar*. As you will see, when you need to make a menu selection, this bar is activated. The title of the editor window is the name of the file currently being edited. At the bottom right of the editor window are displayed the current line and column position of the cursor. Along the right side of the window is the vertical scroll bar and along the bottom is the horizontal scroll bar. The *vertical scroll bar* scrolls text up and down. The *horizontal scroll bar* scrolls text left and right. The scroll bars may only be used by a mouse. (If you don't have a mouse, there are keyboard commands that accomplish the same effects as the scroll bars.)

File Edit Search Options   Help
                    MYTEXT.TXT

MS-DOS Editor <F1=Help> Press ALT to activate menus   00001:001

The EDIT
screen
Figure 7-1.

When you are not in the middle of giving the editor a command, then it is
ready to accept input. This means that when you strike keys on the keyboard
they will appear in the editor window at the current cursor location.

By default, the editor is in *insertion mode*. This means that as you enter text
it will be inserted in the middle of what (if anything) is already there. The
opposite is called *overwrite mode*. In this mode of operation new text will
overwrite existing text. You can toggle between these two modes by
pressing the (Ins) key. You can tell which mode is currently active by the
shape of the cursor. When in insertion mode, the cursor is represented as a
blinking underscore. In overwrite mode, it is a blinking rectangle.

REMEMBER: Insertion mode *inserts* new characters in the middle of
existing text; overwrite mode *replaces* existing characters.

Before proceeding, make sure that the editor window is active. This
means that the cursor should be in the editor window. If this is not the
case, press the (Esc) key. Next, type the following lines:

> This is a
> test of the
> DOS editor.

Be sure to press Enter after the last line. If you make a mistake you can use the Backspace key to correct it. Your screen will now look like that in Figure 7-2. Notice the position of the cursor and the values associated with the line and column display at the lower-right corner of the editor window.

Because EDIT is a *screen editor,* you can use the arrow keys to move the cursor around in the text at random. Also, when you press the left mouse button, the cursor moves to the position of the mouse pointer. At this time, use either the arrow keys or the mouse to position the cursor at the far left side of the line "test of the". Now, type this line: **very small**, followed by Enter. As you do so, watch the way the existing line is moved to the right instead of being overwritten. This is what happens when the editor is in insertion mode. Had you toggled the editor into overwrite mode, the original line would have been overwritten. Your screen will now look like Figure 7-3.

7

```
 File  Edit  Search  Options                                    Help
┌──────────────────────── MYTEXT.TXT ────────────────────────────┐
│This is a                                                       ↑│
│test of the                                                      │
│DOS editor.                                                      │
│                                                                 │
│                                                                 │
│                                                                 │
│                                                                 │
│                                                                 │
│                                                                 │
│                                                                 │
│                                                                 │
│                                                                 │
│                                                                 │
│←                                                               →│
└─────────────────────────────────────────────────────────────────┘
 MS-DOS Editor  <F1=Help> Press ALT to activate menus      00004:001
```

Editor screen
with text
entered
Figure 7-2.

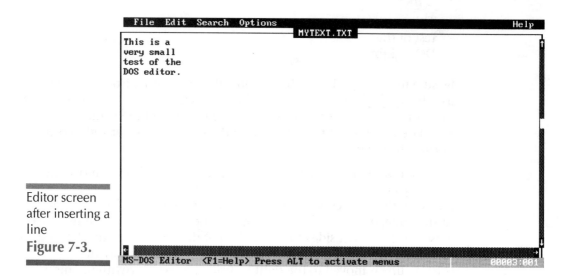

Figure 7-3.

Deleting Characters, Words, and Lines

You can delete a single character to the left of the cursor by pressing the
Backspace key or by pressing Ctrl-H. To delete the character that the
cursor is on press either the Del key or Ctrl-G. To try each method, first
position the cursor on the *i* of "is" in the first line and press Backspace.
Notice that the preceding space is removed. Reenter the space now.
Next, position the cursor on the *i* again and try pressing Del. This time
the *i* is removed. Reenter the *i* at this time.

You can delete an entire word that is to the right of the cursor by
typing Ctrl-T.

You can remove an entire line by typing Ctrl-Y. It does not matter
where the cursor is positioned in the line—the entire line is deleted.
You should try deleting a few lines and words at this time. Before
continuing, however, reenter the lines that you deleted.

If you wish to delete from the current cursor position to the end of the
line, type the sequence Ctrl-Q Y. To see how this works, position the
cursor on the *s* of "small" in the second line and enter the sequence
Ctrl-Q Y. Notice that the word "very" is still there, but the rest of the
line, beginning with the *s* in "small", is deleted.

Activating and Using the Menu Bar

Now that you have seen how text is entered and how some simple text manipulations are performed, it is time to learn to use the menu bar. Many of the commands that follow may be activated by the menu, so you need to know how to use it. The menu bar can be operated using either the keyboard or the mouse. Both methods are discussed here.

Accessing the Menu Bar Using the Keyboard

To activate the menu bar using the keyboard, press the `Alt` key. Try this now. As you can see, File is highlighted. You can use the `←` and `→` keys to move the highlight to different options. Try this now. Finally, return to the File option. To see the menu associated with an option, press `Enter` while that option is highlighted. For example, press `Enter` now. Your screen will look like that in Figure 7-4.

7

The File menu
Figure 7-4.

TIP: When the menu bar is active, you can also select a menu option by pressing the highlighted character associated with that option. For example, pressing Ⓕ causes the File menu to display.

As you can see, File has several menu selections associated with it. To select one, use the Ⓣ or Ⓣ key to move the highlight to the option you want and then press ⌷Enter⌷. (Don't select one at this time.) If a menu option cannot be selected, it will be shown in low intensity. (Some options only apply in certain circumstances.) When a menu is displayed, you can also select a menu option by pressing the highlighted character associated with that option.

To cancel the menu bar, press ⌷Esc⌷. This reactivates the editor window. Press ⌷Esc⌷ at this time.

Accessing the Menu Bar Using the Mouse

Accessing the menu bar using the mouse is somewhat easier than using the keyboard. To activate a menu, simply position the mouse pointer on the option you want and then click the left mouse button. This causes that option's menu to appear. To make a selection from that menu, position the mouse pointer on the desired option and click the left mouse button. To return to the editor window using the mouse, just position the mouse pointer anywhere in the editor window and click the left mouse button. The process of positioning the mouse pointer on an object and then pressing the left button is commonly referred to as "clicking on" the object.

Using Help

If at any time when using EDIT you need help, simply select the Help option in the menu bar. You may also press the ⌷F1⌷ key, which provides information on how to use EDIT. The Help option is straightforward and self-explanatory.

Moving, Copying, and Deleting Blocks of Text

EDIT allows you to manipulate blocks of text. You can move or copy a block to another location or delete it altogether. In order to do any of these things you must first define a block. A *block* can be as short as a single character or as large as your entire file. However, typically, a block is somewhere between these two extremes.

You can define a block of text two different ways: using the keyboard or using the mouse. To define a block using the keyboard, move the cursor to the beginning of the block, hold down the (Shift) key, and use the arrow keys to move the cursor to the end of the block; then release the arrow and (Shift) keys. The block you define will be highlighted. To define a block using the mouse, first position the mouse pointer at the beginning of the block. Next, press and hold the left mouse button and move the mouse to the end of the block. Finally, release the button.

For example, move the cursor to the *t* at the beginning of the third line, press the (Shift) key, and press the (↓) twice. Your screen should look like Figure 7-5.

The clipboard is a region of memory used to temporarily store text.

Once you have defined a block of text, you can move it using the following sequence. First, press (Shift)-(Del). This causes the text to be removed from the screen and put into the *clipboard,* which is a temporary storage area used by the editor. Next, move the cursor to the point in your file where you want to move the text and press (Shift)-(Ins). You may also move text using menu commands. To do this, first define a block, then activate the Edit menu bar option, and select Cut. This removes the selected text and puts it in the clipboard. Move the cursor to the new location, activate the Edit menu again, and this time select Paste. This moves the text to the new location.

7

TIP: Menu commands take more time to use than their keystroke equivalents. Once you have the keystroke commands memorized, they are faster to use than the menu.

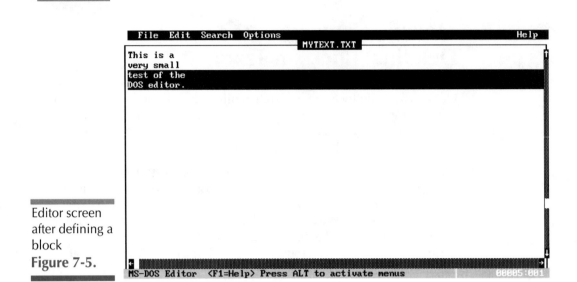

To copy a block, first define the block. Next, press Ctrl-Ins. This copies the block into the clipboard, but does not remove the block from the screen. Then move the cursor where you want the text to be copied and press Shift-Ins. You can also use the Edit menu to copy a block. After you have created a block, first select the Copy option to copy the text into the clipboard. Next, move the cursor to where you want the text copied and select the Paste option.

To delete the currently marked block, either press Del or select the Clear option in the Edit menu. The deleted text is *not* put into the clipboard.

Before moving on, let's copy a block of text. First, define a block of text that consists of the first two lines of the sample text you have in the editor. (To do this, position the cursor at the start of the first line, hold down Shift, and press the ↓ twice.) Next, press Ctrl-Ins. Now, move the cursor to the bottom of the file and press Shift-Ins. Your screen will look like Figure 7-6.

More on the Clipboard

As stated in the previous section, the clipboard is a temporary depository for fragments of text that have been moved or copied. To

```
  File  Edit  Search  Options                              Help
                          MYTEXT.TXT
 This is a                                                       ↑
 very small
 test of the
 DOS editor.
 This is a
 very small




                                                               ▓


                                                               ▓
█                                                              ↓
MS-DOS Editor  <F1=Help> Press ALT to activate menus    00005:001
```

Editor screen
after copying a
block
Figure 7-6.

7

move text into the clipboard you need to mark the region and then
either move or copy that block.

To retrieve a block of text from the clipboard, use the Edit menu's Paste
command or press (Shift)-(Ins). This causes the most recently moved or
copied block of text in the clipboard to be copied into the editor
window at the current cursor location. However, this does not remove
the text from the clipboard. You can press (Shift)-(Ins) as often as you like,
producing multiple copies of the text.

Each time you move or copy a new block of text, that text replaces any
previous text held in the clipboard.

More on Cursor Movement

EDIT has a number of special cursor commands. These commands are
summarized in Table 7-1. You should experiment with these commands
at this time. Of course, you may also move the cursor by positioning
the mouse pointer at the desired location and clicking.

Action	Command
Move left one character	← or Ctrl-S
Move right one character	→ or Ctrl-D
Move left one word	Ctrl-← or Ctrl-A
Move right one word	Ctrl-→ or Ctrl-F
Move up one line	↑ or Ctrl-E
Move down one line	↓ or Ctrl-X
Scroll up	Ctrl-↑ or Ctrl-W
Scroll down	Ctrl-↓ or Ctrl-Z
Move up one page	Pg Up or Ctrl-R
Move down one page	Pg Dn or Ctrl-C
Move to start of line	Home or Ctrl-Q S
Move to end of line	End or Ctrl-Q D
Move to top of screen	Ctrl-Q E
Move to bottom of screen	Ctrl-Q X
Move to top of file	Ctrl-Q R or Ctrl-Home
Move to bottom of file	Ctrl-Q C or Ctrl-End
Move to start of next line	Ctrl-Enter
Scroll screen left	Ctrl-Pg Up
Scroll screen right	Ctrl-Pg Dn

Cursor Commands Table 7-1.

NOTE: By holding down the Shift key you can use any of the cursor commands (except for the scrolling commands) to help define a block. For example, Shift-Ctrl-→ highlights the word to the right of the cursor.

Dialog Boxes

The next few EDIT commands use a dialog box, so a brief discussion of dialog boxes is necessary. A *dialog box* is a special type of window that performs user input related to a specific function. Dialog boxes are used by EDIT to input various types of information and to set or select various options. For the most part, dialog boxes are intuitive to use, and the ones employed by EDIT are particularly straightforward. The dialog boxes used by EDIT are fully described in this chapter, and you will have no trouble using them. However, a complete description of dialog boxes in general is deferred until Part 5, where the Shell is described. (The DOS Shell uses many different types of dialog boxes.) If you don't plan to use the Shell, then the discussion in this chapter is sufficient to allow you full use of the DOS editor.

Finding and Replacing Text

EDIT allows two common text processing operations: finding a specific piece of text and changing one piece of text into another. Both of these actions are examined here.

7

Finding Text

Often, you will want to find a specific sequence of characters in your file. This will be especially true when working with larger files. To find a sequence of characters use the Ctrl-Q F command or select the Find option in the Search menu. You will then be prompted by the dialog box shown in Figure 7-7 for the text you wish to find. The editor will automatically copy the word that the cursor is on or near in your file into the Find What box. If this is the text you want to search for, then you do not need to enter anything. Otherwise, just enter the text you want to find. The sequence of characters you are looking for is generally referred to as a *string* and it may be up to 127 characters long. Once you have entered the text, press Enter and the search will begin. (If you are using a mouse, you can click on the OK button to start the search.)

If you change your mind and don't want to search for a string, you can cancel the Find box by either pressing Esc or clicking on the Cancel button. Also, if you need help, you can click on the Help button. (To select a button using the keyboard, press the Tab key until the desired button is reached and then press Enter.)

```
┌─────────────────────── Find ───────────────────────┐
│                                                     │
│  Find What: ┌──────────────────────────────────┐   │
│             │ This                             │   │
│             └──────────────────────────────────┘   │
│                                                     │
│                                                     │
│      [ ] Match Upper/Lowercase      [ ] Whole Word  │
│                                                     │
├─────────────────────────────────────────────────────┤
│          OK  ■         < Cancel >        < Help >   │
└─────────────────────────────────────────────────────┘
```

The Find
dialog box
Figure 7-7.

If the string you are looking for is found, then the cursor is moved to the start of that string. If no matching string is found, the message "Match not found" is displayed and the cursor remains in its previous location.

You can specify two options that affect how the search for the string you entered is conducted. These options are controlled by check boxes. A *check box* is active if it has an X in it. If the box is empty, then the option is inactive. To activate (or deactivate) a check box, press the Tab key until that box is selected, then press the Spacebar. Pressing the Spacebar alternately selects and deselects a check box item. You can also change the state of a check box by clicking on it with the mouse.

NOTE: In general, to move between items in a dialog box, press the Tab key. Each time you press Tab, a new item is selected.

By default, the search is not case sensitive. This means that for the purposes of the search, "test" and "TEST" will be treated as the same. You can cause the search to be case sensitive by selecting the Match Upper/Lowercase check box. Also, by default, substrings are found. For example, if you search for the word "other", a match will be found with the word "Another" because it contains the word you are looking for. You can prevent these types of matches by selecting the Whole Word option.

The search proceeds from the current cursor location forward (toward the end) in the file.

You can repeat the search by pressing Ctrl-L or F3, or by selecting the Repeat Last Find option in the Search menu. Repeating the search allows you to find multiple occurrences of a string within a file.

Replacing Text

In addition to finding a string, you can change one string into another using the Change option. To do this, type Ctrl-Q A or select the Change option in the Search menu. You will see the dialog box shown in Figure 7-8. Its operation is identical to the Find command except that it allows you to replace the string you are looking for with another. Enter the string that you want to replace in the Find What box and enter the new string in the Change To box.

As you can see, the options available in the Change dialog box are similar to those available with Find, with two additions. By default, the editor will ask you before making a change. (This is why the Find and Verify button is highlighted.) You can turn off this feature by starting the search with the Change All button selected. To again cause the editor to prompt you before each change, select the Find and Verify button.

7

Setting and Finding Place Markers

You can set up to four place markers in your file by typing Ctrl-K *n*, where *n* is the number of the place marker (0-3). After a marker has

```
┌──────────────────────────── Change ────────────────────────────┐
│                                                                 │
│  Find What: ┌─────────────────────────────────────────────────┐ │
│             └─────────────────────────────────────────────────┘ │
│                                                                 │
│  Change To: ┌─────────────────────────────────────────────────┐ │
│             └─────────────────────────────────────────────────┘ │
│                                                                 │
│                                                                 │
│      [ ] Match Upper/Lowercase        [ ] Whole Word            │
│                                                                 │
├─────────────────────────────────────────────────────────────────┤
│   Find and Verify   < Change All >  < Cancel > < Help >         │
└─────────────────────────────────────────────────────────────────┘
```

The Change dialog box

Figure 7-8.

A marker is a
good way to
move between
two points in
a large file.

been set, the command Ctrl-Q *n*, where *n* is the marker number, causes the cursor to go to that marker. Place markers are especially convenient in large files.

Saving and Loading Your File

To save your file using the same name you specified when you executed the editor, activate the File menu and select Save. This is by far the most common method that you will use to save a file.

If you wish to save your file under a different name, activate the File menu and select the Save As option. You will see a dialog box like that shown in Figure 7-9.

You can save the file under the name that you gave it when you invoked the editor, or you can change it by entering a new name in the File Name box and then pressing Enter or selecting the OK button. The directory that the file will be saved to is shown immediately below the File Name box. You can change the directory or the drive your file is

```
┌──────────────── Save As ────────────────┐
│                                          │
│  File Name: ┌────────────────────────┐   │
│             │ MYTEXT.TXT             │   │
│             └────────────────────────┘   │
│  C:\DOS                                  │
│                 Dirs/Drives              │
│              ┌───────────────┐ ↑         │
│              │ ..            │ ▓         │
│              │ [-A-]         │ ▓         │
│              │ [-B-]         │ ▓         │
│              │ [-C-]         │ ▓         │
│              │ [-D-]         │ ▓         │
│              │ [-E-]         │ ▓         │
│              │ [-F-]         │ ↓         │
│              └───────────────┘           │
├──────────────────────────────────────────┤
│    ‹  OK  ›      ‹ Cancel ›    ‹ Help ›   │
└──────────────────────────────────────────┘
```

The Save As
dialog box
Figure 7-9.

saved to by first activating the Dirs/Drives box and selecting the directory or drive from the list. This is accomplished by first pressing [Tab] to activate the Dirs/Drives box and then using the [↑] and [↓] keys to highlight the directory or drive desired. Once the proper item is highlighted, press [Enter]. You can also click on the desired directory or drive using the mouse.

Once you have finished editing one file, you can move on and edit other files without having to leave and reenter the editor. Further, you can edit a preexisting file or create a new one.

To edit a preexisting file select the Open option in the File menu. This causes a dialog box to be displayed, and you are prompted for the name of the file you wish to load. There are two ways that you can specify the file name. First, you can type it in. Second, you can [Tab] to the list of files shown in the dialog box and make a selection. If you have a mouse, you can also double-click on the desired file and it will be loaded. (A *double-click* is accomplished by pressing the left mouse button twice in quick succession.) By default, all files with the .TXT extension are displayed. However, if you change the file name in the File Name box, the file list will reflect those that match the new name. You can use wildcard characters in the file name. For example, to list all files in the current directory, specify *.* as the file name.

You can change the directory or drive the file is to be loaded from using the Dirs/Drives box.

If you try to load a file that is nonexistent, you will receive an error message, and the file currently being edited will be left unchanged in the editor window.

If the file you are currently editing has had changes made to it but has not yet been saved, you will be prompted to save the file before loading another.

If you want to create a new file, select the New option in the File menu. The file will not have a name until you give it one when you save it.

Printing the File

To print the file that is currently being edited, select the Print option in the File menu. You will see the dialog box shown in Figure 7-10.

```
┌──────────── Print ────────────┐
│                                │
│    ( ) Selected Text Only      │
│    (•) Complete Document        │
│                                │
├────────────────────────────────┤
│  < OK >   < Cancel >   < Help > │
└────────────────────────────────┘
```

The Print
dialog box
Figure 7-10.

If no block of text is selected, then the entire file will be printed.
However, if you have defined a block and you select the Selected Text
Only option, then only that block will be printed. Even if you have
selected a block, you can still print the entire file by selecting the
Complete Document option.

REMEMBER: Make sure that your printer is online.

Autoindentation

EDIT includes a feature called *autoindentation*. To understand what it
does, enter this text exactly as it is shown:

```
This
  is
    an
      example of autoindentation.
```

As you enter the text you will notice that the cursor returns to the
position of the previous indentation level. This feature makes the
creation of tables and lists much easier because you don't need to
manually enter several spaces.

When you press Backspace at the start of an indented line, the cursor
moves to the left one full indentation level rather than just one space.

Using the Scroll Bars

If you have a mouse, you can use the scroll bars to move text through the editor window. To do this, position the mouse pointer on the arrow that points in the direction that you want to move the text and press the left mouse button. This will scroll the text one position in the direction of the arrow. If you press and hold the left button, the text will be scrolled continuously. You may also click the mouse anywhere on the scroll bar and the text will move proportionally. The scroll bars only work when the file is larger than will fit in one screen.

TIP: The best way to learn how to use the scroll bars is to experiment with them.

Entering Control Characters

You can enter a control character into a file by first typing Ctrl-P followed by the control character you want. For example, Ctrl-P Ctrl-T inserts a Ctrl-T into your file. It will appear as the paragraph symbol.

7

CAUTION: You should not enter control characters into your file unless an application program requires you to do so.

Exiting EDIT

Once you are finished editing, you can terminate EDIT by selecting the Exit option in the File menu. If you have not already saved the file you have been editing, EDIT will give you a chance to do so before terminating.

Command Summary

Table 7-2 shows all of the EDIT commands.

Action	Command
Cursor Commands	
Move left one character	⬅ or Ctrl-S
Move right one character	➡ or Ctrl-D
Move left one word	Ctrl-⬅ or Ctrl-A
Move right one word	Ctrl-➡ or Ctrl-F
Move up one line	⬆ or Ctrl-E
Move down one line	⬇ or Ctrl-X
Scroll up	Ctrl-⬆ or Ctrl-W
Scroll down	Ctrl-⬇ or Ctrl-Z
Move up one page	Pg Up or Ctrl-R
Move down one page	Pg Dn or Ctrl-C
Move to start of line	Home or Ctrl-Q S
Move to end of line	End or Ctrl-Q D
Move to top of screen	Ctrl-Q E
Move to bottom of screen	Ctrl-Q X
Move to top of file	Ctrl-Q R or Ctrl-Home
Move to bottom of file	Ctrl-Q C or Ctrl-End
Move to start of next line	Ctrl-Enter
Scroll screen left	Ctrl-Pg Up
Scroll screen right	Ctrl-Pg Dn
Insert Commands	
Toggle insertion mode	Ins or Ctrl-V
Insert a blank line	Enter or Ctrl-N
Insert control character	Ctrl-P

EDIT Command
Summary by
Category
Table 7-2.

Action	Command
Delete Commands	
Delete entire line	`Ctrl`-`Y`
Delete to end of line	`Ctrl`-`Q` `Y`
Delete character on left	`Backspace` or `Ctrl`-`H`
Delete character at cursor	`Del` or `Ctrl`-`G`
Delete word to the right	`Ctrl`-`T`
Delete block	`Del` or `Ctrl`-`G`
Delete block and put in clipboard	`Shift`-`Del`
Delete leading spaces	`Shift`-`Tab`
Find Commands	
Find	`Ctrl`-`Q` `F`
Find and replace	`Ctrl`-`Q` `A`
Repeat find	`Ctrl`-`L` or `F 3`
Miscellaneous Commands	
Toggle overwrite/insertion mode	`Ins` or `Ctrl`-`V`
Set a place marker	`Ctrl`-`K` n
Find a place marker	`Ctrl`-`Q` n

EDIT Command
Summary by
Category
(*continued*)
Table 7-2.

Setting Some Editor Options

You can change some aspects of the way the editor operates by selecting the Options menu. This menu contains two selections, Display and Help Path. The Help Path is used to specify the path to the editor help files. If DOS has been installed correctly on your computer, you will not need to use this option.

The Display option lets you change the way some things in the editor work and look. Activate the Display option at this time. You will see the dialog box shown in Figure 7-11. You can change the foreground (text) and background colors used by the editor. If you don't use a mouse, you can remove the scroll bars from the editor window by deselecting the Scroll Bars option. You can also change the size of a tab.

REMEMBER: The Help Path option is rarely, if ever, changed.

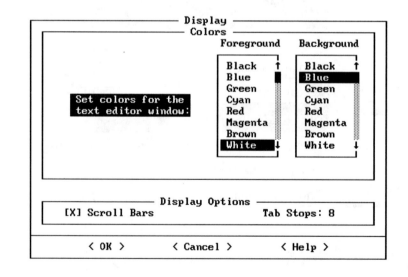

The Display options dialog box
Figure 7-11.

Summary

In this chapter you learned how to

- ◆ Start EDIT and enter text
- ◆ Activate and use the menu bar
- ◆ Delete characters, words, and lines of text
- ◆ Move, copy, and delete blocks of text
- ◆ Use the clipboard
- ◆ Find and replace text
- ◆ Set and find place markers
- ◆ Save and load files
- ◆ Print your files
- ◆ Enter control characters
- ◆ Use the scroll bars
- ◆ Exit EDIT
- ◆ Set various options

In the next chapter you will learn to create your own DOS commands called *batch files*.

7

C H A P T E R

8 BATCH FILES

From time to time you will find that you would like to give the computer a list of commands all at once, and then have the computer whir away on its own without further interaction from you, until the list of commands has finished. For example, you might want to tell the computer to prepare payroll information, print checks, and create weekly backup files, all without having to wait for each task to be completed before giving the next command. The creation of lists of commands is the subject of this chapter.

What Are Batch Files?

DOS allows you to create lists of commands through the use of batch files. A *batch file* is a text file which contains one or more DOS commands. All batch file names must have the .BAT extension. Once you have created a batch file, you cause DOS to execute the commands in the file by entering the name of the batch file at the DOS prompt, as if it were a DOS external command. In fact, you can think of batch files as custom commands which you create.

Two Simple Batch Files

As an easy first example, use EDIT (or your favorite text editor) to create a file called TEST.BAT that contains these lines:

```
DIR
CHKDSK
```

Now, enter **TEST** at the command line. As you can see, DOS first lists the directory and then executes CHKDSK. (Note that you do not use the extension when you enter a batch file's name at the prompt.)

How It Works

When you enter a command at the DOS prompt, a sequence of events begins. First, DOS checks to see if the string of characters you entered matches one of DOS's internal commands. If it does, then that command is executed. Otherwise, DOS checks the current disk to see if what you entered at the prompt matches one of DOS's external commands or an application program. (Remember, all DOS external commands and programs end with the .EXE or .COM extension.) If the command or program is found, it is executed. Otherwise, DOS checks to see if there is a batch file that matches what you entered at the DOS prompt. If one exists, DOS sequentially executes the commands that are in the batch file, starting with the first command and finishing with the last.

TIP: It is important that batch file commands do not have the same name as any other DOS command or application program that you are using. If you do accidentally create a batch file with the same name as a DOS command, DOS will always execute the command—never the batch file.

A Second Example

Often you will find that you execute the same sequence of commands over and over again. For example, if you are using an accounting program, at the end of each day you may make copies of all the data files. Assume that the data files are called REC.DAT, EMP.DAT, INV.UPD, WITHHOLD.TAX, and PAYABLE.DAT. To copy these files from drive C to drive A, you would enter this command sequence:

    COPY *.DAT A:
    COPY INV.UPD A:
    COPY WITHHOLD.TAX A:

However, if you create a batch file that contains these commands and call that file BKUP.BAT, then all you need to enter is **BKUP** to copy the files.

To see how such a command will work, create three files called SAMPLE1.TXT, SAMPLE2.TXT, and SAMPLE3.TXT. Enter a few characters of your own choosing into each. Now, create the BKUP.BAT file that contains these commands:

    COPY SAMPLE1.TXT A:
    COPY SAMPLE2.TXT A:
    COPY SAMPLE3.TXT A:

Place a diskette into drive A and enter **BKUP** at the prompt. You will see DOS copy the files.

8

Although creating a batch file command as described here certainly saves some typing, its main advantage is that it is reliable. Once you have created a batch command, it will always do exactly what you want it to do. You don't need to worry about it accidentally forgetting to copy a file, for example.

Cancelling a Batch Command

The easiest way to cancel a batch command once it begins is to press Ctrl-Break. (Ctrl-C also works.) Depending upon what commands make up the batch command, DOS may wait until the current command finishes before stopping the batch command. DOS will prompt you with this message:

```
Terminate batch job (Y/N)? _
```

If you really want to stop the batch command's execution, press **Y**; otherwise, press **N**, and the command will continue to run. Keep in mind that the effects of any of the commands that make up the batch file that have already been executed by DOS will not be nullified. For example, if the first command in a batch file erases some file, then stopping the batch command at some point after this will not prevent the file from being erased.

Adding Parameters

The COMP command is used in several examples in this chapter. Remember, if you are using DOS 6, you may not have the COMP command. If this is the case, substitute the FC command.

Many times you will want to create a batch command that will operate slightly differently depending upon the situation in which it is used. For example, consider these two batch files:

Batch File 1	**Batch File 2**
COPY SAMPLE1.TXT A:	COPY SAMPLE2.TXT A:
COMP SAMPLE1.TXT A:	COMP SAMPLE2.TXT A:

As you can see, the only difference between file 1 and file 2 is the name of the file used in the COPY and COMP commands. You will learn in this section how to create one batch file that can take the place of these two batch files by using place holders instead of actual file names.

Replaceable Parameters

DOS allows you to use up to 10 *replaceable parameters* as place holders in a batch file. (Sometimes these replaceable parameters are referred to as *dummy parameters*.) These replaceable parameters are referred to as %0 through %9. Each piece of information you pass to the batch file is called an *argument,* and it is placed on the command line immediately after the batch file name. For this reason, these are called *command-line arguments*. Each replaceable parameter in a batch file is replaced by its corresponding argument. Parameter %0 will be replaced by the name of the batch file. Parameter %1 will contain the first argument on the command line, %2 contains the second argument, and so on. For example, create a batch file called CPYFILE.BAT that contains this line:

    COPY %1 %2

When you enter this at the DOS prompt,

    CPYFILE SAMPLE1.TXT TEMP

parameter %1 will contain SAMPLE1.TXT and %2 will have the value TEMP. (In this, and the rest of the examples in this book, the %0 parameter is not needed and is not used.) Try this now.

The single most important thing that you can remember about the command-line arguments used in a batch command is that they must be separated by spaces, tabs, commas, or semicolons. DOS does not recognize any other character as a separator. This means that the string,

    this+is+a+test

will be seen by DOS to be one argument, not four. Also, the fact that the space, tab, or other separator is used means that you will not be able to use an argument that contains these characters. For example, this will be seen as four separate arguments by DOS:

    this is a test

Special Batch File Commands

DOS allows you to use some special commands in batch files which give you greater control over how a batch file is interpreted or how it operates. These special commands allow you to create batch files that are actually a little like programs. The commands are

ECHO
PAUSE
REM
IF
GOTO
CALL
FOR
SHIFT
CHOICE

Each command is discussed here.

ECHO

The ECHO command has two uses. First, it is used to control whether DOS displays the commands in a batch file as each is executed. By default, ECHO is on, which means that DOS displays each command in the batch file as it is executed. If ECHO is turned off, the batch commands will not be displayed, but any output produced by the commands is still shown. The second use of the ECHO command is to print messages to the screen.

The ECHO batch command takes this general form:

ECHO *on/off/message*

To turn ECHO off you enter

ECHO OFF

To turn it on, use

ECHO ON

For example, create a file called E.BAT and enter these lines into it:

```
ECHO OFF
VER
```

When you execute this batch file (by entering **E** at the prompt), you will see the output of the VER command, but you will not see DOS actually execute the command. The output displayed by this batch file looks like this:

```
C>ECHO OFF

MS-DOS Version 6.00
C>
```

For comparison, remove the ECHO command and try the batch command again. This time each command is displayed as it is executed. The output now looks like this:

```
C>VER

MS-DOS Version 6.00
```

As you can see, this time the C>VER was displayed.

When a batch file command sequence concludes, ECHO is automatically turned on.

REMEMBER: When you turn ECHO off, only the output of the commands is displayed on the screen. When ECHO is on, DOS also displays itself executing each command.

You can use ECHO to display a message on the screen. To do this, place the message after the ECHO command. For example, this batch file tells the user what to do if errors are found in a file comparison operation:

8

```
ECHO OFF
COMP %1 %2
ECHO If errors have been reported, call the office manager.
```

Keep in mind that the message will be displayed whether ECHO is on or off.

Suppressing ECHO One Line at a Time

If you only wish to suppress the display of certain batch commands, it may be easier to accomplish this on a line-by-line basis. To prevent a batch command from displaying when executing, simply place an @ in front of it. For example, DOS will echo all commands in this batch file except the second one:

```
DIR
@COPY %1 %2
CHKDSK
COMP %1 %2
```

The PAUSE Command

You can temporarily stop a batch command through the use of the PAUSE command, which takes this general form:

PAUSE *message*

The *message* is optional. When a PAUSE is encountered, DOS displays the message, if present, and then displays its own message:

```
Press any key to continue . . .
```

DOS will now wait until any key is pressed on the keyboard. You can cancel the batch command by pressing Ctrl-Break.

TIP: If you are using an early version of DOS, the PAUSE message will be "Strike a key when ready...". Either way, the message means the same thing.

The PAUSE command is very useful when a precondition must be met before processing can continue. For example, the following batch file can be used to copy the files on the disk in drive A to the disk in drive B. It first prompts you to place the proper diskettes in the drives.

```
ECHO OFF
PAUSE Put source diskette in A and destination diskette in B
COPY A:*.* B:
```

Your screen will look like this:

```
Put source diskette in A and destination diskette in B
Press any key to continue . . .
```

Adding Remarks with the REM Command

Remarks are completely ignored by DOS.

Sometimes it is helpful to imbed messages and/or notes to yourself (or others) in the batch file to help you remember precisely what the file does. You can do this with the REM command. The REM command has this general form:

REM *remark*

The *remark* can be any string from 0 to 123 characters in length. No matter what the remark contains, it will be completely ignored by DOS.

This batch file command uses remarks to show who created the file and what it is used for:

8

REM Purpose: weekly accounting backup batch file
REM Author: Herbert Schildt
REM Date of creation: 11/16/93
COPY *.DAT A:
COPY *.INV A:
COPY *.BAK A:

Identifying your more important batch file commands as shown in this example is a good idea—especially when several people will be sharing the same system.

As you begin to write larger batch file command sequences, you will find that remarks can help you remember the what and why behind them. Sometimes it is useful to use remarks to give a "play-by-play" description of what a batch file is doing.

The IF Command

The IF command can be confusing at first, but it is one of the most powerful batch commands.

Many times it is useful to create a batch command that does different things depending upon certain conditions. To accomplish this, DOS supports the IF batch file command. The IF takes this general form:

IF *condition command*

Here, *condition* is one of three possible types of conditions and *command* is any other DOS command—batch or standard. If the condition evaluates to true, the command that follows the condition is executed. Otherwise, DOS skips the rest of the line and moves on to the next line (if there is one) in the batch file.

DOS allows the IF to use three different types of conditional expressions. First, you may test two strings for equality. Second, you can check to see if a file exists. Finally, you can see if the previously executed program (or command) terminated because of an error. We will look at examples of these now.

Check Strings for Equality

In DOS, a string is simply a sequence of characters. You can use the IF to check two strings for equality using this general form:

IF *string1* == *string2 command*

If *string1* equals *string2* then the condition is true; otherwise it is false. To see a simple example, create a file called CHKSTR.BAT that contains these lines:

```
IF RED == YELLOW ECHO This will not be printed.
IF RED == RED ECHO This you will see.
```

Try this batch command now. As you can see, only the second ECHO statement is executed.

Of course, comparing two strings as shown in the previous example is of little practical value. However, you can use this feature to compare command-line arguments. For example, change the CHKSTR.BAT file like this:

```
IF %1 == YELLOW ECHO The color is yellow.
IF %1 == RED ECHO The color is red.
```

Now, try executing CHKSTR with an argument of RED. As you can probably guess, it reports that the color is red.

For a more useful example, imagine that a computer in a small office is used by three different people called George, Fred, and Mary. Assume further that Mary does word processing, George is in charge of accounting, and Fred uses a spreadsheet. You could write one backup batch file that will back up the files in the proper directory given the name of the person. This batch command could look like this:

```
IF %1 == MARY COPY \WP\*.* A:
IF %1 == FRED COPY \SPSHEET\*.* A:
IF %1 == GEORGE COPY \ACC\*.* A:
```

Assuming this file is called BK.BAT, then all Mary has to do to back up her files is place a diskette into drive A and enter

```
BK MARY
```

Checking for a File

You can check to see if a file or set of files exists by using the EXIST condition of the IF, which takes this general form,

8

IF EXIST *file-name command*

where *file-name* is the name of the file you are checking for. The *file-name* may include both a drive specifier and a path name. Also, you may use the ? and * wildcards if desired.

For example, enter these lines into a file called EXTEST.BAT:

```
IF EXIST GARBAGE.FIL ECHO This should not be found.
IF EXIST SORT.EXE ECHO SORT.EXE is on the disk.
```

Run this now. As you can see, only the message "SORT.EXE is on the disk." is displayed.

You can make use of the EXIST condition to provide a double check when copying files. If the file already exists on the destination diskette, the batch file will allow the user to cancel the command if the file should not be overwritten.

```
IF EXIST B:%1 PAUSE B:%1 exists - press Ctrl-Break to cancel
COPY %1 B:
```

Checking for Errors

It is possible for an application program to set an internal DOS variable that indicates whether the program terminated normally or because of an error. For the sake of discussion, call this variable the *error variable*. If a program terminates normally, it sets the error variable to 0, which indicates that everything went right. If it terminates because of an error, it sets the error variable to a number greater than 0. If a program does not actually set the value of the error variable, it is 0 by default. DOS lets you check this variable through the use of the ERRORLEVEL condition in the IF command. It takes this general form,

IF ERRORLEVEL *n command*

where *n* is a number greater than or equal to 0 and represents the error number set by the application program. If the value of the error variable is equal to or greater than *n*, the condition is true.

Frankly, the use of ERRORLEVEL is somewhat complicated and the command is used most frequently by programmers. However, all programs will set the ERRORLEVEL to 0 if they terminate normally. This means that you can use the following form of the IF command in any batch file you create to check for normal program termination before proceeding. (Keep in mind that not all application programs will set this variable when they terminate because of an error—so some errors could be missed.)

```
REM Check to see that the previous program terminated
REM normally.
IF ERRORLEVEL 1 PAUSE Abnormal program termination.
```

Using NOT

You can precede the IF condition with the word NOT, which will then reverse the outcome of the condition. For example, if

```
EXIST TEST.DAT
```

is true, then

```
NOT EXIST TEST.DAT
```

is false.

To understand the operation of the NOT, assume that you have an application program that requires the file INFO.DAT to be present on the current disk. You could use this batch command to check for the file before the program is run:

```
IF NOT EXIST INFO.DAT PAUSE Insert the program disk.
```

The GOTO Command

The GOTO batch command is used to direct DOS to execute the commands in a batch file in a nonsequential order. The general form of the GOTO is

```
GOTO label
```

where *label* is a label that is defined elsewhere in the batch file. When the GOTO is executed, it causes DOS to go to the specified label and begin executing commands from that point. Using the GOTO, you can cause execution to jump forward or backward in the file.

 REMEMBER: By default, batch files are executed from the top down. The GOTO allows you to execute a batch file in a different order.

For example, create a file called GOTOTEST.BAT and enter these lines:

```
IF %1 == RED GOTO RED
IF %1 == BLUE GOTO BLUE
:RED
ECHO You chose the color red.
DIR
GOTO DONE
:BLUE
ECHO You like blue.
CHKDSK
:DONE
REM The batch file is now finished.
```

Try this batch command with the arguments of BLUE and RED now.

As you can see by the previous example, all labels must begin with a colon. A label may be up to 125 characters long, but DOS will only use the first 8. In the language of computers, only the first 8 characters of a label's name are significant. This means that these labels will appear the same to DOS:

```
:longlabel1
:longlabel2
```

You may not use a period in a label name.

As the example illustrated, you can use the GOTO in conjunction with the IF to create *blocks of commands* that will only be executed if the condition controlling the IF is true. Notice that you must provide a GOTO around other blocks of commands, as is done with the GOTO

DONE in the RED block, if you don't want execution to "fall through" into the next block.

You can use the GOTO and label to create a loop. For example, this batch file continues to list the directory until you press a [Ctrl]-[Break] to cancel the command:

```
:ONE
DIR
GOTO ONE
```

CAUTION: Loops are easy to accidentally create when using the GOTO command. If this happens to you, just press [Ctrl]-[Break] to cancel the batch file.

CALL

Sometimes you will want to execute another batch file from within a batch file. The best way to do this is through the use of the CALL command. The general form of CALL is

CALL *batch-file*

where *batch-file* is the name of the batch file you wish to execute.

As a first simple example, create a file called ONE.BAT containing these lines:

```
ECHO OFF
ECHO This is in batch file ONE
CALL TWO
ECHO This is back in batch file ONE
```

Now, create the file TWO.BAT which contains these lines:

```
ECHO This is in batch file TWO
```

8

Now, execute batch file ONE. After it has run, your display will look like this:

```
This is in batch file ONE
This is in batch file TWO
This is back in batch file ONE
```

CAUTION: It is possible for a batch file to call itself, but you must make certain that some terminating condition eventually stops the process. If you don't, the process will continue indefinitely.

A good use for CALL is to allow the creation of master batch files, which simply consist of calls to other batch files. In this approach the master file looks somewhat like an outline and provides a quick way to see what is actually happening. (As you create your own batch files, you will be surprised at how long and complicated they can become.) For example, a master batch file for word processing might look like this:

```
REM First create the document
CALL WORDPROC
REM Next, check it for spelling
CALL SPELL
REM Now, print it
CALL PRNT
```

You can pass arguments to the called batch file by specifying them after the name of the called file. These arguments are received by the called file as if they had been command-line arguments. For example, this CALL statement passes the arguments **one** and **two** to the file MYBATCH:

```
CALL MYBATCH one two
```

One final point about calling other batch files: cancelling a called file cancels all batch files. This includes the one currently executing as well as the one that called it.

Repeating Commands with FOR

It is possible to repeat a series of commands using different arguments through the use of the FOR command. The FOR command takes this general form,

FOR %%*var* IN (*argument list*) DO *command*

where *var* is a single-letter variable that will take on the values of the arguments. The arguments must be separated by spaces. The FOR will repeat *command* as many times as there are arguments. Each time the FOR repeats, *var* will be replaced by an argument moving from left to right. The FOR continues to repeat until the last argument is used.

For a first simple example, create a file called SIMPFOR.BAT containing these commands:

```
ECHO OFF
FOR %%I IN (%1 %2 %3) DO ECHO %%I
```

This batch file will print the first three command-line arguments it is called with. For example, execute it with the arguments ONE TWO THREE. The output produced by the FOR command will look like this:

```
ONE
TWO
THREE
```

Here, the %%I is the variable that will be replaced by the command-line arguments specified in %1, %2, and %3. In this case, as the output shows, these are ONE, TWO, and THREE.

As a second example, create a file called FORTEST.BAT containing these commands:

```
ECHO OFF
FOR %%H IN (FORTEST.BAT ONE.BAT TWO.BAT) DO DIR %%H
```

Run FORTEST now. As you can see, the DIR command is executed three times, each time with a different file name. Each time the FOR repeats, %%H is replaced by the next argument in the list. That is, the first time,

%%H equals FORTEST.BAT, the second time, %%H equals ONE.BAT, and so on.

You can use the FOR command to execute a list of commands by placing the commands in the argument list. For example, this command will first clear the screen, then list the directory, and finally, check the disk:

FOR %%C IN (CLS DIR CHKDSK) DO %%C

You may not use a FOR command as the object of the DO. That is, FOR cannot be used to execute another FOR command.

REMEMBER: The FOR command continues to execute until the last argument is processed.

The SHIFT Command

As you know, there are only ten replaceable parameters, %0 through %9. You can use the SHIFT command to gain access to command-line arguments greater than ten. Each time the SHIFT command is executed, the contents of the replaceable parameters are shifted down one position, with whatever was in %0 being lost and %9 containing a new argument if one exists. For example, given these beginning values,

Replaceable Parameter	Value
%0	TEST
%1	A
%2	B
%3	C
%4	<empty>

after one SHIFT they will have the following values:

Replaceable Parameter	Value
%0	A
%1	B
%2	C
%3	<empty>

As a first example, create a file called SHFT.BAT that contains these commands:

```
ECHO OFF
ECHO %0 %1 %2 %3
SHIFT
ECHO %0 %1 %2 %3
```

Execute this command as shown here:

```
SHFT ONE TWO THREE
```

You will see this output:

```
SHFT ONE TWO THREE
ONE TWO THREE
```

You can use a loop to make accessing a large number of arguments easier. For example, change the SHFT.BAT file so that it contains these commands:

```
ECHO OFF
:LOOP
ECHO %1
SHIFT
IF NOT %1 == END GOTO LOOP
REM This will loop until an argument containing
REM the word END is reached.
```

Now, execute this batch file as shown here:

```
SHFT THIS IS A TEST THAT ACCESSES EACH ARGUMENT END
```

This will display the following:

```
THIS
IS
A
TEST
THAT
ACCESSES
EACH
ARGUMENT
```

Processing User Choices

CHOICE is only available if you are using DOS version 6.

If you are using DOS version 6, you can present the user with a choice and obtain a response to which your batch file can respond. This is accomplished using the CHOICE command. CHOICE is a powerful and flexible command that has several forms and options. Let's begin with its most basic form, as shown here:

CHOICE *prompt*

Here, *prompt* is a message that is displayed on the screen. The prompt may be either quoted or not. (Generally, quoted prompts are used.) After the prompting message, [Y,N]? is displayed. When executed, the CHOICE command displays the prompt and then waits until the user presses either **Y** or **N**. For example, this CHOICE command,

CHOICE "Do you want to continue "

causes this prompt to be displayed on the screen:

```
Do you want to continue [Y,N]?
```

The command will then wait for you to press either **Y** or **N**. Any other key will cause the console to beep, and the keypress will be ignored.

The choice that the user selects is returned to your batch file as an ERRORLEVEL value. This means that the value can be tested using an IF statement. If the user presses **Y**, then the error value 1 is returned. If the user presses **N**, then the error value 2 is returned. To see how these values can be used, try this batch file:

```
REM A simple example of CHOICE
ECHO OFF
CHOICE "Which Key "
IF ERRORLEVEL 2 GOTO TWO
IF ERRORLEVEL 1 GOTO ONE

:ONE
ECHO You pressed Y
GOTO DONE

:TWO
ECHO You pressed N
GOTO DONE

:DONE
```

When run, this file displays the following prompt:

```
Which key: [Y,N]?
```

Depending upon which key you press, the appropriate response is displayed. By default, CHOICE lets you enter the response in either upper- or lowercase.

Notice how the IF statements are arranged in the preceding example. Remember, an IF ERRORLEVEL will be true if the error value is equal to or greater than the value specified in the statement. This means that your batch files must always test for the larger values first.

TIP: Technically, the prompting string is optional. When not used, only the [Y,N]? is displayed. From a practical point of view, however, the prompting string is almost always needed.

Using Case-Sensitive Responses

As mentioned, by default, you may enter your response in either upper- or lowercase. However, if you want the response to be case sensitive, then specify the /S option. To see its effect, change the CHOICE line in the foregoing example so that it looks like this:

    CHOICE "Which Key " /S

Now, try the batch file. As you will see, you must enter the response in uppercase.

Using Other Responses

By default, CHOICE requests either a Y or N (corresponding to a Yes or No) response. However, you can specify the letters that you want CHOICE to respond to. Also, you can prompt the user for more than two possibilities. This allows CHOICE to respond to something other than Yes or No. To specify the letters CHOICE will accept, use the /C option. It has this general form,

    /C*chars*

where *chars* are the letters that you want to use. You may use as many characters as you like. For example, here is a batch file that lets the user choose among three options represented by the letters A, B, and C:

```
REM Respond to three choices.
ECHO OFF
CHOICE "Press a key now: " /CABC
IF ERRORLEVEL 3 GOTO THREE
IF ERRORLEVEL 2 GOTO TWO
IF ERRORLEVEL 1 GOTO ONE

:ONE
ECHO You pressed A
GOTO DONE

:TWO
ECHO You pressed B
GOTO DONE
```

```
:THREE
ECHO You pressed C

:DONE
```

In this example, A has the value 1, B has the value 2, and C has the value 3. More generally, the first character specified in the /C option returns the error value 1, the second character returns 2, and so on.

TIP: You are not limited to only letters of the alphabet when using the /C option. You can also use numbers and certain punctuation characters. However, don't use these characters (DOS reserves them for special purposes): <, >, and |.

Suppressing the Character Prompt

In some cases you might not want CHOICE to display the response letters (the characters inside the square brackets). You can suppress this prompt by specifying the /N option. For example, change the CHOICE line in the preceding example so that it looks like this:

```
CHOICE "Press a key now: " /CABC /N
```

When you run the file, only the message "Press a key now:" will be displayed—no prompting letters will be shown.

Using a Timeout

Sometimes you will want to give the user a chance to make a selection, but if the user does not make a choice in a reasonable length of time, you want the batch file to continue on, using a default selection. To accomplish this, use the /T option. Its general form is shown here:

/Tchar,seconds

8

Here, *char* is the character that will be used by default if the user does not make a selection within the specified number of seconds. The number of seconds to wait is given in *seconds*. Here is an example that uses a timeout:

```
REM A timeout example.
ECHO OFF
CHOICE "Select now (timeout in 3 secs.): " /CABC /TC,3
IF ERRORLEVEL 3 GOTO THREE
IF ERRORLEVEL 2 GOTO TWO
IF ERRORLEVEL 1 GOTO ONE

:ONE
ECHO You pressed A
GOTO DONE

:TWO
ECHO You pressed B
GOTO DONE

:THREE
ECHO You pressed C

:DONE
```

In this example, if the user does not make a selection within 3 seconds, the default value linked to C (in this case, the value 3) is returned automatically and the batch file continues execution.

TIP: Once the user presses any key (even if invalid) in response, the /T is disabled and the timeout feature is no longer active.

Using CHOICE to Build Menu Batch Files

One excellent use of the CHOICE command is to create menu batch files that allow the user to choose between two or more selections. Although your own situation and work environment will dictate what type of menu-based batch files are appropriate, the following short example gives the flavor of their use. This file allows the user to either display the DOS version number, check the disk, or display the directory tree:

```
REM A simple menu file.
ECHO OFF
CHOICE "Version, Check-disk, or Tree: " /CVCT
IF ERRORLEVEL 3 GOTO TREE
IF ERRORLEVEL 2 GOTO CHKDSK
IF ERRORLEVEL 1 GOTO VER
GOTO DONE

:VER
VER
GOTO DONE

:CHKDSK
CHKDSK
GOTO DONE

:TREE
TREE

:DONE
```

Your use of menu files is limited only by your imagination.

Executing a Batch File from Within a Batch File

It is possible to start another batch file from within a batch file without the use of the CALL command. However, executing a batch file without the use of CALL produces different results than when the CALL is used. To cause one batch file to execute another, simply use the name of the batch file like any other command. When the batch file's name is encountered, DOS will automatically stop executing the first batch file and begin executing the second. However, when the second batch file

8

terminates, control returns to DOS and the prompt is displayed; DOS does not return to the original batch file.

For example, assume that BKUP is the name of a batch file. Then given this batch file,

```
CLS
CHKDSK
BKUP
DISKCOMP A: B:
```

the final line will never be executed. If you want control to return to the original batch file, use the CALL command.

 ## AUTOEXEC.BAT

AUTOEXEC.BAT is executed when DOS first begins running.

There is one very special batch file which you will probably want to create. It is called AUTOEXEC.BAT, and it is this batch file that DOS automatically executes at startup. Often, you will want DOS to perform one or more tasks when the computer is first started. These tasks can be placed in the AUTOEXEC.BAT file.

A very simple AUTOEXEC.BAT file might look like this:

```
DATE
TIME
CLS
VER
```

This AUTOEXEC.BAT file first prompts for the date and time. Then it clears the screen and, finally, it displays the DOS version number.

You can use the AUTOEXEC.BAT file to create a custom look to your system. For example, a computer dedicated to word processing may use this AUTOEXEC.BAT file:

```
CLS
ECHO WELCOME TO WORD PROCESSING
ECHO          AT WIDGET CORP.
PAUSE
CD \WP
```

You can also use the AUTOEXEC.BAT file to confirm that the proper programs are available for use. For example, assume that the program ACCOUNT.EXE is required for the operation of the computer and it must be located on drive A. This AUTOEXEC.BAT file will wait until you put a diskette containing ACCOUNT.EXE into drive A:

```
ECHO OFF
:LOOP
IF EXIST A:ACCOUNT.EXE GOTO OK
ECHO  Insert program diskette into drive A
PAUSE
GOTO LOOP
:OK
```

Later in this book you will learn that there are several ways to customize DOS, and some of these customization commands make perfect candidates for inclusion in the AUTOEXEC.BAT file.

TIP: The AUTOEXEC.BAT file is a perfect place to put commands that you always execute when your computer starts running.

8

Summary

In this chapter you learned

✦ How to create custom DOS commands through the use of batch files

✦ How to parameterize a batch file

✦ About the special batch file commands:

ECHO
PAUSE
REM
IF
GOTO
CALL
FOR

SHIFT

CHOICE

◆   About the AUTOEXEC.BAT file and its special purpose in DOS.

In the next chapter you will learn some advanced commands that will give you even greater power over your computer.

CHAPTER

DOS DOS DOS DOS DOS DOS DOS DOS

≈MADE EASY≈

9 MORE DOS COMMANDS

Now that you know the basics of DOS, it is time to learn about more DOS commands that give you greater control over your computer. Some of these commands are fairly complicated but they yield great returns for the time you invest.

ATTRIB

DOS associates a set of file attributes with each file on disk. Most of these attributes are for DOS's internal use and may not be examined or modified. However, you can examine and set the *archive, read-only, system,* or *hidden* attributes using the ATTRIB command. ATTRIB is an external command.

All files have attributes that affect their capabilities.

The general form of the ATTRIB command is this:

ATTRIB *attribute file-name*

where *attribute* is either not present or one of the following:

Attribute	Effect
+R	Turn on read-only attribute
–R	Turn off read-only attribute
+A	Turn on archive attribute
–A	Turn off archive attribute
+H	Turn on hidden attribute
–H	Turn off hidden attribute
+S	Turn on system attribute
–S	Turn off system attribute

The *file-name* is the name of the file—which may include a drive and path specifier—that will have its attributes changed. Before going on, let's discuss what these attributes do.

The *archive* attribute is used primarily by DOS to streamline the process of backing up the fixed disk. Although this attribute will be examined more closely later in this book when fixed disk backup is discussed, the following brief discussion will give you the general idea.

Each time a file is created or modified, the archive attribute is turned on. During the backup process, the archive attribute is turned off. During subsequent backups, it is possible to copy only those files that have changed since the last backup because only those that have changed will have the archive attribute on. You generally don't need to change the archive attribute, and it is best left alone.

The *read-only* attribute is used to determine whether a file can be modified. A file that has the read-only attribute turned on can be read but not written to—that is, it cannot be changed. When the read-only attribute is turned off, the file can be read or written to. Generally, when a file is created, the read-only attribute is turned off. The main reason that you would want the read-only attribute on is to prevent someone from accidentally or maliciously tampering with an important file.

The state of the *hidden* attribute determines whether a file will appear in a directory listing. If it is off (the default), then the file is visible. If it is set, the file is hidden from view.

The *system* attribute is set if a file is part of the DOS system. Otherwise, that attribute is cleared. System files are also hidden.

TIP: Most users will only want to change the archive and read-only attributes. The other two are primarily used by system managers and programmers.

You will need a file to use with the following examples, so create a text file called TEST that contains a few characters of your own choosing. You can examine the attribute setting of TEST with the ATTRIB command by not specifying an attribute. For example, enter this command:

ATTRIB TEST

DOS will respond with this message:

A C:\TEST

The "A" signifies that the archive attribute is turned on, as you would expect, since TEST is a new file that has not been backed up.

To set a file to read-only mode, use the +R argument. For example, enter this:

ATTRIB +R TEST

9

Examine the attribute settings again by using ATTRIB without any attribute arguments. You will see this message:

```
A   R  C:\TEST
```

This tells you that TEST is now in read-only mode. To summarize: When an attribute is turned on, its first letter is displayed. If it is turned off, nothing is displayed.

To see the effect of read-only, first try to erase the file. DOS will respond with this message:

```
Access denied
```

Because the file is marked read-only, it may not be modified or erased. However, try this command:

    TYPE TEST

Since typing a file involves only reading it, DOS lets you look at it. You also can use PRINT to print it and COPY to copy it. You simply cannot change it.

To turn off the read-only attribute, use this command:

    ATTRIB –R TEST

Now, try erasing the file. As is evident, the file is now erased.

You can change the attributes of several files at the same time by using wildcard characters in the file name. For example, this turns on the hidden attribute of all files that begin with FORM:

    ATTRIB +H FORM*.*

CAUTION: You can use the wildcard characters * and ? with ATTRIB, but do so with caution since you will be setting the attributes of all the files specified.

You can change the attributes of all files in a directory plus those in any subdirectories by placing a /S after the end of the file name. (Be sure to leave a space between the file name and the /S.) For example, this command will set the archive attribute of all files with the .TXT extension on a disk in drive A. *Don't try this example.*

ATTRIB +A A:*.TXT /S

REMEMBER: To turn on an attribute, use the + sign. To turn it off, use the – sign.

LABEL and VOL

When you list the directory of a diskette, if the diskette does not already have a volume label, the first line looks like this:

```
Volume in drive A has no label
```

If the diskette already has a label, the first line looks something like this:

```
Volume in drive A is WORKDISK
```

Until now, we have ignored this message. Here you will learn what a volume label is and how to give a disk a volume label or change an existing one.

What Is a Volume Label?

A volume label is essentially a name for a disk—either floppy or fixed. A volume label can be up to 11 characters long and may consist of any characters allowed in a file name. Note, however, that no period is allowed in the volume label.

A volume label is the name of a disk.

There are three reasons why you should give a disk a volume label. The first is that it helps to positively identify the disk. This can be useful when you are trying to remember which disk is which. However, the volume label should never take the place of the external stick-on label.

9

The second reason to give a disk a volume label is that at some point in the future, new versions of DOS may allow you to access a disk by its volume label instead of by drive letter. Third, it is possible that an application program may make use of a disk's volume label.

Using LABEL

The DOS LABEL command is used to give a disk a name. To see how LABEL works, let's begin with an example. Put a blank formatted disk in drive A and switch to drive A now. To execute LABEL simply enter **LABEL** at the DOS prompt. You will see the following:

```
Volume label (11 characters, ENTER for none)?_
```

At this point, enter the label **MYDISK**. Now, try the DIR command. The first line will look like this:

```
Volume in drive A is MYDISK
```

As you can see, the volume now has the label MYDISK.

You also can change an existing volume label by using LABEL. Simply enter the new label when prompted. The label you enter will replace the previous label on the disk.

To remove a volume label, press [Enter] instead of specifying a new name when prompted for the volume label. DOS will then prompt you as shown here:

```
Delete current volume label (Y/N)?
```

At this point you can either go ahead and remove the volume label by answering Yes or abort the LABEL command by answering No.

You can specify the volume label on the command line as an argument to LABEL. For example, this changes the volume label to MYDISK:

```
LABEL MYDISK
```

In this form of the command, DOS does not display any messages.

You can place a drive specifier in front of the label in the command line version to change the volume label of a disk other than the current one. For example, this sets the volume label of the diskette in drive B to SAMPLE:

    LABEL B:SAMPLE

Using VOL

If you just want to see the volume label of a disk and don't want to change it, use the VOL command. For example, if you still have the disk used in the previous examples in drive A, then enter **VOL** at this time. You will see this message:

```
Volume in drive A is MYDISK
```

You can use a drive specifier with VOL to see the volume label of a disk in a drive other than the current one. For example, this command displays the volume label for drive B:

    VOL B:

A Closer Look at FORMAT

Although you learned the basics of the FORMAT command earlier, now is the time to become familiar with some of its many options. All the FORMAT options use the same form—a forward slash followed by the option character. There can be more than one option present.

9

NOTE: If you are using a version of DOS prior to 5, then some of the options described here will not be available.

Specifying a Volume Label

As you know, FORMAT requests a volume label when you format a diskette. It is possible to specify the volume label on the command line by using the /V option. For example, the following lets you add a volume label to the diskette that will be formatted in drive A:

FORMAT A: /V:*name*

Here, *name* becomes the volume label of the diskette. (When using this method, you won't be prompted for a label.) If you don't specify *name*, then FORMAT prompts you for a label name, as it does by default.

NOTE: When formatting, versions of DOS prior to 5 do not automatically prompt for a volume label, so you must specify /V on the command line if you want to give a disk a label.

Putting the System Files on a Diskette

These three files must be present on the disk in order for a diskette to be able to load DOS:

✦ COMMAND.COM

✦ IO.SYS

✦ MSDOS.SYS

Collectively, these files are referred to as the *DOS system files*, or *system* for short. (Some versions of DOS will call these files by slightly different names.) Loosely, they form different parts of the DOS program. The only one that will show up when the directory is listed is COMMAND.COM; the other two will be hidden. You can have FORMAT copy these files onto the newly formatted diskette by using the /S option. Once the formatting has been completed, in addition to the other messages, the message "System transferred" will be displayed.

CAUTION: In older versions of DOS, COMMAND.COM will not be transferred by FORMAT when the /S option is used. You must copy this file manually after the formatting has concluded using the COPY command.

FORMAT must have access to the system files in order to transfer them to the new diskette. If they are not on the current disk, you will be prompted to insert a system diskette so that the system files can be copied.

Although a diskette that has been formatted using the /S option can start the computer and load DOS, you will only have access to DOS's internal commands because the external commands are not transferred to the new diskette. You can copy the external commands onto the diskette, however.

Leaving Room for the System Files

DOS is a copyrighted program that you may use, but may not give or sell to anyone else except as described in the DOS license agreement. For this reason, you may need to create a diskette that reserves room for the DOS system files but does not actually copy them to the diskette. For example, you might wish to prepare a diskette for a friend that contains several of your files, but you want to make sure that he or she can put a system on it if necessary. (This is done with the SYS command, which will be discussed a little later in this chapter.) If you don't reserve room for the system, it cannot be put on the diskette.

To cause storage for the system to be reserved, use the /B option during formatting. Room will be set aside for the system files.

Two Ways to Format

The FORMAT command has two options that allow you to format a disk in radically different fashions. (These options only apply if you are using DOS version 5 or later.) The first is the /Q option, which causes a disk to be formatted very quickly. When a *quick format* is performed, the only thing done to the disk is that the file allocation table is cleared. In simple terms, this means that all files on the disk are erased, including hidden and system files. Because a quick format simply clears the file allocation table, it must be used on a previously formatted diskette. In other words, you cannot quick format a previously unformatted diskette.

The opposite of the quick format is the *unconditional format*. An unconditional format performs an actual, low-level format of the diskette. An unconditional format irretrievably destroys all information on the diskette. To unconditionally format a disk, specify the /U option.

Transferring the System with SYS

If a diskette has been formatted using the /B option or if there is sufficient room on a diskette, you can copy the system files to it using the SYS command. SYS has this general form:

SYS *drive-specifier*

where *drive-specifier* determines the drive that will receive the system files. SYS is an external command.

To see how SYS works, format a fresh diskette using no options whatsoever and put it in drive A. Next, enter this command:

SYS A:

SYS will respond with the message "System transferred". This means that the system files have been copied to the disk in drive A.

CAUTION: If you use an older version of DOS (version 4 or earlier), you need to know about one little wrinkle in the way the SYS command works. As stated in the previous section, there are three system files: MSDOS.SYS, IO.SYS, and COMMAND.COM. For some reason, COMMAND.COM is not transferred by the SYS command. However, if the target diskette will be used to start the computer and load DOS, COMMAND.COM must be present because it is the part of DOS that interprets your commands. Without it, there is no way for you to communicate with DOS. To install COMMAND.COM on the diskette, simply copy it there. (It must go in the root directory.) One final point: when using early versions of DOS (prior to 5), the diskette must have been formatted using the /B option in order for SYS to work properly in all situations.

The VERIFY Command

Most of the time, disk write operations are successful. However, on rare occasions, such as a power surge, an error can occur, in which case the contents of the disk file will not be exactly what they are supposed to be. You can have DOS verify that the data has been written correctly. To do this, DOS actually reads the section of the file just written and compares it to what is in memory. If a discrepancy is found, a write error is reported.

VERIFY takes this general form:

VERIFY on/off

By default, VERIFY is off. To turn it on, enter this command:

VERIFY ON

You might think that it is a good idea to always have VERIFY turned on, but it generally isn't. With VERIFY on, each write operation will take about twice as long because of the extra work DOS is doing. Generally, it is a good idea to turn on VERIFY only when working with very important files. Remember, disk errors are quite rare. If you experience frequent errors, your computer probably needs to be checked by a qualified service technician.

You can see if VERIFY is on or off by entering **VERIFY** with no argument. For example, entering this:

VERIFY

results in this message:

```
VERIFY is on
```

(assuming that verify is on).

Using MEM

If you have DOS version 4 or later you can use the MEM command to determine the amount of memory in your system, the amount of it that is free, and how it is organized. What this command displays depends upon the version of DOS you are using as well as how your system is configured. However, you should have no trouble understanding the essence of it. MEM has several options, but they are intended for use mostly by programmers and system integrators.

9

Using MOVE

If you have DOS version 6, you will be able to move files using the MOVE command. Moving a file first copies the file to the new destination and then erases it from its original location. While you can move a file manually by first using COPY and then using ERASE, using the MOVE command automates the process. Here is the general form of MOVE:

MOVE *source destination*

Here, *source* is the file or files that you want to move, which may include wildcard specifiers, and *destination* is a drive specifier and/or directory. You also can specify a new file name if you are moving only one file. For example, this moves the file TEMP from the C drive to the A drive:

MOVE C:TEMP A:

You also can use MOVE to change the name of a directory. To do this use this general form:

MOVE *old-dir-name new-dir-name*

where *old-dir-name* is the full path name of the directory to be renamed and *new-dir-name* is its new name.

XCOPY: An Expanded Copy Command

There are some situations in which COPY is less than perfect. For example, assume that you have a diskette with directories organized like this:

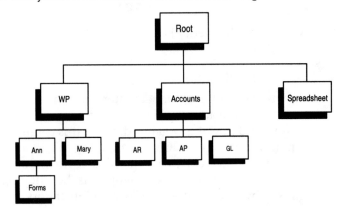

How can you copy the entire contents of the WP directory including the contents of the ANN and MARY subdirectories plus ANN's subdirectory FORMS, and still maintain the directory structure? Using the COPY command you will have to copy each directory individually, making sure that all the files are copied into the correct destination directory. This approach is clearly error prone and tedious. For this reason DOS versions 3.0 and greater include the XCOPY command which, in addition to having many other useful features, lets you copy complete sets of directories and subdirectories automatically.

XCOPY is an external command. In its simplest form it works much like COPY. For example, to copy a file called SAMPLE from drive A to drive B you could use this command:

    XCOPY A:SAMPLE B:

However, XCOPY goes far beyond this. XCOPY takes this general form:

    XCOPY *source destination options*

where *source* and *destination* may be either a drive specifier, a file name, or a directory name, or any combination of the three. The *options* let you control exactly what and how XCOPY copies.

Let's look at how XCOPY functions with its various options.

9

Copying Files

Although it is faster to copy files with the internal COPY command, you can copy files using XCOPY. The wildcard characters * and ? are allowed. The option /V (verify) is also supported.

Copying Groups of Directories

You can use XCOPY to copy the contents of the current directory plus the contents of any subdirectories. To see how this works, format two diskettes and label them ONE and TWO. On diskette ONE, create these two subdirectories using these commands. (Fixed disk users: do *not* use your fixed disk for this example.)

MKDIR WP
MKDIR ACCOUNTS

Switch to the WP directory and issue this command:

MKDIR LETTERS

The directory structure of diskette ONE should now look like this:

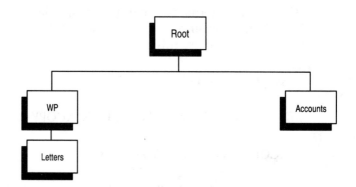

Create a short text file called SAMPLE.TXT containing whatever you like in the root directory. Create another file called SAMPLE2.TXT in the WP directory. Next, create a file called SAMPLE3.TXT in the WP\LETTERS directory. Finally, copy XCOPY.EXE into the root directory of diskette ONE. Put diskette ONE in drive A. If you have a dual floppy system, put diskette TWO into drive B. Otherwise, you will need to swap it in and out of drive A as prompted by DOS.

To begin, first try this command:

XCOPY A: B:

If you have only one floppy drive, DOS will alternately call it A and B, allowing you a chance to swap in the correct diskette. After the command is finished, only the file SAMPLE.TXT from the root directory will have been copied to diskette TWO. You can confirm this by displaying the directory of diskette TWO.

In order for XCOPY to copy the contents of a group of directories, you need to use the /S option. Try this command now:

XCOPY A: B: /S

After the command has finished, list the directory of diskette TWO. As you can see, the directory WP has been created. If you change to WP, you will see that SAMPLE2.TXT has been copied to that directory and that the subdirectory LETTERS has been created. SAMPLE3.TXT will be found in WP\LETTERS.

The /S option tells XCOPY to copy the contents of the current directory plus all of its subdirectories. If necessary, it will create the subdirectories on the destination diskette.

You might be wondering why the ACCOUNTS directory was not found on diskette TWO. The reason is that ACCOUNTS had no files in it. If a directory contains no entries, then XCOPY will not create it on the destination diskette. If you want all directories created, whether empty or not, you must specify the /E option. For example, this command will cause the ACCOUNTS directory to be created on diskette TWO:

XCOPY A: B: /S /E

By default, XCOPY uses the current directory. However, you may specify a different starting directory. For example, this:

XCOPY A:\WP B: /S

will only copy the contents of the WP directory plus its subdirectory.

Using the Archive Attribute

You can use XCOPY to copy only those files that have the archive attribute turned on by using either the /A option or the /M option. Remember that the archive attribute is turned on whenever a file is created or changed. The difference between the two options is what happens to the archive attribute on the source files.

If you use the /A option, the archive attribute is not changed on the source file. This means you could make repeated copies of those files with the archive attribute turned on. However, the /M option causes the archive attribute of the source files to be turned off after they are copied. The reason for this is to allow you an easy way to copy only those files that have changed since the last time a copy was made.

The main purpose of the /A and /M options is to allow XCOPY to automatically copy those files that have changed since the last copy operation took place. The most common reason for using these options is to automate the backing up of important files.

TIP: Frankly, the /A and /M options to XCOPY are not often used because DOS provides a better command, which also uses the archive attribute to perform backup operations. (You will learn about it a little later.) It is best to leave this sort of backing up to a command, which is designed expressly for this purpose.

Using the Date Option

You can use XCOPY to copy files based upon their creation dates by using the /D option. The /D option takes this general form:

/D:*mm-dd-yy*

Only those files with creation dates the same as or later than the specified date will be copied. For example, this:

XCOPY A: B: /S /D:12-12-93

will copy all files with creation dates beginning with 12-12-93 and later.

The /D option only applies to files. Directories will be established on the destination disk without regard to their creation dates.

Query Before Copy

The /P option causes XCOPY to prompt you before each file is copied. The message will take this general form:

file-name (Y/N)?

If you answer "Y", the file is copied. Answering "N" causes that file to be skipped.

Using the /W Option

As you have noticed, XCOPY begins to copy files immediately. If you need to switch diskettes before the copying takes place, specify the /W option, which causes XCOPY to issue this prompt prior to starting the copying process:

```
Press any key to begin copying file(s)
```

Replacing Files

As you continue to use DOS you will find that there are two very common situations that involve copying files that neither COPY nor XCOPY can handle. The first is when you want to replace the files on the destination disk by files of the same name from the source disk. For example, a work disk may contain several files for which a new version exists. The second situation is the opposite of the first. Sometimes you will want to add files to a disk without overwriting any file already on the disk. You can accomplish both of these activities with REPLACE.

This is the general form of REPLACE:

REPLACE *source destination options*

where *source* and *destination* specify the source and destination file names, directories, or drives, and may include the wildcard characters * and ?. REPLACE is an external command.

In its simplest form, REPLACE replaces existing files on the destination disk. For example, this command:

REPLACE A:SAMPLE B:

replaces the file SAMPLE on drive B (which must already exist), with the one on drive A. However, REPLACE really shines when wildcards and options are used.

Using the two diskettes you created for the XCOPY examples, create the text file called RPLCTEST.TXT containing anything you like on disk ONE. Also, copy the file REPLACE.EXE to diskette ONE. Now, insert diskette ONE in drive A and, if you have two floppies, diskette TWO in drive B. If you have only one floppy, DOS will alternate that drive between A and B and you will be prompted to swap the two diskettes. Now, enter this command:

9

REPLACE A:*.* B:

Your screen will look like this:

```
A>REPLACE A:*.* B:

 Replacing B:\SAMPLE.TXT

 Replacing B:\XCOPY.EXE

2 File(s) replaced
```

As you can see, the REPLACE command copied SAMPLE.TXT and XCOPY.EXE but did not copy RPLCTEST.TXT. The reason is that RPLCTEST.TXT did not exist on the destination diskette. Remember, by default, REPLACE will only copy those files it finds on the destination diskette. In this example, only the files in the root directory were replaced. However, if you specify the /S option, then all files in all subdirectories will also be examined and replaced if possible. For example, try this command now:

REPLACE A:*.* B: /S

This replaces all files on the destination diskette in all directories.

You can use REPLACE to add to a disk only those files that are not currently on the destination disk. This prevents existing files from being overwritten. To do this, use the /A option. Try this command now:

REPLACE A:*.* B: /A

This time you will see this:

```
 Adding B:\REPLACE.EXE

 Adding B:\RPLCTEST.TXT

2 File(s) added
```

The only files copied were those that did not already exist on diskette TWO.

If you need to insert a different diskette before REPLACE begins, use the /W option. This causes REPLACE to wait until you press a key before beginning.

The /P option causes REPLACE to ask you before a file is replaced. For example, try this:

    REPLACE A:*.* B: /P

You will see this prompt:

```
Replace B:\SAMPLE.TXT? (Y/N)
```

If you answer "Y" the file will be replaced; otherwise it will not.

You can replace only those files on the target diskette that are older than the ones on the source diskette by using the /U option.

By default, REPLACE will not replace files that are marked as read-only on the target. However, if you specify the /R option, then read-only files will also be replaced.

Some points to remember: You cannot use the /A and /S options together. You cannot use the /U and the /A options together. Keep in mind that the source and destination need not be on different disks—they may simply be different directories on the same disk.

Printing Graphics Images

When you press the [Prt Sc] key, whatever is on the screen is printed on the printer. However, this will only work correctly for screens that contain text and no graphics. Here, the term *graphics* is used to mean things like lines, circles, boxes, charts, and the like. Although DOS does not generate graphics displays, many application programs do. If you want to be able to print a screen that contains graphics to the printer you must first execute the GRAPHICS command. GRAPHICS is an external command.

The GRAPHICS command has this general form:

    GRAPHICS *printer option*

where the name of *printer* is determined according to Table 9-1. (Not all versions of DOS will support all printers shown in the table.) If *printer* is not specified, then it defaults to GRAPHICS.

If no printer name is specified, the IBM Personal Graphics Printer is assumed. The Epson series printers are quite commonly used with microcomputers and also work with the default GRAPHICS setting.

9

TIP: If in doubt about which printer to specify, use the default setting.

For example, to allow graphics to be printed on a color printer with a red, green, blue, and black ribbon, enter this:

GRAPHICS COLOR4

Printer Type	Name
IBM Personal Graphics Printer	GRAPHICS
Wide-carriage IBM Personal Graphics Printer	GRAPHICSWIDE
IBM Proprinter	GRAPHICS
IBM PC Convertible Printer	THERMAL
IBM Color Printer with black ribbon	COLOR1
IBM Color Printer with red, green, blue, and black ribbon	COLOR4
IBM Color Printer with black, cyan, magenta, and yellow ribbon	COLOR8
Any Hewlett-Packard DeskJet printer	DESKJET
Hewlett-Packard LaserJet	LASERJET
Hewlett-Packard LaserJet II	LASERJETII
Hewlett-Packard PaintJet	PAINTJET
Hewlett-Packard QuietJet	QUIETJET
Hewlett-Packard QuietJet Plus	QUIETJETPLUS
Hewlett-Packard PCL printer	HPDEFAULT
Hewlett-Packard Rugged Writer	RUGGEDWRITER
Hewlett-Packard Rugged Wide Writer	RUGGEDWRITERWIDE
Hewlett-Packard ThinkJet	THINKJET

Printer Names for use with the GRAPHICS Command
Table 9-1.

By default, white on the screen is printed as black on the printer and black on the screen is printed as white. The /R option causes black to print as black and white to print as white. This option is seldom used.

The background color of the screen is usually not printed. However, if you have a color printer, you can print the background by specifying the /B option.

If you have an IBM PC Convertible Liquid Crystal Display, use the /LCD option.

Finally, the GRAPHICS command includes the /PRINTBOX option. This option requires significant technical knowledge to use. However, if you have an application program that requires this option, just follow that application program's instructions.

Summary

This chapter introduced a number of powerful DOS commands that expand the control you have over the system. These commands are listed here:

+ ATTRIB
+ LABEL
+ VOL
+ SYS
+ VERIFY
+ MEM
+ MOVE
+ XCOPY
+ REPLACE
+ GRAPHICS

9

You also learned how to install the DOS system files on a diskette using the FORMAT command.

In the next chapter, you will learn about filters, pipes, and how to redirect input and output. These things give you control over how information moves about inside the computer.

CHAPTER

10

REDIRECTING I/O

Data goes into the computer via input devices and leaves by way of output devices. The transfer of information to or from these devices is called an input/output operation, or I/O operation for short. The computer has several I/O devices, including the keyboard, the monitor, the printer, and the disk drives. Using some special DOS commands it is possible to reroute the flow of data. This is called redirecting I/O.

Standard Input and Standard Output

You might be surprised to learn that DOS does not "know" where its commands come from or where its output is sent. That is, DOS does not know, or care, that you use a keyboard to enter commands and that you see DOS's response on a monitor. The reason for this is that DOS does not deal directly with the I/O devices. Rather, it works through two special internal pseudo-devices called *standard input* and *standard output*. These pseudo-devices provide the programming support for the various I/O devices supported by the computer. Hence, DOS itself does not know precisely what device sent it a command or where its output is displayed.

When DOS begins execution, standard input is linked to the keyboard and standard output is linked to the monitor. However, it is possible to change which device is linked with which pseudo-device. For example, you can think of standard input and standard output as depicted in Figure 10-1.

We will look first at the redirection of I/O to and from a disk file. Later, you will see how to redirect I/O to the other devices supported by the computer.

Redirecting Output to a File

DOS uses the > and >> operators to redirect the output generated by a DOS command or an application program that would normally be

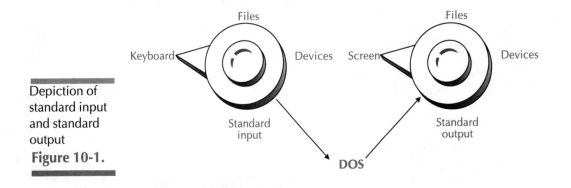

Depiction of
standard input
and standard
output
Figure 10-1.

shown on the screen. The most common usages of these operators with files are

command > *filename*
command >> *filename*

where *command* is either a DOS command or an application program, and *filename* is the name of the file that will receive the output generated by *command*. For example, enter this command:

DIR > OUT.DIR

Nothing is displayed on the screen. Now, list the file OUT.DIR on the screen using the TYPE command. You will see that the output of the DIR command is contained in the file OUT.DIR. That is, output from DIR has been *redirected* to the file OUT.DIR.

The difference between the > and >> operators lies in how the output file is handled. The > operator always creates a new, empty file to hold the output information. If a file by the specified name already exists on the disk, it is first erased and then a new, empty one is created. That is, if OUT.DIR had already existed on your work disk, the previous example would have erased it, destroying its contents, and then recreated it and put the new information into it. However, the >> operator does not destroy an existing file. If the specified file already exists, the >> operator causes the output to be placed on the end of the file. If the file does not exist, however, it will still be created.

To understand the difference, try this command:

DIR SORT.EXE > OUT.DIR

If you now enter **TYPE OUT.DIR**, you will see something similar to this (remember, the exact information will vary slightly):

```
Volume in drive C is CDISK
Volume Serial Number is 1968-89D8
Directory of C:\DOS

SORT     EXE      6922 01-28-93   6:00a
        1 file(s)          6922 bytes
                        5054464 bytes free
```

As you can see, the old contents of OUT.DIR are no longer present. Now try this command:

DIR SORT.EXE >> OUT.DIR

Enter **TYPE OUT.DIR** to display the following:

```
Volume in drive C is CDISK
Volume Serial Number is 1968-89D8
Directory of C:\DOS

SORT      EXE      6922 01-28-93   6:00a
        1 file(s)        6922 bytes
                       5054464 bytes free


Volume in drive C is CDISK
Volume Serial Number is 1968-89D8
Directory of C:\DOS

SORT      EXE      6922 01-28-93   6:00a
        1 file(s)        6922 bytes
                       5054464 bytes free
```

This time the previous contents of the file were preserved and the new output placed on the end.

REMEMBER: The > redirects output to a file which is newly created each time. Any existing file by the specified name will be erased. The >> puts redirected output on the end of an existing file. Any previous contents are preserved.

It is important to understand that only the output that would normally go to the screen is being redirected. Other I/O operations performed by the command are not affected. For example, try this COPY command:

COPY OUT.DIR TEST > OUTPUT

This command correctly copies the contents of OUT.DIR into TEST. Only the information that COPY sends to standard output will be placed into the file OUTPUT. In this case, OUTPUT will only contain the message "1 file(s) copied."

A log file records computer activity while you are away.

One of the most common uses of redirected output is to create a *log file*, which records the activity of the computer when you are not physically in attendance. For example, the end-of-month phase of an accounting package might include several lengthy operations which are best run overnight. If you place all the commands in a batch file with output redirected into a log file using the >> operator, then when you come in the next morning you can check to see that all went well.

Redirecting Input to a File

You can redirect standard input using the < operator. Instead of causing the command to send its output to a file, < causes a command to use the contents of a file as input. When input is redirected, information that is normally entered at the keyboard is read from the specified file.

Although you will seldom need to redirect the input to a file, it is easy enough to do if you are careful. To see a simple example in action, first create a file called INPUT.DAT that contains the word "SAMPLE" followed by a blank line. Now, execute this command exactly as shown:

LABEL < INPUT.DAT

Recall that LABEL sets the volume label name of the disk. As you can see, it no longer pauses and waits for you to enter the label name. Instead, it reads the name from the file INPUT.DAT. To confirm that this actually happened, use VOL to display the volume label. (You can change the label back to what it was previously, now.)

10

CAUTION: You must be very careful with redirecting input to a file because if the file fails to contain sufficient input to satisfy the command, the computer will effectively stop running and lock up. If this happens, the only thing you can do is restart the system.

Although all of DOS's commands allow their input and output to be redirected, some application programs do not. Certain programs bypass DOS's standard I/O routines and communicate directly with the hardware—generally to achieve improved performance. In this situation, the redirection operators will not be effective. If you attempt to redirect I/O to an application program and it doesn't work, this is probably the reason.

Redirecting I/O to Other Devices

You can redirect I/O operations to devices other than disk drives by using their DOS *device names*. These device names and what they refer to are shown in Table 10-1. You cannot create disk files with names that are the same as any device name. For traditional reasons, you may place a colon after the device name. However, this book will not do this because it is superfluous.

Device	Description
CON	The console, either keyboard or screen
AUX	The first asynchronous serial port
COM1	Same as AUX
COM2	The second asynchronous serial port
COM3	The third asynchronous serial port
COM4	The fourth asynchronous serial port
PRN	The first printer—output only
LPT1	Same as PRN
LPT2	The second printer—output only
LPT3	The third printer—output only
NUL	A nonexistent device used by programmers for testing software

DOS Device Names
Table 10-1.

You can use the device names any place you would use a file name. For example, create a short text file called MYNAME that contains your name. Now, try this command:

COPY MYNAME PRN

Your name will be printed on the printer.

Think back to the early chapters in this book before you knew how to use EDIT (or EDLIN, if you are using an early version of DOS). Now you can understand why you used COPY commands like this to create short text files:

COPY CON MYFILE

This tells COPY to read the keyboard for input and to put that data in a file. The reason that you had to enter a [Ctrl]-[Z] at the end of the text is that [Ctrl]-[Z] is DOS's end-of-file marker. The only way the COPY command knows that it is to stop reading input is when it encounters the end-of-file marker.

As another example, an alternative to the TYPE command to display the contents of a text file on the screen is to simply COPY it to CON. For example, this prints your name on the screen:

COPY MYNAME CON

10

TIP: A really slick trick that allows you to use your computer like a very expensive typewriter is this command:

COPY CON PRN

Now, whatever you type will be printed on the printer. However, COPY will wait until you enter a [Ctrl]-[Z] before printing begins.

You can use the I/O redirection operators on device names as well as file names. For example, this command shows a handy way to print a copy of the directory listing:

DIR > PRN

CAUTION: When redirecting to a device, make sure that the device exists and is online. If either condition is not met, your command may "hang up" the computer.

Using CTTY

DOS allows you to redirect both the input and output to a different device by using the CTTY command. The command name, which probably seems strange, is a traditional name derived from the early days of computing when Teletype machines were used instead of terminals. The command name is short for Change TeleTYpe. It is possible to hook up a remote terminal to a DOS-based computer and then switch control of the computer to that terminal. For example, if the terminal were connected to the COM1 serial port, you would enter the following command to switch control to it:

CTTY COM1

Don't try this, however, unless you know that the device you are switching to is actually capable of controlling the computer. For example, a printer isn't.

To switch control back to the console, enter

CTTY CON

Unless you have a remote terminal attached to your computer, don't use the CTTY command.

Filters

Filters are
special DOS
commands
that modify
(filter) data
and then
pass it along.

DOS has three special commands called *filters*. They are called filters because they read standard input, perform some manipulations on the information, and write it to standard output. The three filter commands are MORE, FIND, and SORT. Let's look at these now.

MORE

The MORE filter reads standard input, displays 24 lines at a time on the screen, and waits for you to press a key before displaying the next screen full of information. To see how MORE works, create a text file call BIG.TXT that is 50 lines long with each line containing its line number. That is, the first ten lines of the file will look like this:

```
1
2
3
4
5
6
7
8
9
10
```

Now, try this command:

```
MORE < BIG.TXT
```

As you can see, the first screen full of lines of the file is displayed. On the bottom line is the prompt:

```
— More —
```

To see more of the file, press any key.

The general form of MORE is

```
MORE < filename
```

10

where *filename* is the name of the file to be processed. You can also use a device name. Actually, the < and the file name are optional. However, if they are left off, MORE will simply read characters from the keyboard and display them on the screen, which is not very useful.

TIP: MORE provides a better way to browse through large text files than TYPE does because it automatically pages through them 24 lines at a time.

FIND

The FIND filter searches a list of files for occurrences of a specified string and displays each line where a match occurs. FIND has this general form:

FIND *options* "*string*" *file-list*

The *string* is the sequence of characters that you are looking for. It must be enclosed in double quotes. The *file-list* is the list of files that FIND will search. You may not use the wildcard characters in the file names.

Before you can try the examples, you must create a file called SAMPLE.TXT and enter these lines into it:

    This is a sample text
    file that illustrates
    the use of the FIND filter command.
    Notice that upper CASE
    and lower case
    are considered separately by FIND.

Now, try this command:

    FIND "that" SAMPLE.TXT

FIND will respond with this output:

```
---------- SAMPLE.TXT
file that illustrates
Notice that upper CASE
```

Each time an occurrence of the search string is found, FIND responds by printing the line in which the match occurs.

As the contents of the file suggest, FIND treats upper- and lowercase letters separately. For example, try this command:

FIND "CASE" SAMPLE.TXT

FIND will only report a match in the line "Notice that upper CASE"; it will not find the line with "lower case" in it.

You can specify more than one file to search. To see how this works, copy SAMPLE.TXT to SAMPLE2.TXT and change the first line so that it reads as follows:

This is a second sample text

Now, try this command:

FIND "second" SAMPLE.TXT SAMPLE2.TXT

FIND will respond like this:

```
---------- SAMPLE.TXT

---------- SAMPLE2.TXT
This is a second sample text
```

10

Notice that the files are searched in the order in which they appear on the command line. In this case, the word "second" occurs only in SAMPLE2.TXT. However, if you enter this command:

FIND "text" SAMPLE.TXT SAMPLE2.TXT

FIND will respond with:

```
---------- SAMPLE.TXT
This is a sample text
```

```
---------- SAMPLE2.TXT
This is a second sample text
```

You may have any number of files in the list, as long as the total length of the command line does not exceed 128 characters.

Sometimes all you will want to know is if there are any occurrences of the string, and if so how many times it appears in the file. To do this, use the /C option. For example, try this command:

> FIND /C "that" SAMPLE.TXT

FIND responds like this:

```
---------- SAMPLE.TXT: 2
```

As you can see, only the number of occurrences is reported—the line containing the string is not shown.

You can use the /N option to show the relative line number of each occurrence. Try this:

> FIND /N "that" SAMPLE.TXT

The output now looks like this:

```
---------- SAMPLE.TXT
[2]file that illustrates
[4]Notice that upper CASE
```

The line numbers are shown between square brackets. You cannot use the /N and the /C options together.

Finally, you can have FIND report all lines that do *not* contain the string by using the /V option. For example, this command,

> FIND /V "that" SAMPLE.TXT

produces this output:

```
This is a sample text
the use of the FIND filter command.
and lower case
are considered separately by FIND.
```

REMEMBER: You must specify each file to be searched by FIND separately. You may not use wildcard characters.

SORT

The SORT filter command sorts information read from standard input and writes the sorted version to standard output. SORT has this general form,

SORT   *option*   *<input*   *>output*

where *input* and *output* are either file or device names. If they are not specified, then the screen is used for output and the keyboard for input. It is not uncommon to have SORT display its output on the screen.

SORT works by sorting information on a line-by-line basis. It treats upper- and lowercase as the same. Unless you specify otherwise, sort arranges the information in ascending alphabetical order.

As a simple first example, create a file called SORTTEST.TXT and enter these lines:

    one
    two
    three
    four
    five
    six
    seven
    eight
    nine
    ten

Now, try this command:

    SORT < SORTTEST.TXT

This will cause SORT to display the sorted file on the screen. The output will look like this:

10

```
eight
five
four
nine
one
seven
six
ten
three
two
```

You can have the sorted information placed in a file by specifying the file name. For example, this command places the information in the file TEMP:

SORT < SORTTEST.TXT > TEMP

You can sort in reverse order by specifying the /R option. This displays the SORTTEST.TXT file in reverse alphabetical order:

SORT /R < SORTTEST.TXT

One good use for SORT is to sort the directory. To do this, first create a file called OUT.DIR that contains the directory listing, using this command:

DIR > OUT.DIR

Now, try this command:

SORT < OUT.DIR

A sorted directory will be displayed.

REMEMBER: If you use DOS version 5 or later, you can sort the directory using the DIR command with the /O option.

Sorting on a Specific Column

Tables of information are very common. Sometimes it is useful to sort a table using information other than the first column. Unless directed otherwise, SORT begins sorting with the first character of each line. However, you can tell SORT what character to begin sorting on with the /+ *n* option, where *n* is the column to begin with.

For example, a hardware store might keep its inventory in a file similar to the one shown here:

```
item     cost on-hand
pliers   10    10
hammers  8      3
nails    1    100
screws   1      0
```

The store manager could use SORT to sort the data based on the on-hand column to provide an easy way to see which items are out of stock or running low. The command would look like this, assuming the file is called SORTTEST.TXT:

> SORT /+13 < SORTTEST.TXT

The output is

```
screws   1      0
hammers  8      3
pliers   10    10
nails    1    100
item     cost on-hand
```

The number 13 is used in the command because that is the character position that starts the on-hand column. If you try this example, do not use any tabs in the file.

 ## Pipes

It is possible to route the output of one command into the input of another. This process is called *piping* because you can conceptually think of the information flowing from one command to the next through a pipe. To create a pipe between two programs, you use the | operator, which uses this general form:

10

command1 | command2

The output of *command1* is automatically redirected to the input of *command2*. For example, try this command:

DIR | MORE

This causes the directory listing to be sent as input to MORE instead of to the screen. MORE then displays the directory 24 lines at a time.

In the previous section you saw one way to produce a sorted directory listing, however there is an easier way, as this command illustrates:

DIR | SORT | MORE

Try this. As you can see, the directory is displayed in sorted order. In this case, two pipes were used. The output of DIR was used as input by SORT whose output was, in turn, used as input by MORE. You can visualize the way this command operates as shown in Figure 10-2. In general, you can have as many pipes as can fit on the command line.

When a pipe is created, a temporary disk file is established that is automatically erased when the commands are completed. Therefore, there must be room on your disk for this temporary file. The size of the file is governed by the amount of output generated by the command

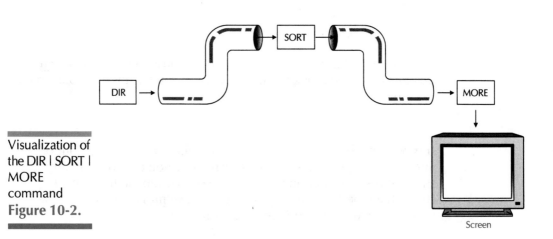

Visualization of the DIR | SORT | MORE command
Figure 10-2.

that is putting data into the pipe. Generally, a few thousand free bytes are sufficient.

Here is another example that uses a pipe to help you find a "lost" file. From time to time, a file will accidentally get placed into the wrong directory of a disk. If there are a great many subdirectories it can take a long time to find the file by manually searching each directory. However, this command will search all directories on a disk and report the path to the file. The file is called TEST here, but in reality, you would substitute the name of the file you are looking for.

CHKDSK /V | FIND "TEST"

If you remember, when CHKDSK is used with the /V option, it displays all the files on the disk in this basic form:

drive:path\filename

Hence, when a match is reported, the path to the file is also shown.

REMEMBER: If you have DOS version 5 or later, you can also search all directories for a file by using the /S option to DIR.

Putting It All Together— Creating Simple Databases

10

You can use I/O redirection and pipes to create simple but effective databases. You can use the FIND command to locate information, the SORT command to sort the database, and the MORE command to browse through it. You can use EDIT, or any other editor, to enter information into the database. The only restriction is that each entry in the database be on one line.

As a simple example, a quick-reference telephone directory database of frequently called numbers will be developed. The database will use this basic format:

Last-name, First-name area-code number

For example,

    Bell, Alexander 123 555-1010

For the sake of the examples, enter the following information into PHONE.DAT:

    Washington, George 111 555-1111
    Bell, Alexander 222 555-2222
    Newton, Isaac 333 555-3333
    Nietzsche, Friedrich 444 555-4444

To find Newton's telephone number you would use this command:

    TYPE PHONE.DAT | FIND "Newton"

Newton's phone number will appear.

You can sort your phone list using this series of commands:

    SORT < PHONE.DAT > TEMP
    COPY TEMP PHONE.DAT
    ERASE TEMP

You can list the numbers for groups of people based on the beginning letters in their names. For example, the following command lists the telephone numbers for both Newton and Nietzsche.

    TYPE PHONE.DAT | FIND "N"

You can expand the telephone directory to include addresses or perhaps remarks, as long as everything fits on one line.

You can use the same basic approach to create databases for other items. The possibilities are limited only by your imagination.

Summary

In this chapter you learned

✦   About standard input and output

◆ How to redirect I/O

◆ About DOS devices

◆ About the filter commands SORT, FIND, and MORE

◆ About pipes

◆ How to create simple databases using DOS

In the next chapter you will learn how to expand DOS's command-line capabilities by using the DOSKEY command.

10

PART

3

ADVANCED DOS
FEATURES

CHAPTER

11

USING DOSKEY TO EXPAND THE COMMAND-LINE INTERFACE

In this chapter you will learn about a command that greatly enhances the command-line interface. Although DOS's editing keys make using the command line a little easier, DOS includes a command that lets you take full control. This command is called DOSKEY, and it allows you to reuse previous commands and to give a name to a series of commands. As you will see, DOSKEY is a powerful addition to the command-line interface.

NOTE: DOSKEY is only available with DOS version 5 or later.

DOSKEY is an external command. Also, DOSKEY is an installed command. To install it, simply enter **DOSKEY** at the command line. (Do this now so that you can follow along with the examples.)

Accessing Your Command History

Your command history is a record of what you enter at the command prompt.

As you know, when you press F3 the last command you entered is redisplayed and may be used again. DOSKEY expands this concept by letting you reuse not only the previously entered command, but any of the last several commands you gave DOS. (The exact number of commands that DOSKEY remembers varies, depending on several factors, but generally you can count on at least the last 25 commands.) DOSKEY records your commands as you enter them, creating a *command history*.

To see how DOSKEY works, give DOS the following commands, one at a time. (Be sure that DOSKEY is installed.)

        DIR
        CHKDSK
        VER

Once you have entered these commands, press the ⬆ key one time. You will see VER redisplayed. Now, press the ⬆ key a second time; this time CHKDSK is shown. Press ⬆ a third time and DIR is displayed. Each time you press the ⬆ key DOSKEY displays the command you entered before the one currently shown. When a command is shown, it may be executed again by pressing Enter.

As stated, each time you press the ⬆ key the next earlier command in your command history is displayed. In essence, pressing ⬆ moves backwards through your command history. To move in the forward direction, press the ⬇ key. For example, if DIR is currently displayed, then pressing ⬇ causes CHKDSK to be shown.

To display the first (oldest) command in your command history, press [Pg Up]. To display the last (newest) command you entered, press [Pg Dn].

You can display your command history by pressing the [F7] key. Try this now. You will see output similar to this:

```
1: DIR
2: CHKDSK
3:>VER
```

As you can see, all commands are numbered. (You will see how to make use of this fact later on.) Also, notice that VER is preceded by a >. The command that is preceded by the > is the one that will be displayed next.

As you can see from the foregoing examples, access to your command history can save you considerable time and effort when you need to reissue the various commands repeatedly. However, your command history also provides another valuable service: it lets you verify what commands you actually gave DOS. This can be important when something goes wrong, and you think you may have issued a command in error. Using DOSKEY you can find out if that is the case. Also, with DOSKEY installed, you can find out if anyone has tampered with your system by checking the command history, looking for commands that you did not give.

As you know, when you press [F7] your command history is displayed with a number associated with each command. You can execute any command in that history by specifying its number. To do this, first press [F9]. You will see this prompt:

```
Line number:
```

Enter the number of the command. The command associated with the number appears on the command line. To execute that command, press [Enter].

11

REMEMBER: The [↑] key moves backwards through your command history; the [↓] key moves forward.

DOSKEY's Expanded Editing Keys

In addition to the editing keys supported by DOS, new editing keys are available when DOSKEY is installed. These are shown in Table 11-1.

To try these new editing keys, enter the following on the command line (but don't press (Enter)):

This is a test

Now, press the (Home) key. The cursor jumps to the *T* at the start of the line. Press (End). Now the cursor moves to the end of the line.

You can move the cursor forward one word by pressing (Ctrl)-(→). To move back one word, press (Ctrl)-(←). Try both of these keys now.

As you know, pressing (Backspace) erases the character to the left of the cursor. However, you can move the cursor to the left without erasing the character by pressing the (←) key. Try this now. You can also move forward nondestructively by pressing the (→) key. One reason you might want to move the cursor nondestructively is to fix a typing error.

By default, DOS uses overwrite mode in editing. This means that when you nondestructively move the cursor into the middle of the command line and then type a character, the character you type overwrites the character that was previously there. However, it is possible to switch

Key	Action
(Home)	Positions the cursor at the start of the current command line
(End)	Positions the cursor at the end of the current command line
(←)	Nondestructively moves the cursor back one character
(→)	Nondestructively moves the cursor forward one character
(Ctrl)-(←)	Nondestructively moves the cursor back one word
(Ctrl)-(→)	Nondestructively moves the cursor forward one word
(Ins)	Toggles between insert and overwrite modes
(Ctrl)-(T)	Allows multiple commands to be entered on a single command line

DOSKEY's Expanded Editing Keys
Table 11-1.

DOSKEY can
alternate
between
overwrite and
insert modes.

DOS to insert mode by pressing the [Ins] key. When you do this, the shape of the cursor will also change. When using insert mode, each time you type a character, any characters to the right of the current location are *shifted right* and not overwritten. Thus, insert mode allows you to insert text in the middle of the command line. Insert mode only lasts until you press [Enter]. Then overwrite mode is resumed.

Without DOSKEY, you can enter only one command at a time on the command line. However, after installing DOSKEY it is possible to specify several commands on a single command line. To do this, each command must be separated by a [Ctrl]-[T], which will be displayed as a paragraph symbol. For example, try the following command line. It executes the DIR, CHKDSK, and VER commands.

DIR ¶ CHKDSK ¶ VER

One thing to remember when you string commands together using [Ctrl]-[T] is that you need to press [Ctrl]-[C] for each command that you want to cancel. That is, in the foregoing example, if you want to cancel all three commands, you press [Ctrl]-[C] three times.

TIP: Putting multiple commands on one line is very useful when you want to execute a command sequence in quick succession.

Using Macros

A macro is a
name that
stands for
one or more
commands.

Another major feature of DOSKEY is the macro. A *macro* is a name that you define that represents one or more commands. In essence, by defining a macro, you are defining a new command that consists of one or more other DOS commands or your own application programs.

To define a macro, use this general form of DOSKEY:

DOSKEY *macro* = *command sequence*

For a simple first example, execute this command now:

DOSKEY TOM = DIR

11

Now, enter **TOM** on the command line. As you might expect, the directory is listed. What has happened is that now TOM is another name for DIR. DIR is still present, it is just that now TOM also causes the directory to be listed. Although this simple first example provides no tangible benefit, the next few examples reveal some of the power of using macros.

To create a macro that stands for a series of commands, you need to specify a list of commands. Each command must be separated by the character combination, $T. (The *T* may be in either upper- or lowercase.) For example, try this command:

DOSKEY MYCOM = DIR $T VER $T CHKDSK

The $T is the command separator used within a macro.

Once you have entered this command, enter **MYCOM** on the command line. As you will see, this causes the directory to be listed, the DOS version number to be displayed, and the CHKDSK command to be executed. In essence, the $T is similar in operation to the [Ctrl]-[T] command separator used with the command line. You can specify as many commands as you like, but no command line can exceed 127 characters.

To see a list of all the macros currently available, use this form of the DOSKEY command:

DOSKEY /MACROS

Try this now to see the definitions of the two macros that you just created.

To remove a macro, use this general form of DOSKEY:

DOSKEY *macro* =

When no command sequence is specified, the macro is removed from the system.

To remove all macros, press [Alt]-[F10].

It is important to understand that all macros are held in the memory of the computer and are lost when the computer is turned off. Therefore, they must be reentered each time the computer is turned on.

TIP: You can put frequently used macro definitions into the AUTOEXEC.BAT file so that they are automatically generated each time you turn on the computer.

Increasing the Power of Macros

You can increase the power of your macros in three ways: by adding pipes, by redirecting I/O, and by using arguments. These functions are accomplished using the $ commands shown in Table 11-2. As you proceed you will see several similarities between the operation of a DOSKEY macro and a batch file. Let's see how these functions work.

The $B is DOSKEY's way of specifying the | (pipe) operator. As you should recall from the previous chapter, the | causes the output of the command on the left to be fed into the input of the command on the right. For example, the following macro uses $B to display a sorted directory listing:

DOSKEY SORTDIR = DIR $B SORT

Command	Purpose
$B	Creates a pipe and stands for the	symbol
$G	Redirects output and stands for the > symbol
$L	Redirects input and stands for the < symbol
$1 through $9	These are the replaceable parameters that will receive the values of any arguments specified on the command line. They are similar in function to the batch file parameters %1 through %9
$*	A special replaceable parameter. It will contain all the information you specify after the macro name on the command line
$$	Produces a single $ (dollar sign) symbol

DOSKEY's $
Commands
Table 11-2.

11

When you execute the SORTDIR macro, you will see the following displayed on the command line just before the sorted directory is displayed:

```
C:\DOS>DIR | SORT
```

When DOSKEY actually executes the macro, the $B is translated into the | that DOS can understand.

The $G redirects the output of a command. It is equivalent to the > DOS operator. Typically, output is redirected into a file or to another device. For example, the next macro definition directs the output of the CHKDSK command to a disk file called CHKOUT.

DOSKEY CDSK = CHKDSK $G CHKOUT

TIP: To generate the >> operator specify two $G's together. That is, GG.

The $L redirects input and is the same as the < input operator.

The replaceable parameters $1 through $9 operate just the way the batch file parameters %1 through %9 work. The arguments you enter after the macro name on the command line are copied into the parameters. For example, given this macro definition,

DOSKEY CPY = COPY C:$1 D:$2

the command line shown next causes the file called HERE on drive C to be copied to the file THERE on drive D.

CPY HERE THERE

The $* parameter is replaced by everything that follows the macro name on the command line. For example, given this definition,

DOSKEY PR = PRINT $*

the following command line will cause the files ONE, TWO, and THREE to be printed on the printer:

    PR ONE TWO THREE

In this case, the $* is replaced by "ONE TWO THREE." This means that you can specify as many files as you want without knowing the exact number in advance. Although $* is seldom used with DOS commands, you may have application programs for which the $* parameter is appropriate.

Since the $ is used to signal the beginning of a DOSKEY command, if you actually want a $ (dollar sign) to appear, use $$.

Some DOSKEY Options

To save your command history, DOSKEY allocates 512 bytes of memory. Because the lengths of the commands differ, you cannot know precisely how many commands can be stored in that amount of memory. A reasonable estimate is between 40 and 50, unless all of your commands are very long. Once the memory set aside for your command history is full, each new command eliminates one or more of the oldest commands. If you think that you will need DOSKEY to remember more commands than will fit in 512 bytes, you can specify the amount of memory set aside for DOSKEY using this general form when you first install DOSKEY:

    DOSKEY /BUFSIZE = *number-of-bytes*

For example, this sets aside 2000 bytes for DOSKEY to use:

    DOSKEY /BUFSIZE = 2000

The minimum amount of memory that you can specify is 256 bytes. To specify the amount of memory used by DOSKEY, you must do so when you first install it. You cannot change the amount of memory set aside for DOSKEY once it is installed.

Another way to display your command history uses this form of DOSKEY:

DOSKEY /HISTORY

The list produced by this form of DOSKEY differs from the one produced by pressing F7 in that it does not display any line numbers.

You can reinstall DOSKEY using this command:

DOSKEY /REINSTALL

You may need to reinstall DOSKEY when working with certain types of programs, but this will be very rare.

As you know, by default, the DOS command line uses overwrite input mode. You can change this to insert mode using this form of DOSKEY:

DOSKEY /INSERT

To change it back to overwrite mode, use this command:

DOSKEY /OVERSTRIKE

Summary

In this chapter you learned to use DOSKEY to

✦ Reuse previous commands

✦ Expand your command-line editing capabilities

✦ Create macros

✦ Switch between overwrite and insert modes

In the next chapter you will learn how DOS can help you recover from mistakes and accidents.

C H A P T E R

≋MADE EASY≋

12

RECOVERING FROM MISTAKES

Things in real life seldom proceed along the path of perfection. Being human means that we will make mistakes. Fortunately, relative to DOS, many mistakes can be remedied before any real harm has been done. In this chapter you will learn about some important DOS commands that help you undo two common errors: accidentally erasing a file and accidentally reformatting a disk.

NOTE: The commands discussed in this chapter are supported only by DOS version 5 and later. Previous versions of DOS do not have these important commands. Further, the way these commands operate differs between DOS versions 5 and 6. When differences apply, each version will be discussed.

To follow along with the examples in this chapter, put a blank, formatted diskette into drive A. Also, remember that all the commands discussed here are external commands.

Undeleting a File

By far the most common error that occurs when using DOS is accidentally erasing an important file. For example, this can happen when you erase using wildcard characters, and a file that you didn't intend to erase matches the wildcard. Other times, a file is erased and later you realize that you need that file. Also, newcomers to DOS sometimes just do the wrong thing and accidentally erase one or more files. Whatever the reason, in many cases, DOS will let you recover a file using the UNDELETE command. The UNDELETE command has this general form,

> UNDELETE *path*

When erasing a file, DOS does not actually physically destroy its information. It simply marks it as deleted.

where *path* specifies the drive and path name of the directory that contains the file or files that you want to undelete. If you do not specify a drive or path, the current drive and directory are used.

Before trying UNDELETE, it will be useful for you to understand how and why a file can be undeleted. When you remove a file using ERASE (or DEL), the information in the file is not physically destroyed. Instead, the file is marked as deleted in the directory. When a file is marked as deleted, DOS is free to use that part of the disk for other purposes. However, as long as no other file has overwritten the erased file, it is possible to recover the file by simply restoring its directory entry.

Let's try the UNDELETE command now. First, create a small text file, called TEST.TXT, containing anything you like. Next, copy the file to the diskette in drive A. This should be the only file on the disk. Next, erase TEST.TXT on drive A. Now, enter this command:

UNDELETE A:

You will see something similar to the following:

```
Directory: A:\
File Specifications: *.*

    Delete Sentry control file not found.

    Deletion-tracking file not found.

    MS-DOS directory contains     1 deleted files.
    Of those,    1 files may be recovered.

Using the MS-DOS directory method.
    ?EST      TXT       15  1-16-93  4:09p  ...A Undelete (Y/N)?
```

Before continuing, note these two lines:

```
Delete Sentry control file not found.
Deletion-tracking file not found.
```

As you will learn later, it is possible to help UNDELETE do a better job by using a Delete Sentry and a tracking file, but you don't need to worry about this now.

NOTE: If you are using DOS 5, the output displayed by UNDELETE will be slightly different. Also, you will not see the "Delete Sentry" line. The Delete Sentry is added in version 6 of DOS.

12

Notice also that the first letter of TEST now contains a question mark. When you erase a file, the first character of the file name is destroyed.

As you will soon see, UNDELETE will prompt for the correct first letter when you undelete the file.

UNDELETE prompts you before undeleting each file. The reason for this is that by default UNDELETE restores all deleted files in the directory. However, it is likely that you want most of the files you have deleted to stay deleted. By prompting you, UNDELETE allows you to decide on a file-by-file basis which files you want to undelete. Since you want to undelete the file, press **Y**. (You don't need to press [Enter] after pressing **Y**.) Next, you will see the following prompt. (This message will be slightly different for DOS 5 users, but the meaning is the same.)

```
Please type the first character for ?EST    .TXT:
```

Since the first character is *T*, press **T** once now. (Again, you won't need to press [Enter] after pressing **T**.) Assuming that everything worked correctly (which it should have if you followed the directions), you will see this message:

```
File successfully undeleted.
```

If you list the directory of the disk in drive A, you will see that, indeed, TEST.TXT has been restored.

NOTE: As stated earlier, when a file is erased, DOS is free to reuse the portion of the disk that held the file. Therefore, if you erase a file and then create new files, copy additional files to the disk, or alter the contents of one or more files, it is possible that the erased file will actually be physically overwritten. If this occurs, you will not be able to successfully restore the deleted file. For this reason, if you accidentally erase a file, use UNDELETE immediately. Do not perform any other operations on that disk until you have undeleted the file.

In some cases, you will be able to restore only part of a file. If the restored file is a text file, you may be able to use the part that was restored. However, if the file is a program or data file, it is best to use a backup copy of the file instead of the partially undeleted file. (Trying to use a partially restored program will almost certainly crash your computer!)

Undeleting Specific Files

Instead of having UNDELETE attempt to restore all erased files on a disk, you can specify exactly which ones to undelete using this general form:

UNDELETE *filename*

The *filename* may include wildcard characters, a drive specifier, and/or a path name.

For example, this command undeletes only TEST.TXT:

UNDELETE A:TEST.TXT

On your own, you might want to copy several files to the disk in drive A, delete a few, and try various forms of the UNDELETE command, studying their effects.

NOTE: Up to this point, the discussion of UNDELETE has applied to both DOS 5 and DOS 6. However, from this point on, the discussion of error recovery diverges. Please read those sections that apply to the version of DOS you are using.

Using MIRROR to Help UNDELETE (for DOS 5)

This section applies only to DOS 5 users. If you are using a later version, skip to the next section.

You can greatly improve the operation of UNDELETE by maintaining a tracking file. A *tracking file* keeps track of which files are deleted. This information is used by UNDELETE to restore an erased file. To cause a tracking file to be created, use the MIRROR command. As you will see, MIRROR has several uses, but the one that causes a tracking file to be maintained has this general form,

MIRROR *drive:* /T*x*

where *drive* specifies the disk for which unformatting information will be saved (discussed later), and *x* is the letter of the drive that you want to track.

12

For example, the next command creates a tracking file for drive A and stores unformatting information about drive C:

MIRROR C: /Ta

If the drive specifier is not present, unformatting information about the current drive is saved.

It is important to understand that each disk that you track must be specified individually. That is, all drives are not automatically tracked. You can specify as many drives as you like on the same command line. For example, this tracks drives A and C:

MIRROR /Ta /Tc

You will need to specify all drives that you want to track the first time you execute this command because you cannot execute it a second time just to track another disk. The reason for this is that MIRROR is an *installed command.* This means that part of it remains in memory after it is first executed. Once this part of MIRROR is installed, you cannot "reinstall" it. It is the part of MIRROR that remains in memory that monitors all disk operations and records which files are deleted.

The MIRROR command creates two files on the disk. The first is called MIRROR.FIL, which is used to repair a diskette that is accidentally reformatted or to help restore accidentally erased files in the root directory. (You will see how this works later in this chapter.) The second file, which is created the first time you erase a file, is called PCTRACKR.DEL. This is the tracking file that contains information about erased files and is used by UNDELETE if it is present on the disk. This file is hidden and will not show in a normal directory listing.

To see how MIRROR can help UNDELETE, execute this command:

MIRROR /Ta

Next, erase TEST.TXT and then execute the UNDELETE command. You will see the following output:

```
Directory: A:\
File Specifications: *.*

     Deletion-tracking file contains     1 deleted files.
     Of those,    1 files have all clusters available,
                  0 files have some clusters available,
                  0 files have no clusters available.

     MS-DOS directory contains     1 deleted files.
     Of those,    1 files may be recovered.

Using the deletion-tracking file.

TEST    EXE    15  1-16-93  4:09p  ...A  Deleted: 1-16-93  5:43p
All of the clusters for this file are available. Undelete (Y/N)?
```

Files that have all clusters available will be fully recovered. Those with some clusters missing will only be partially recovered. Files with no clusters cannot be recovered. Now, press **Y** to undelete the file. This time, UNDELETE is able to use the information in the tracking file to undelete TEST.TXT. Specifically, you do not need to specify the first letter of the file name. Notice that the date and time when the file was deleted are also displayed.

By default, MIRROR will store information for 25 to 303 deletions, depending upon the size of the disk. If the limit is reached and you erase another file, MIRROR removes the information about the oldest deletion and replaces it with the current deletion. You can specify the number of deletions that MIRROR will store by including a number after the /T option, using this general form:

MIRROR /Tx-*num*

Here, *num* is the number of deletions that will be stored. For example, this command specifies that 50 deletions will be stored for drive C:

MIRROR /Tc-50

12

The number of files tracked must be in the range 1 through 999.

At first thought, it might seem like a good idea to always use the 999 default. However, the more deletions that you track, the larger the tracking file becomes. In general, room for 50 to 100 is probably sufficient.

Some Additional MIRROR Options

MIRROR contains three other options. They are /1, /U, and /PARTN. Each will be examined here.

Each time you execute MIRROR, MIRROR.FIL is created. By default, any preexisting MIRROR.FIL is renamed MIRROR.BAK as a safeguard against the new MIRROR.FIL containing an error. For example, MIRROR.FIL could be damaged by an error in a program. However, if you don't feel that this added measure of safety is warranted, then specify the /1 option, which causes MIRROR to not create the backup file.

To remove MIRROR from memory, specify the /U option. For example, this unloads MIRROR:

> MIRROR /U

One reason you might want to remove MIRROR is so that you can reinstall it using a different set of options. As stated, MIRROR cannot be installed a second time because the first installation is still in memory. But unloading it clears it from memory and allows you to install it again.

You can have MIRROR save information about the partitions of a fixed disk by specifying the /PARTN option. Fixed disks that can hold more than 32 megabytes may be *partitioned* into two or more logical drives. For example, it is quite possible that your computer only has one fixed disk, but that you access it as C and D. It is information about how your disk is partitioned that MIRROR saves using the /PARTN option. It creates a file called PARTNSAV.FIL. You should store PARTNSAV.FIL on a floppy disk because you will need it if you ever have to rebuild the directory structure of your fixed disk. (Rebuilding damaged disk directories is discussed later in this chapter.)

Using Deletion Tracking to Help UNDELETE (for DOS 6)

This section applies only to DOS 6 users. If you are using DOS 5, refer to the previous section.

You can greatly improve the operation of UNDELETE by maintaining a tracking file. A *tracking file* keeps track of which files are deleted. This information is used by UNDELETE to restore an erased file. To cause a tracking file to be created, you must execute the UNDELETE command using the /T option. This causes part of UNDELETE to remain resident in memory and to keep track of files that are erased. The general form of UNDELETE that is used to load the memory-resident part is shown here:

UNDELETE /T*x*

Here, *x* is the letter of the drive that you want to track. After this command has executed, UNDELETE creates a hidden system file called PCTRACKR.DEL on the specified drive. PCTRACKR.DEL stores recovery information about each file erased on that drive. For example, this command creates a tracking file for drive A:

UNDELETE /Ta

To see how a deletion-tracking file can help UNDELETE, execute the previous command now. Next, erase TEST.TXT and then unerase it using UNDELETE. You will see the following output:

```
Directory: A:\
File Specifications: TEST.TXT

    Delete Sentry control file not found.

    Deletion-tracking file contains    1 deleted files.
    Of those,    1 files have all clusters available,
                 0 files have some clusters available,
                 0 files have no clusters available.

    MS-DOS directory contains    1 deleted files.
    Of those,    1 files may be recovered.

Using the Deletion-tracking method.
```

12

```
TEST    TXT    15  1-16-93   4:09p  ...A  Deleted: 1-16-93  5:43p
All of the clusters for this file are available. Undelete? (Y/N)
```

Files that have all clusters available will be fully recovered. Those with some clusters missing will only be partially recovered. Files with no clusters cannot be recovered. Now, press **Y** to undelete the file. This time, UNDELETE is able to use the information in the tracking file to undelete TEST.TXT. Specifically, you do not need to specify the first letter of the file name. Notice that the date and time when the file was deleted are also displayed.

It is important to understand that each disk that you track must be specified individually. That is, all drives are not automatically tracked. You can specify as many drives as you like on the same command line. For example, this tracks drives A and C:

    UNDELETE /Ta /Tc

Because the /T option causes part of UNDELETE to be installed in memory, you will need to specify all drives that you want to track the first time you execute this command. You cannot use the /T option a second time just to track another disk. Once this part of UNDELETE is installed, you cannot "reinstall" it. It is the part of UNDELETE that remains in memory that monitors all disk operations and records which files are deleted.

By default, the /T option automatically gives you room to store information for 25 to 303 deleted files. The actual number depends on the size of the disk that you are tracking. If the limit is reached and you erase another file, then UNDELETE removes the information about the oldest deletion and replaces it with the current deletion. You can specify the number of deletions that UNDELETE will store by including a number after the /T option, using the general form:

    UNDELETE /T*x-num*

Here, *num* is the number of deletions that will be stored. For example, this command specifies that 50 deletions will be stored for drive C:

    UNDELETE /Tc-50

The number of files tracked must be in the range 1 through 999.

At first thought, it might seem like a good idea to always specify 999 files to track. However, the more deletions that you track, the larger the tracking file becomes. In general, room for 50 to 100 is sufficient.

NOTE: If you previously used DOS 5 and have just upgraded to DOS 6, it is important to understand that this new form of DELETE takes the place of the MIRROR command. (In fact, MIRROR is no longer included.)

Using a Delete Sentry to Help UNDELETE (for DOS 6)

This section applies only to version 6 of DOS.

Although using a tracking file enhances the performance of UNDELETE, there is an even better way to help improve its reliability. Called a *Delete Sentry*, it is the highest level of protection that you can obtain using the DOS error recovery system. The Delete Sentry maintains a special directory called SENTRY into which erased files are copied. That is, when a Delete Sentry is on duty, each time you delete a file, it is copied into the SENTRY directory. Using this method, if you need to undelete a file, the file is simply copied back into your working directory. Remember, when you use either a tracking file or UNDELETE unaided, it is still possible that your erased file will be overwritten by some other file sometime between when the file was erased and when you try to recover it. Using a Delete Sentry prevents this.

The SENTRY directory will use about seven percent of each protected disk's space. If you delete more files than will fit, the oldest files are removed to make room for the new ones. This means that it is still possible to permanently erase a file. However, the level of protection offered by the Delete Sentry is still very significant.

To use a Delete Sentry, use this general form of UNDELETE:

UNDELETE /S*drive*

Here, *drive* specifies the drive to be used. If *drive* is not specified, the current drive is assumed. This form of UNDELETE installs part of itself

12

in memory. The memory-resident portion provides the sentry. Because the Delete Sentry is memory-resident, you must specify all the drives you want to monitor when you first install the sentry.

The Delete Sentry provides the highest level of file recovery protection. It is the best protection to use if you have the disk space available to support it. Remember, the Delete Sentry trades away seven percent of your disk space for the added protection. If you cannot spare the space, then you will need to use either deletion tracking or no UNDELETE enhancements at all.

Some UNDELETE Options

UNDELETE has several options that affect how it operates. The /LIST option lists all erased files that will be recovered. (The files are not actually recovered, however). The /ALL option undeletes files automatically, without prompting. (That is, you won't be asked if you want to undelete the file or files.) The /DT option causes UNDELETE to use only the tracking file when undeleting. The /DOS option tells UNDELETE to ignore the tracking file.

If you are using DOS 6, you will have five additional UNDELETE options available. The /DS option causes UNDELETE to recover only those files stored in the SENTRY directory. The /U option removes (unloads) the memory-resident portion of UNDELETE. This is useful when you need to reinstall it using a different set of options. The /PURGE option erases all files in the SENTRY directory. You may want to do this to free disk space. The /STATUS option shows the protection method in effect for each drive. The /LOAD option causes UNDELETE to load its memory-resident portion using the information in the UNDELETE.INI file. This option is generally used only by system integrators.

Unformatting a Disk

Perhaps the most catastrophic error that you can make is to accidentally reformat a disk that contains important information. Prior to DOS 5, accidentally reformatting a disk meant that all data on that disk was, for all practical purposes, irretrievably gone. However, beginning with version 5, DOS contains the UNFORMAT command, which unformats the disk and returns it to its previous state.

The reason that a disk can be unformatted is because reformatting does not necessarily destroy the preexisting information on the disk. Instead, it simply reconstructs the file allocation table. The old information is still physically present on the disk. (However, disks that have been reformatted using the /U option to the FORMAT command cannot be restored.) Keep in mind that you can only successfully unformat a disk that has *just* been accidentally reformatted. Once that disk has been used, any attempt to unformat it will only be partially successful because new information has replaced the old.

NOTE: The exact method of unformatting a disk varies between DOS versions 5 and 6. Both versions are examined here.

CAUTION: Unformatting a disk destroys its current state and returns the disk to its original condition. This implies that any information you currently have on the disk will be destroyed. Therefore, don't UNFORMAT disks that haven't been accidentally reformatted because you will lose data. Further, for safety *do not* try any of the examples in this section. UNFORMAT is a valuable command, but it must only be used if you have actually accidentally reformatted a disk.

Unformatting Using DOS 5

When using DOS 5, UNFORMAT, like UNDELETE, works best in conjunction with MIRROR because it uses the information in the MIRROR.FIL file to unformat your disk.

The general form of UNFORMAT is

UNFORMAT *drive*:

where *drive* is the drive specifier of the disk that you want to UNFORMAT.

UNFORMAT first looks on the disk to be unformatted for the MIRROR.FIL file. Even though this file will not show up in a directory

12

listing after reformatting, UNFORMAT can still find it by searching the disk directly, bypassing DOS. If it finds the file, you will see a prompt similar to this:

```
The last time MIRROR or FORMAT command was used was
at hh:mm on mm-dd-yy.
The prior time MIRROR or FORMAT command was used was
at hh:mm on mm-dd-yy.

If you wish to use the last file as indicated
above, press L. If you wish to use the prior
file as indicated above, press P. Press ESC
to terminate UNFORMAT.
```

Because it is possible that two MIRROR files will be on the disk (MIRROR.FIL and MIRROR.BAK), UNFORMAT gives you the chance to choose which one you want to use. In general, you should use the newest file, by pressing **L**.

Assuming that you have a MIRROR.FIL file, UNFORMAT will return your disk to its original state prior to the accidental reformatting. As long as MIRROR.FIL is up-to-date, the restoration will be complete.

If the disk that you are unformatting does not have a MIRROR.FIL file, then UNFORMAT will do its best to restore the disk, but you should expect that some files will not be fully restored.

UNFORMAT has a number of options. You can have UNFORMAT simply confirm that the contents of MIRROR.FIL agree with the current state of the disk by using the /J option. When you specify /J, the disk is not reconstructed.

When unformatting a disk without the benefit of a MIRROR.FIL file, you can see how the disk will be rebuilt without actually unformatting it by specifying the /TEST option. You might want to use this option if you think that the result of an UNFORMAT will be less desirable than what you currently have.

You can have UNFORMAT display all files and directories on the disk by specifying the /L option.

The /PARTN option unformats a fixed disk's partition table. When the /L is used in conjunction with /PARTN, the current partition table is displayed. Frankly, the actual contents of the partition table are useful only to programmers, so you will probably not need to use this option.

You can have all output from the program directed to a printer by specifying the /P option.

You can have UNFORMAT ignore the MIRROR.FIL file by specifying the /U option.

Unformatting Using DOS 6

Using the DOS 6 version of UNFORMAT is straightforward and takes this general form,

UNFORMAT *drive*:

where *drive* is the drive to unformat. For example, to unformat the diskette in drive A, use this command:

UNFORMAT A:

The DOS 6 version of UNFORMAT uses the information still present in the root directory and the disk's file allocation table to unformat your disk. (Remember, the old information about your disk is not necessarily destroyed by reformatting.) If the disk has not been used since it was accidentally reformatted, then UNFORMAT can use this information to successfully restore your disk. If the disk has been used, only a partial restoration is possible.

UNFORMAT has three options. The first is /L, which causes all the files and subdirectories to be displayed as the disk is unformatted. The /TEST option causes UNFORMAT to display how the disk will be unformatted, but does not actually do it. You might want to use this option if you think that the result of an UNFORMAT will be less desirable than what you currently have. Finally, the /P option sends the output of the UNFORMAT command to the printer.

12

Summary

In this chapter you have learned

✦ How to undelete a file using UNDELETE

✦ To use MIRROR when using DOS 5

✦ How to unformat a disk using UNFORMAT

In the next chapter you will learn how to customize DOS to best fit your personal needs.

C H A P T E R

DOS DOS DOS DOS DOS DOS DOS DOS

≈ MADE EASY ≈

13

CONFIGURING DOS

There are several things about DOS that you can change. Some affect the way DOS operates or appears, while others alter the way DOS accesses disk drives or defines devices. You can also configure DOS for use in a foreign country. In this chapter you will learn the commands that let you configure DOS to best meet your needs.

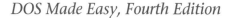

NOTE: If your computer is working just the way you like it and you
have no other reason to change its basic operation, then you will
probably not want to change its configuration. However, read this
chapter anyway so that you are familiar with the different
configurations that are possible. Also, you may need to change your
configuration when you install a new application program.

Using the MODE Command

As you know, DOS controls the devices that constitute the computer.
Some of these devices have various modes of operation. When DOS
starts, these devices are set to operate in a way that applies to the widest
range of situations. However, you can change how some of the devices
operate to best take advantage of your system's configuration. One of
the most versatile configuration commands is MODE. You can use
MODE to change the operation of the video adapter, the keyboard, the
serial communication ports, and the printer. MODE is an external
command.

MODE has many forms—some of which apply only to very specialized
situations. Here, we will look at the most commonly used ones.

Controlling the Video Adapter

The *video adapter* is a circuit card inside the computer that controls the
monitor. Its purpose is to generate and maintain the text and graphics
that you see on the screen. There are two basic types of video adapters:
the monochrome adapter, which can only display text characters in
black and white, and the various color/graphics adapters, which can
display text and graphics in color. Though uncommon, it is possible for
both of these adapters to be in your computer. You can use MODE to
select a video adapter or set how it displays information. This is the
general form of MODE that you would use to do this:

MODE *video-mode*

where *video-mode* is one of the adapter codes shown in Table 13-1.

Video-mode	Effect
40	Sets a color/graphics adapter display width to 40 columns
80	Sets a color/graphics adapter display width to 80 columns
BW40	Activates the color/graphics adapter and sets the width to 40 columns and the display mode to black and white
BW80	Activates the color/graphics adapter and sets the width to 80 columns and the display mode to black and white
CO40	Activates the color/graphics adapter and sets the width to 40 columns and the display mode to color
CO80	Activates the color/graphics adapter and sets the width to 80 columns and the display mode to color
MONO	Activates the monochrome adapter—the display width is always 80 columns

The Video
Adapter Codes
Table 13-1.

If you have a color/graphics adapter, you can set it to either 40- or 80-column mode and to display in either color or black and white. For example, if you have a color/graphics adapter, enter this:

    MODE CO40

The screen will clear, and you will see the DOS prompt displayed at twice its usual size. In 40-column mode the letters are twice as big, so only 40 can fit from side to side. For this reason, 40-column mode is almost never used. To reset the display to the normal 80-column mode, enter this:

    MODE CO80

13

> **T**IP: If you need to see the computer's screen from a distance, try switching to 40-column mode.

If you have a monochrome adapter, you cannot change its mode of operation. However, if you have two adapters in your system, you can enter the following to switch to the monochrome adapter:

    MODE MONO

Although fairly rare, there can sometimes be a mismatch between the color/graphics video adapter and the monitor, which causes the image not to be centered (left and right) on the screen. You can shift the display left or right by using the following form of MODE:

    MODE *video-adapter*, R/L, T

Use "R" to shift the display to the right or "L" to shift it to the left. The display is shifted two spaces in 80-column mode and one space in 40-column mode. The "T" is optional; when present, it causes a test pattern to be displayed and asks you whether the screen is correct. For example, this command:

    MODE CO80, L, T

produces this display:

```
01234567890123456789 0/.../01234567890123456789
Do you see the rightmost 9 (Y/N)?
```

If you type **N**, the display is shifted left and you are reprompted.

> **T**IP: Modern computers will not require the type of adjustment performed by MODE.

Setting the Autorepeat Rate and Delay

You can control both the rate at which characters are automatically repeated when you hold a key down and the length of the delay before the autorepeat begins. (DOS refers to the autorepeat rate as the *typematic rate*.) You do these things using this form of the MODE command:

MODE CON RATE=*rate* DELAY=*delay*

The typematic rate governs how fast keys repeat when you hold down a key.

Here, *rate* is the number of characters generated per second and *delay* is the number of quarter seconds before the autorepeat begins. The maximum value for *rate* is 32. The maximum value for *delay* is 4. You must always specify both the rate and the delay value—you cannot leave one off.

The following command sets the autorepeat feature to 25 repetitions per second with a delay of 1/4 second:

MODE CON RATE=25 DELAY=1

The typematic rate will not be able to be changed on all computers.

Configuring the Printer

You can set the maximum number of characters per line and the number of lines per vertical inch that the printer will display with the following form of MODE:

MODE LPT# COLS=*length* LINES=*lines-per-inch*

The # must be printer number 1, 2, or 3 (there can be up to three printers on the system). The *length* must be either 80 or 132, and *lines-per-inch* must be either 6 or 8. When DOS begins, the line length is 80 with 6 lines per inch. Note that when you select 132, the printer automatically makes each character smaller so that 132 characters can fit on one line. Selecting 8 lines per vertical inch simply puts the lines closer together.

13

For example, the following configures the first printer for 132 columns, 8 lines per inch:

MODE LPT1 COLS=132 LINES=8

This form of MODE can also accept an option called RETRY, which takes this form:

RETRY=*x*

where *x* is either e, b, p, r, or n. (The meaning of these options requires a technical knowledge beyond the scope of this book.) This option is generally used only by system integrators. However, if an application program tells you to use this option, simply append it to the end of the MODE LPT# command. Don't change this option without reason.

Configuring the Serial Port

A serial port transfers data to an external device.

To transfer data to external devices, a computer can use two types of ports: *parallel* and *serial*. The parallel ports are usually used for printers, and the serial ports are used for such things as modems, plotters, and other special devices. However, a printer can be connected to a serial port. The full name for the serial port—and the way it is referred to in the IBM user manuals—is the asynchronous serial communications adapter. But *serial port* is much shorter and is the commonly used term. The most important difference between the two is that a parallel port transmits 8 bits of data (1 byte) at a time, while the serial port transmits data 1 bit at a time (hence the name serial). The rate at which the bits are transmitted is measured in *bits per second* and is abbreviated as *baud*. In order for the serial port to communicate with an external device, the baud of the device must match the baud of the serial port. This is usually done for you automatically by the application programs you are using, but you may occasionally be told to manually set the baud. You do this by using the MODE command with this general form:

MODE COM# *baud*

where # is the adapter number 1 through 4, and *baud* is the baud setting, which must be one of the following numbers: 110, 150, 300, 600, 1200, 2400, 4800, 9600, 19200. The larger the number, the faster the transfer rate. Though only the first two digits are actually necessary, you can use the whole number if you like. For example, to set COM1 to 9600 baud, enter this:

MODE COM1 9600

The default setting for serial ports is 1200 baud.

Serial ports have several other attributes that may need to be set to something other than their default values. Occasionally you may have to set these values. Though it is beyond the scope of this book to explain the technical details of these attributes, we will present a brief overview.

A serial port uses one of the following: even, odd, or no parity. The *parity* setting determines if and how error checking will be performed. No parity means that no error checking occurs. The parity of the serial port and the external device communicated with must be the same. The default setting is even. The number of *data bits* determines how many bits are used to transfer information. This number can be between 5 and 8, with the default value being 7. The number of *stop bits* determines how many nondata bits occur between the data bits. This can be either 1 or 2; the default is 2 for 110 baud and 1 for the others. This is the general form of MODE that you use to set all the information for the port:

MODE COM# *baud, parity, data-bits, stop-bits*

where *parity* is "E" for even, "O" for odd, or "N" for none. The *data-bits* and *stop-bits* are numbers. For example, to set the COM1 to 300 baud, even parity, 8 data bits, and 2 stop bits, enter this:

MODE COM1 300, E, 8, 2

Tip: Some computers also allow the parity value to be specified as M (mark) or S (space), but this is quite rare.

13

NOTE: A final parameter that you can optionally specify when configuring the serial port follows the stop-bits. This value is called *retry*. It may have these values: E, B, P, R or N. (An explanation of these parameters is beyond the scope of this book.) You should only specify the retry parameter if instructed to do so by either a knowledgeable coworker or by the instructions that accompany your computer or an application program.

Redirecting Printer Output

If you have a serial printer, you can redirect all printer output to it by using this form of MODE:

MODE LPT#=COM#

where # is the number 1 through 3 for LPT, or 1 through 4 for COM. For example, the following command switches the default printer to COM1:

MODE LPT1=COM1

Redirecting the printer is most useful when you have two or more printers attached to your computer.

Now all printer output, including that produced by the PRINT SCREEN command, will be directed to COM1.

To reset the printer to its default, use this form:

MODE LPT#

where *n* is a number between 1 and 3. For example, entering this resets LPT1:

MODE LPT1

Checking Status

You can see the status of each device controlled by MODE by entering MODE by itself. To see the status of a specific device, use this form:

MODE *device*

For example, to see the status of COM1, use this command:

MODE COM1

Changing the DOS Prompt

By default, the DOS system prompt displays the current drive followed by a > symbol. However, you can change the prompt to display practically anything you want by using the PROMPT command. This is the general form of the PROMPT command:

PROMPT *message*

where *message* is a string that will become the new system prompt. For example, if you enter this:

PROMPT My Computer:

DOS displays the prompt as this:

```
My Computer:
```

To return the DOS prompt to its default message, enter **PROMPT** without a message.

Though short prompts are usually the best, the prompting message can be up to 128 characters long. For example, you might use a prompt like the following to discourage unauthorized use:

```
PROMPT Warning: authorized users only!
```

You can include special characters and other information in the prompt by using one or more of the codes shown in Table 13-2. All PROMPT codes begin with a dollar sign. Because the characters >, <, |, and = have special meanings when they appear on a DOS command line, you must use the proper code if you want one of these characters to appear in the prompt.

One of the most popular prompts is created with the following command:

PROMPT PG

13

Code	Meaning
$$	dollar sign
$b	| character
$d	system date
$e	escape character
$g	> character
$h	a backspace
$l	< character
$n	current drive letter
$p	current directory path
$q	= character
$t	current time
$v	DOS version number
$_	carriage return-linefeed sequence

The PROMPT
Codes
Table 13-2.

This causes the current directory path name to be displayed, followed by the > standard DOS prompt. For example, if the current path is C:\ACCOUNTS\AP, the DOS prompt will look like this:

```
C:\ACCOUNTS\AP>
```

This prompt is so popular because it makes it easy to tell which directory you are in. You might want to put this prompt command into the AUTOEXEC.BAT file so that it automatically executes upon startup.

Another popular prompt is formed with the following command:

```
PROMPT $D $T $P$G
```

This causes the current system date and time to be displayed along with the directory path. If the date were 12/3/93, the time noon, and the root directory were current, the prompt would look like this:

```
Fri 12-03-93 12:00:00.00 C:\>
```

Experiment to see which prompt you like best and then place that
PROMPT command into the AUTOEXEC.BAT file.

TIP: A custom prompt is a good way to personalize your system.

Using the CONFIG.SYS File

DOS has a number of features that can only be set when it begins
execution. That is, some aspects of DOS may not be changed after the
DOS prompt has been displayed because they affect the fundamental
operation of the system. To alter these types of attributes, you must use
a special configuration file called *CONFIG.SYS* and some special DOS
configuration commands.

When DOS begins execution, it looks in the root directory of the disk
from which it was loaded for the file CONFIG.SYS. If it is present, DOS
reads the given configuration commands and sets the specified
parameters accordingly. If CONFIG.SYS is not found, DOS uses its
default settings. When you create or alter the CONFIG.SYS file, none of
the changes will take effect until you restart DOS.

If DOS was installed on your computer in the normal way then you will
already have a CONFIG.SYS file. In general, you will not want to
remove anything from the file. The instructions contained in the file
are necessary to support the operation of DOS and other application
programs you may have. However, you may want to change a few of
the commands to work differently as you will see in the next few
sections. You also may want to add one or more commands to this file.
The common configuration commands are discussed next.

CAUTION: Many configuration commands are intended only for
programmers or people specifically in charge of configuring a
system. For example, several configuration commands deal with
networks, extended memory management, and work groups. All of
these areas require specialized knowledge that is beyond what the

13

average user has. Also, changing your CONFIG.SYS file incorrectly can cause your system to malfunction. Therefore, if you have any reservations about using the commands discussed in this section, consult a knowledgeable person before proceeding. This book explains those configuration commands that you, personally, are likely to need to use.

BREAK

As you know, the Ctrl-Break (or Ctrl-C) key combination is used to cancel a command or application program and return to DOS. However, DOS's default method of operation only checks for a Ctrl-Break when I/O operations take place to the standard input, output, or printer devices, or the serial port. Some programs may not perform any of these operations for quite some time and therefore may not respond quickly to a Ctrl-Break command. For example, a database program that is doing a sort operation on a very large file may not perform any I/O operations for several minutes. You can instruct DOS to check for a Ctrl-Break more frequently by placing the following command in the CONFIG.SYS file:

    BREAK=ON

Keep in mind, however, that this will cause all commands and programs to run slower because DOS is spending more time checking to see if you have pressed Ctrl-Break.

COUNTRY

As you may know, different countries and different languages may vary in how they display and define the time, date, and currency symbols. Also, collating sequence and certain capitalization conventions may differ. For example, in Europe the comma is used as a decimal separator instead of the period. Generally, if you live in a country other than the United States, your computer will, by default, be configured to that country's standards. However, should you need to change DOS to conform to the conventions of a different country, you can accomplish this using the COUNTRY command. The COUNTRY command takes this general form:

COUNTRY = *code*

where *code* must be one of the codes listed in Table 13-3. (If you are using a version of DOS prior to 6, then not all of the countries listed in the table will be available.)

For example, the following command configures DOS for Spain:

COUNTRY = 034

If the country you want is not listed, choose the one whose conventions are the closest to what you need.

DOS contains extended support for countries with special character requirements, and you can specify a character set definition with the COUNTRY command. This issue is covered at the end of this chapter when we discuss foreign language versions of DOS.

DEVICE

A device driver is a piece of software that controls a device.

The parts of DOS that control the various devices of the computer are called *device drivers*. All the drivers necessary for the operation of a standard configuration of the computer are included in DOS when it begins execution. However, some special device drivers are optional, and you must tell DOS to load them if you want to use them.

Some device drivers are supplied by application programs and some are included with DOS. Several of the ones supplied by DOS are shown here. If you are using a version of DOS prior to 6 then you will not have all of these drivers (also, some may be called by different names):

- ANSI.SYS
- DISPLAY.SYS
- DRIVER.SYS
- DBLSPACE.SYS
- EGA.SYS
- EMM386.EXE
- HIMEM.SYS

13

Country/Language	Code
Arabic	785
Australia	061
Belgium	032
Brazil	055
Canada—English	001
Canada—French	002
Czechoslovakia	042
Chinese	086
Chinese (Taiwan)	088
Chinese (mainland)	086
Denmark	045
English (generic)	061
Finland	358
France	033
Germany	049
Hungary	036
Israel—Hebrew	972
Italy	039
Japan	081
Korea	082
Latin American	003
Netherlands	031
Norway	047
Poland	048
Portugal	351
Spain	034
Sweden	046
Switzerland	041
United Kingdom	044
United States	001
Yugoslavia	038

The DOS
Country Codes
Table 13-3.

+ POWER.EXE

+ RAMDRIVE.SYS

+ SETVER.EXE

+ SMARTDRV.EXE

Also, you may have other device drivers to handle special hardware. For example, a mouse typically requires a special device driver. This section presents an overview of the most commonly used device drivers. Other drivers, such as EMM386.SYS, HIMEM.SYS, and POWER.EXE are discussed later in this book, in conjunction with other commands to which they relate.

To tell DOS to load a device driver, use the DEVICE command, which takes this general form:

DEVICE = *device-driver*

ANSI.SYS

Occasionally, an application program will instruct you to load the ANSI.SYS device driver, which enables DOS to understand an additional method of controlling the cursor's position on the screen. ANSI.SYS can make it easier for some types of application programs to use the screen. It also can give you some additional control over your screen. (Refer to your DOS user manual for details.)

If you need to load this driver, use the following command in the CONFIG.SYS file:

DEVICE = ANSI.SYS

NOTE: If your device drivers are not in the root directory, then be sure to specify the correct path so that DOS can locate them. For example, if they are in the DOS directory on drive C, then use **DEVICE = C:\DOS\ANSI.SYS** Since all modern versions of DOS store the DOS files in the DOS directory of drive C, the commands in this section will reflect this. However, if your computer is organized differently, be sure to make the appropriate corrections.

13

RAMDRIVE.SYS

A RAM-disk simulates a disk drive by using the memory in your computer.

The one device driver that you will really want to use is RAMDRIVE.SYS, which is used to create a virtual disk drive in RAM (sometimes referred to as a *RAM-disk*). A virtual disk simulates the operation of a disk drive using RAM rather than the magnetic surface of the disk to hold the files.

As far as your programs are concerned, a virtual disk looks and acts just like a regular disk drive with one big difference that you will see and appreciate: virtual disks are much faster than standard disk drives because they run at the speed of the computer's memory, which is always faster than the transfer rate of a disk drive. However, this speed has its price. The virtual disk effectively reduces the amount of available memory of the system. While this is often not a problem, some application programs may require so much memory that a virtual disk cannot be used. You should also be aware that when the power is turned off, or if the computer is restarted, anything stored on the virtual disk is lost. So be sure to copy files that you wish to save to an actual disk before concluding a session at the computer.

This is the basic form of the RAMDRIVE.SYS command:

DEVICE = RAMDRIVE.SYS *total-size sector-size entries*

where *total-size* is the size of the virtual disk in kilobytes, which must be in the range of 4 through 32,767. The default value is 64K, but this is usually too small. If you specify a value larger than can be allocated, RAMDRIVE adjusts it to the largest amount that will fit in memory. The *sector-size* specifies how large to make the sector size and must be 128, 256, or 512 bytes. The default value is 512, which is generally adequate. The *entries* argument specifies the number of directory entries to be allowed in the root by the virtual disk. This value is 64 by default, which is usually a good choice, though you can specify any number between 2 and 1024.

The following command in CONFIG.SYS creates a virtual disk 384K bytes in size, uses 128-byte sectors, and has 64 root directory entries:

DEVICE = C:\DOS\RAMDRIVE.SYS 384 128 64

Several computers have what is called *extended memory*, which is memory that is not directly usable by DOS but may be used by programs running under DOS. (You will learn more about extended and its close cousin, expanded, memory in the next section.) If you have extended memory, you can use it for the virtual disk by placing the /E option at the end of the RAMDRIVE command. For example, the following command tells RAMDRIVE to use the 512K bytes of extended memory:

    DEVICE = C:\DOS\RAMDRIVE.SYS 512 /E

If your computer has *expanded memory*, which is another form of memory not normally usable by DOS but which RAMDRIVE can use, then you can tell RAMDRIVE to use it by specifying the /A option.

When RAMDRIVE.SYS is installed during startup, you will see a message similar to this one:

```
Microsoft RAMDrive version 3.07 virtual disk X:
```

where *X* will be the letter of the virtual disk.

C AUTION: Use of a virtual disk is highly recommended because of the dramatic increase in speed. However, once you turn the computer off or restart DOS, anything stored on a RAM disk is lost unless previously copied to a real disk.

SMARTDRV.EXE

Another device driver that you will probably want to add to your CONFIG.SYS file is called SMARTDRV.EXE. SMARTDRV.EXE speeds up disk operations. After it is installed, some of your application programs that make heavy use of the disk will run faster. This device driver requires extended memory.

To speed up disk operations, put this line in your CONFIG.SYS file:

    DEVICE = C:\DOS\SMARTDRV.EXE

13

SMARTDRV.EXE has several options that can affect its performance. However, the use of these options requires significant knowledge about how your computer and DOS function. As such they are best left to specialists.

FILES and FCBS

You can specify the number of files that may concurrently be open and the number of file control blocks (FCBS) that may concurrently be in use. (A *file control block* is a region of memory used by DOS to store information about an open file.) The default values given to these items are acceptable in most cases, but some application programs may require you to change them in order to run correctly.

A file control block (FCB) is a region of memory that contains information about an open disk file.

The number of concurrently open files is 8 by default. If you need to change this, use the FILES command, which has this general form:

FILES = *num*

where *num* is a number between 8 and 255. For example, the following command sets the number of files to 10:

FILES = 10

To change the number of file control blocks, use the FCBS command, which has this general form:

FCBS = *num*

where *num* is the total number of file control blocks. It must be between 1 and 255; the default is 4. For example, the following command tells DOS to allow 12 file control blocks:

FCBS=12

NOTE: Frankly, many application programs require 20 or more files or FCBS, so don't be surprised if you need to change these values in your CONFIG.SYS. (Only do so if the instructions that accompany your application program tell you to do so.)

INSTALL

You use the INSTALL command to install the following DOS commands from within your CONFIG.SYS file:

✦ FASTOPEN.EXE

✦ KEYB.COM

✦ NLSFUNC.EXE

✦ SHARE.EXE

SHARE is used in networking, and NLSFUNC is used to provide extended foreign language support. We will look at KEYB later in this chapter and FASTOPEN in another chapter. Depending upon how you use your computer there may be other commands that you will need to install using INSTALL.

The commands installed by INSTALL may also be executed at the DOS prompt. Thus, the use of INSTALL is largely a convenience.

This is the general form of the INSTALL command:

INSTALL *filename*

where *filename* is the name of the file to be installed.

LASTDRIVE

DOS automatically knows how many *physical* disk drives are on your system. However, because it is possible to have more *logical* drives—such as those created using RAMDRIVE—you can use the LASTDRIVE command to increase the number of drives allowed. This is the general form of LASTDRIVE:

LASTDRIVE = *letter*

where *letter* is the drive letter and must be between "A" and "Z."

13

REM

You can put a comment into your CONFIG.SYS file by preceding it with the REM command. Whatever follows REM on the same line is ignored when DOS processes the file.

Bypassing the CONFIG.SYS File

If you are using DOS version 6 you can cause DOS to ignore the configuration file when your computer starts. There is one good reason why you might want to do this: If you incorrectly change the CONFIG.SYS file, your computer may not work at all! Therefore, if you make a change to CONFIG.SYS and your computer will not work, press and hold the F5 key after DOS prints the message "Starting MS-DOS". Hold the key until the command prompt is displayed. Once you see the command prompt, you can correct your CONFIG.SYS file and then restart your computer.

NOTE: Pressing F5 also causes the AUTOEXEC.BAT file to be skipped. Because both the CONFIG.SYS and AUTOEXEC.BAT have been bypassed, your computer will be configured in only its default state. Therefore, some things will function or look different than normal.

If you know which configuration command is causing the trouble, you can still have DOS execute the rest of the CONFIG.SYS file by pressing and releasing the F8 key when the "Starting MS-DOS" message is displayed. This causes DOS to ask you before executing each command, which allows you to manually bypass the incorrect command while leaving the rest of the configurations intact.

Configuration Menus

Beginning with DOS 6, it is possible to define a menu in a configuration file that allows two or more different configurations to be selected when your computer is turned on. The creation of multiple configurations and menus is technical in nature and beyond the scope of this book. Just be aware that some computers may ask you to choose a configuration when the system is started.

Using NumLock

Users with version 6 of DOS can control whether NumLock
is on or off when DOS begins running. As you know, the numeric
keypad generates either numbers or arrow keys, depending upon the
state of the (Num Lock) key. Generally, NumLock is on by default.
However, to turn NumLock off when DOS begins, include this line in
your CONFIG.SYS file:

    NUMLOCK = OFF

If, for some reason, NumLock is off by default on your computer and
you want it on, use this command to turn it on when DOS starts:

    NUMLOCK = ON

 ## Using Extra Memory

In its default mode of operation, DOS can only utilize 640,000 bytes of
memory in your computer. However, it is possible for your computer to
actually contain far more memory than this. In fact, many application
programs routinely use this extra memory.

The extra memory can take three forms: extended, expanded, and the
upper memory area. Extended memory follows normal memory. Most
computers come with extended memory. Expanded memory is
specialized memory that is accessed only as needed and requires special
software drivers. (Only a few computers come with expanded memory.)
The upper memory area is the 384K of memory that is left over in the
first 1 megabyte of RAM in your system. Some of this memory is used
by the computer to support the video adapters, but some is generally
free for other uses. DOS version 5 and later have some options that
allow you to utilize more that just the first 640K of memory.

 NOTE: The commands and device drivers discussed here are
technical in nature. For this reason, they are presented with little
discussion of the details to their operation. However, you should feel
free to use them—they will increase the efficiency of your computer.

13

The device driver HIMEM.SYS aids in the management of your extended memory, and is required by other memory management commands. To use HIMEM, put this line in your CONFIG.SYS file:

DEVICE=C:\DOS\HIMEM.SYS

NOTE: HIMEM can only be used if your computer has an 80286, 80386, or 80486 processor that has extended memory. Specifically, HIMEM will not work with an original IBM PC or XT.

You can have the resident portion of DOS loaded into extended memory by putting this command in your CONFIG.SYS file:

DOS=HIGH

This command must follow HIMEM.SYS. The advantage of loading DOS into extended memory is that it frees normal memory, allowing your application programs more memory.

The DOS configuration command has a second function, which has this form:

DOS=UMB

This command is used to help DOS manage extended memory and is required by some other DOS commands.

NOTE: If you use the UMB option, you also will need to use the EMM386 device driver, described shortly.

You can combine both HIGH and UMB by putting this command in your CONFIG.SYS:

DOS=HIGH,UMB

If your computer has an 80386 or an 80486 processor, you can use the EMM386.EXE command to allow programs that use expanded memory to be run in extended memory by simulating expanded memory. This command also helps DOS manage extended memory and the upper memory area. It is also needed if you use the DOS=UMB command. To use expanded memory, put this line in your CONFIG.SYS file:

    DEVICE=C:\DOS\EMM386.EXE

Once you install the DOS and EMM386 configuration commands, you can use the LOADHIGH (LH for short) command to run programs in your computer's upper memory area. It takes this general form:

    LOADHIGH *filename*

where *filename* is the name of the program you want to run. (It can include a path and drive specifier, too.) For example, to run CHKDSK in the upper memory area, use this command:

    LOADHIGH CHKDSK

Keep in mind that if, for any reason, LOADHIGH cannot load the specified program into upper memory, it is loaded into normal memory and executed.

REMEMBER: LOADHIGH is used to execute a program in the upper memory area. However, from your point of view, the following two command lines will produce identical results:

C>CHKDSK
C>LOADHIGH CHKDSK

The only difference is where the programs reside while executing.

After you have installed EMM386, you can use the DEVICEHIGH configuration command to load device drivers into the upper memory area. Unlike LOADHIGH, DEVICEHIGH works only in your CONFIG.SYS file. DEVICEHIGH uses the same syntax as DEVICE. If it cannot load a device driver into extended memory, it will load it into normal memory.

13

TIP: Because memory management varies widely between computers, consult your owner's manual for further instructions about managing and maximizing memory.

 # PATH

Until now, whenever you needed to execute a command or program, the file had to be in the current working directory. However, if you are using the command prompt, you can tell DOS to look in other directories for external commands, programs, and batch files by using the PATH command. This is the general form of PATH:

PATH *path-list*

where *path-list* is a list of paths, separated by a semicolon, that will be searched. You cannot use spaces in the path list.

To understand how PATH works, assume that a disk has the directory structure shown here:

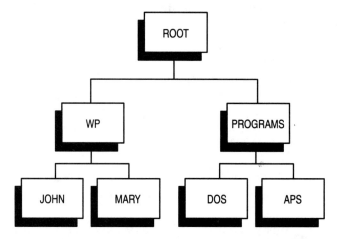

Further assume that all DOS external commands are in the DOS directory and all application programs are in the APS directory. To allow the access of any DOS external command or application program from any directory, enter this:

PATH \PROGRAMS\DOS;\PROGRAMS\APS

Now, whenever a command is given to DOS that is not internal, DOS will first check the current directory. If the command is not found, DOS then begins checking, in order, those directories specified by the PATH command, beginning with the \PROGRAMS\DOS directory. If the command is not found there, DOS then searches the \PROGRAMS\APS directory.

To see what the current path is, simply enter PATH with no arguments. To reset the path to its default, enter this:

PATH ;

Remember, setting a search path with PATH causes DOS to search the specified directories only for .EXE, .COM, and .BAT files. You cannot access data files with the PATH command.

APPEND

The APPEND command gives you access to files in other directories and operates much like PATH except that it can work with any type of file. This is the general form of APPEND:

APPEND *path-list*

where *path-list* is a semicolon-separated list of paths. APPEND is both an internal and external command. The first time that APPEND is executed, it is loaded from disk. Afterward, however, it becomes part of DOS's internal commands. As with PATH, there can be no spaces in the path list.

Assume the same directory structure that we used with the PATH command. APPEND allows you to access data files in the JOHN and MARY directories:

APPEND \WP\JOHN;\WP\MARY

Now the data files in these directories can be accessed from any other directory. However, they will not show up in the directory listing of any other directory, nor can you execute commands or programs in the appended directory.

13

To see which directories are currently appended to the current one, enter APPEND with no arguments. To cancel an APPEND, enter this:

APPEND ;

The APPEND command has several options. To allow application programs to be executed from an appended directory, specify the /X:ON option. To prevent this, use /X:OFF. The default is off. This option must be specified the first time you execute APPEND.

The /PATH:ON option allows a program to search the appended directories even if a specific directory is specified. This option is on by default. /PATH:OFF suspends searching when a full path is specified.

Finally, the /E option gives the environment access to the appended directory list. The /E option may only be used the first time APPEND is executed. It is primarily used by programmers, but you might have an application program that requires this option. If so, just follow the instructions that come with that program.

CAUTION: At this point you might be tempted to simply APPEND all directories together so that you can reach any file in any directory at any time. But this is a bad idea for two reasons. First, it negates the basic philosophy of tree-structured directories and can make it impossible for you to correctly manage your files. Second, although you can read a file from any directory, if an application program writes a file, it will be written in the current directory. This means that if you edit a file in the JOHN directory while the current directory is MARY, saving that file writes it to MARY, leaving the original version in JOHN unchanged.

ASSIGN

You can cause DOS to reroute an I/O request for one drive to another by using the ASSIGN command. For example, you can make all disk I/O options that specify drive A actually go to drive B. This is the general form of ASSIGN:

ASSIGN is included only in DOS versions 5 and earlier.

ASSIGN *old-drive = new-drive*

ASSIGN is an external command.

If you have two floppy drives, try the following command:

    ASSIGN A = B

Now put your DOS work disk in B and enter this:

    DIR A:

As you can see, the B drive is activated.

If you have a fixed disk, put a DOS diskette in A and try this sequence of commands:

    ASSIGN C = A
    DIR C:

This activates the A drive.

You can specify more than one drive reassignment at a time. For example, the following command switches drives A and B:

    ASSIGN A = B B = A

To reset the drive assignments to their original values, enter ASSIGN with no arguments. To see the current drive reassignments, use this form of ASSIGN:

    ASSIGN /STATUS

The ASSIGN command's principal use is to allow application programs originally written under the assumption that the computer would have two floppy drives called A and B to take advantage of a fixed disk.

SUBST

The external command SUBST lets you specify a drive specifier that may refer to either another drive or a directory. This drive specifier is conceptually similar to a nickname. SUBST has this general form:

    SUBST *nickname*: *drive-name*:*path*

13

where *nickname* is the new drive letter that can be used to refer to *drive-name:\path*. For example, the following command allows you to refer to the A drive as E (as well as A):

SUBST E: A:\

You also can substitute a drive specifier for a subdirectory that is on the same disk. For example, assume you have the directory structure shown here on drive C:

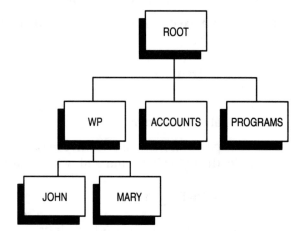

After executing the following command, you may refer to the \WP\MARY directory as if it were drive E:

SUBST E: C:\WP\MARY

The drive letter that you select as a nickname must be less than or equal to E unless you have used a LASTDRIVE command in your CONFIG.SYS file.

You can display the current substitutions by entering SUBST with no arguments. If the substitution of E for \WP\MARY has been made, for example, SUBST will display the following:

```
E:  => C:\WP\MARY
```

To remove a substitution, use this general form:

SUBST *nickname* /D

The SUBST command exists to allow the use of application programs that do not recognize path names. Although most programs available today recognize the full DOS path name, very early programs did not. But these early programs do recognize drive specifiers, so you can use SUBST as a way of making a program work correctly with directories. However, the likelihood of your encountering a program that does not recognize path names is becoming increasingly low.

JOIN

The JOIN command allows the directory of one disk to be connected to a directory on a different disk so that the second directory can access the first disk's files. JOIN is an external command with this general form:

JOIN is included only in DOS versions 5 and earlier.

JOIN *first-drive joined-drive\directory*

where *first-drive* is the drive specifier of the drive that will be joined to *joined-drive* as directory *directory*.

For example, the following command joins the A drive to the B drive in the directory B\ADRIVE:

JOIN A: B:ADRIVE

If drive B is made current, a directory listing will show the directory ADRIVE. You can switch to this directory just as you would switch to other directories—by using the CD command. To put it differently, after the preceding JOIN command, all references to files on A will be made as if they are in the ADRIVE directory of B.

You can see what is joined to what by entering JOIN with no arguments. To cancel a JOIN, use this general form:

JOIN *first-drive* /D

JOIN has a number of restrictions. The directory name that you specify for access to the joined drive must be empty or nonexistent. You cannot join the currently selected drive because the drive name for the joining drive becomes invalid immediately following the JOIN command. Further, do not use JOIN if SUBST or ASSIGN has been used

13

on either of the drives participating in the command. Finally, do not use the commands BACKUP, DISKCOPY, FORMAT, RESTORE, LABEL, RECOVER, CHKDSK, SYS, FDISK, or DISKCOMP when one drive has been joined to another.

TIP: The commands ASSIGN, JOIN, and SUBST are largely obsolete. It is possible that your version of DOS no longer includes them. These commands are included in this book for users who have older versions of DOS.

International Configurations

As you learned when reading about the CONFIG.SYS file, several conventions differ among countries, such as how the time, date, and currency symbols are defined. However, beyond that, several non-English languages require some additional characters, some accented characters, or both. Also, the exact layout of keyboards differs from country to country because of the inclusion of these different characters. (To see the keyboard layouts for other countries and languages, refer to your DOS manual.) DOS allows you to change the configuration of the keyboard and which characters are actually displayed through the use of the KEYB command.

Keep in mind that configuring DOS for a language other than English *does not* cause DOS to translate any messages—all DOS prompts and commands remain in English.

NOTE: If you will never need to alter the country-related configurations of your computer, there is no reason to read this section.

The KEYB Command

Using the KEYB command, you can change how DOS interprets the signals from the keyboard to allow alternate layouts used by foreign countries. Fortunately, if you live in the country in which the computer was purchased, the proper keyboard layout has, most likely, been correctly configured by the dealer. This section presents a brief overview just so you know something about the KEYB command.

DOS supplies several files with the extension .CPI. These are *code page information* files, which hold the codes for the various keyboard and printer character sets. Table 13-4 shows the countries supported along with their keyboard and code page codes. (Because this list is frequently updated, it is quite possible that your copy of DOS will be somewhat different from that listed here.)

If you live in a country that uses code page 437, you needn't worry about code page switching. If you do not, refer to your DOS user manual for explicit instructions on how to switch to the proper code page. (Generally, if you live in one of these countries, your computer will be preconfigured for you, and you won't need to worry about it.)

This is the general form of the external KEYB command:

KEYB *keyboard, code-page, path*

where *keyboard* is a keyboard code for the country desired, *code-page* is the proper code page, and *path* is the path to the KEYBOARD.SYS file. You don't usually specify the last two arguments, allowing them to default to the current code page and the root directory. For example, to switch to a French-speaking Swiss keyboard, enter the following command:

KEYB SF

Try this now. Notice that the positions of the "Y" and the "Z" are reversed on the French keyboard.

TIP: If you have used the KEYB command to switch the keyboard for use in another country, you can switch back to the U.S.-style keyboard at any time by pressing [Ctrl]-[Alt]-[F1]. To return to the other language, press [Ctrl]-[Alt]-[F2].

13

If you want to put KEYB in your CONFIG.SYS file, use this form:

INSTALL=C:\DOS\KEYB.COM *keyboard, code-page, path*

Country	Keyboard Code	Code Page Code
Australia	US	437
Belgium	BE	437
Brazil	BR	437
Canada—English	US	437
Canada—French	CF	863
Czechoslovakia	CZ	850
Denmark	DK	865
Finland	SU	437
France	FR	437
Germany	GR	437
Hungary	HU	850
Italy	IT	437
Latin America	LA	437
Netherlands	NL	437
Norway	NO	865
Poland	PL	850
Portugal	PO	860
Spain	SP	437
Sweden	SV	437
Switzerland—French	SF	437
Switzerland—German	SG	437
United Kingdom	UK	437
United States	US	437
Yugoslavia	YU	850

Countries
Supported with
Keyboard and
Code Page
Codes
Table 13-4.

If the KEYBOARD.SYS file is not in the root directory, then be sure to specify its location. For example, the following KEYB configuration command sets DOS for French-Canadian use; it assumes that KEYBOARD.SYS is in the C:\DOS directory:

INSTALL=C:\DOS\KEYB.COM CF, 863, C:\DOS\KEYBOARD.SYS

You also can specify a keyboard ID code using the KEYB command. The reason for this is that some foreign countries use more than one keyboard. These countries and codes are shown in Table 13-5. In most cases you will never need to use them. To specify a code, use the /ID option, which takes this general form:

/ID:*nnn*

where *nnn* is the keyboard ID. For example, this specifies the French keyboard using the ID 120:

KEYB FR /ID:120

Using SETVER

SETVER is included in versions of DOS 5 and later.

For somewhat complex, technical reasons, some programs are very sensitive to the version of DOS being used to run them. In some cases, a program that is designed to run using DOS version 3.3, for example, will not work correctly with DOS 6. To circumvent this problem, DOS includes the SETVER command, which allows you to tell DOS which version it is supposed to act like when running a specific program. It takes this general form:

SETVER *filename version*

The KEYB
Keyboard ID
Codes
Table 13-5.

Country	Keyboard ID
France	120 and 189
Italy	141 and 142
United Kingdom	168 and 166

13

Here, *filename* is the name of the program, and *version* is the DOS version number that the specified program requires. For example, if your word processor is called WP.EXE and requires DOS version 4 to run correctly, then specifying this command will allow you to use the word processor with DOS 6:

SETVER WP.EXE 4.00

When you use SETVER as shown here, you are making a change to DOS's *version table*. However, DOS only reads this table when it first begins execution, so you will need to restart your system in order for the command to be effective. You can add as many programs as you like to the version table.

You can view the version table by simply entering SETVER without any parameters. Most likely, you will see some predefined entries, which are provided by DOS.

You can remove a program from the version table by using this general form:

SETVER *filename* /DELETE

If you want no output displayed when deleting a file from the version table, add the /QUIET option. (This may be useful in batch files.)

CAUTION: It is best not to "fool" your program into working correctly. Undesired or harmful side effects may occur. It is better to obtain a new version of a troublesome program that runs correctly with your version of DOS. In general, avoid old versions of either DOS or your application programs. The best procedure to follow is to keep your computer's software current. The reason for this is simple, if aggravating: software vendors typically only provide customer support for their latest versions. If you have an old version, you might be out of luck if you encounter trouble!

 ## Summary

In this chapter you learned a number of ways to configure your system, including these:

+ Using the MODE command

+ Changing the DOS prompt

+ Creating a CONFIG.SYS file

+ Setting up a virtual disk

+ Using PATH and APPEND

+ Changing the way that DOS accesses the disk drives

+ Using extended and expanded memory

+ Using KEYB

+ Using the SETVER command

In the next chapter you will learn about protecting your computer from viruses.

13

CHAPTER

14

DEFENDING AGAINST VIRUSES

In recent years, the computer virus has caused more fear and controversy than any other type of potential trouble that can befall a system. The term computer virus refers to a program that belongs to a class of programs that can be accurately called malicious! A virus is differentiated from other programs by two characteristics. First, it is harmful, or at the very least, annoying, to your computer. Second, it is capable of reproducing itself and spreading from machine to machine. Viruses are created

A virus is a malicious program that causes harm to your computer.

by deviant programmers who derive some demented delight from inflicting suffering on others. However, beginning with version 6, DOS has included a powerful tool to help you combat viruses. This tool is called MSAV (Microsoft Anti-Virus), and its diligent use can avoid a disastrous virus attack.

How a Virus Infection Takes Place

As with human diseases, the first line of defense against a virus is avoiding infection. To begin, it is important to understand the following: Your computer will never get a virus if

✦ Your computer is currently free from all viruses

✦ You never (NEVER) put any foreign disk into your computer

✦ Your computer is not part of a network

✦ You never connect a modem to your computer

However, a computer that meets these restrictions is rare, indeed. Short of complete isolation, a computer system is vulnerable to a virus infection two ways: by coming into contact with an infected disk or by communicating with another infected computer either via a network or a modem. From a practical point of view, the most likely method of acquiring a virus is by inserting an infected diskette into your computer and then copying the file or files that contain the virus to your system. It is this route of infection that makes putting unknown diskettes into your computer so risky.

Once a virus has access to your computer, the infection will generally occur in one of three ways. First, some viruses attach themselves to one of DOS's system files, which contains the initial part of DOS that is loaded when your computer is first turned on. This is called a *boot-sector virus*. (In the old days of computing, starting a computer was called *boot strapping* the system, and the term *boot sector* is commonly used to refer to that part of a disk on which the initial part of DOS resides.) Once a boot-sector virus is loaded, it is free to perpetrate its harm. It is also free to copy itself to any other diskette that is inserted into the system.

Another type of virus attaches itself to one of your programs. When the program is executed, the virus takes over. It can then perform its malicious acts as well as copy itself to other programs on your disk or other diskettes inserted into the computer. This type of virus is called a *file-infector virus*.

The third basic type of virus is called a *Trojan horse*. A Trojan horse looks like a legitimate program and, in some cases, will even act like a legitimate program in certain situations. However, the program is really a virus that is generally up to no good when it is executing in your system. Once the Trojan horse is executed, it is free to copy itself to other diskettes.

Once a virus has infected your system it will act one of two different ways. First, the virus may damage your system as soon as it is executed. For example, a virus may erase files or corrupt files each time it is run. A second type of virus will wait until some predetermined event occurs before it harms your system. For example, a virus may wait until a certain date or until you run a certain sequence of DOS commands. This type of virus is particularly infectious, because its infection potentially goes unnoticed for a long period of time.

Whatever the type of virus, if you have DOS version 6, you can mount an effective defense by following the procedures described in this chapter.

Using MSAV

MSAV is the command that checks your computer for viral infections.

Your first line of defense against viruses is MSAV. This command searches for viral infections on your drives and reports any that it finds. It can also remove a virus. There are two general methods that MSAV uses to search for viruses. First, it has a list of known viruses that it looks for. Second, it watches for signs of virus infection. Signs of infection include changes to the boot sector, changes to your DOS files, and changes to other executable programs. To look for changes, MSAV maintains a checksum of each program (and program-related) file on your disk. Loosely, a *checksum* is a number that is derived from a file by adding together the values of each byte in the file. The next time you run MSAV it again computes the checksum for each file. If the new checksum does not agree with the previous checksum, it means that the file has been changed. If you did not alter this file, then the file was altered by some outside entity (probably a virus) for potentially malicious purposes. MSAV also looks for other suspicious activity.

NOTE: The MSAV command supports a large number of options to handle a number of different unusual situations. However, you will generally want to use MSAV in its default mode of operation. It is this operation that is discussed in detail here.

The simplest way to execute MSAV is to enter it without any options on the command line. For example, enter **MSAV** now. You will see the screen shown in Figure 14-1.

As you can see, MSAV is a window-based command that provides a menu of options from which you may select. You may select an option using either the keyboard or the mouse. To select an option using the keyboard, use the arrow keys to position the highlight on the desired option and then press ⌈Enter⌉. To select an option using the mouse, position the mouse pointer over the option you want and then press the left mouse button. (That is, you "click" the mouse on the option you want.) You may also select an option by pressing its associated function key. The function keys are shown on the bottom of the screen. For example, to select Detect & Clean, press the ⌈F5⌉ key. The drive that

```
 ─                   Microsoft Anti-Virus                    8:46a
 ┌──────────────────────────────────────────────────────────────┐
 │ ─                        Main Menu                            │
 │  ┌──────────────────┐   ┌─ ──────────── Detect ───────────┐   │
 │  │ Detect          ▪│   │                                 │   │
 │  ├──────────────────┤   │  • The Detect option scans the  │   │
 │  │ Detect & Clean  ▪│   │    current drive for viruses.   │   │
 │  ├──────────────────┤   │                                 │   │
 │  │ Select new drive▪│   │  • If any viruses are detected  │   │
 │  ├──────────────────┤   │    you have the option to clean │   │
 │  │ Options         ▪│   │    the infected file, continue  │   │
 │  ├──────────────────┤   │    without cleaning, or stop the│   │
 │  │ Exit            ▪│   │    scanning process.            │   │
 │  └──────────────────┘   └─────────────────────────────────┘   │
 │                          Work Drive:        C:                │
 │  Microsoft               Last Virus Found:  None              │
 │  ▶▶▶ Anti-Virus ───────  Last Action:       None              │
 └──────────────────────────────────────────────────────────────┘
  Help   Drive  Exit    Detect  Clean   Delete  Options List
```

The MSAV
main screen
Figure 14-1.

will be checked for viruses is shown as the Work Drive. By default, this will be the drive that was current when you executed MSAV.

If you want to scan your drive for viruses, but not necessarily remove any, select the Detect option. There are two reasons to select this option. First, you might simply want to know if the drive is infected with a virus, but leave the actual disinfection to a specialist. Second, when a virus is found, the Detect option asks if you want it removed. You may not want to remove a virus until you have shown it to a system manager, for example. Also, rarely, a file can be modified in a way that MSAV thinks is a viral infection when it isn't. In this unusual case, using Detect allows you to tell MSAV to skip a file that is not actually infected.

To automatically check and remove viruses from your disk, use the Detect & Clean option.

After either Detect or Detect & Clean has concluded, you will see a report on the status of your drive, similar to the one shown in Figure 14-2.

C**AUTION:** If your office has a virus specialist, contact him or her to remove a virus if MSAV detects one. This may help head off a large-scale infection from occurring in your office.

A sample
MSAV status
report
Figure 14-2.

```
 ─                Viruses Detected and Cleaned
                       Checked        Infected       Cleaned

        Hard disks   :     1              0             0
        Floppy disks :     0              0             0
        Total disks  :     1              0             0

        COM Files    :    49              0             0
        EXE Files    :   251              0             0
        Other Files  :   920              0             0
        Total Files  :  1220              0             0

        Scan Time    : 00:01:33
                                                    ┌─────────┐
                                                    │   OK    │
                                                    └─────────┘
```

14

To select a different drive to scan for viral infection, select the Select new drive option. You will see a list of drives in your system, and you can select a new drive by using either the keyboard or the mouse. To use the keyboard, use the arrow keys to move the highlight to the desired drive and then press (Enter). Alternatively, simply press the letter of the drive you want. To use the mouse, click on the new drive. (To leave the drive unchanged, press (Esc).)

For most users, the default settings for MSAV are correct and there is no reason to set additional options.

MSAV allows you to set a number of options by selecting Options. For the vast majority of users, the default settings will be appropriate and there is no reason to change them. (Also, some options are best used only by system managers.) However, feel free to explore these options on your own. You can obtain a description for each option by first highlighting it and then pressing the (F1) (Help) key. To change the state of an option, position the highlight over that option and press the (Spacebar). (You can also change the state of an option by clicking on it using the mouse.)

To exit MSAV, either press the (Esc) key or position the mouse pointer on the small box in the upper-left corner of the MSAV screen, and press the left mouse button. Then, select the Close option. You will then be prompted by the Close confirmation box, shown here:

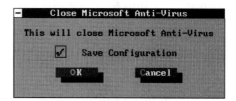

To terminate MSAV, press (Enter) or select the OK box using the mouse. To cancel, press (Esc) or select the Cancel box. If you have changed an option, you can save this change by checking the Save Configuration check box. To do this, either click on it using the mouse or move the highlight to it (by pressing the (Tab) key), and then press the (Spacebar). Saving the configuration causes your changes to become part of MSAV's default operation when you next execute it. (Most of the time, Save Configuration should not be checked.)

How to Use MSAV

For MSAV to be effective, it must be run whenever your computer is vulnerable to infection. This generally means on a daily basis if your computer is used in an office environment. You can either run MSAV manually or include it in your AUTOEXEC.BAT file. If you do the latter, you might want to use the /P option, which suppresses the graphical display. MSAV will then check your disk and report any problems, but it does not require any user interaction.

If you want to check more than one drive when using the /P option, specify the drives on the command line. For example, this causes MSAV to check drives C and D:

MSAV C: D: /P

T**IP:** If, in the normal course of using your computer, things begin to act abnormally, try running MSAV. Your problems may be due to a virus.

New viruses will always be invented. Understand that it is possible to create a virus that will circumvent MSAV's protection capabilities. Therefore, it is always a good idea to be careful about what software enters your computer. Frankly, if you don't know where a diskette or program came from, don't put it in your computer.

Listing Known Viruses

When running MSAV, you can obtain a list of those viruses that MSAV knows about by pressing the F9 key. This causes a window to be shown that displays the viruses of which MSAV is aware. To move through the list of viruses, use the ↑ and ↓ keys or use the mouse to operate the scroll bar. The scroll bars here work just the same as they do in the DOS editor, EDIT (described in Chapter 7). To receive information about a virus, first highlight it and then press (Enter). You can also click on the desired virus using the mouse.

The virus window contains several command buttons. These buttons work like command buttons you encountered when using EDIT. To select a button, first move the highlight to it by pressing (Tab) and then pressing (Enter). Or, you can select a button by clicking on it using the mouse. (You can also select a button by holding down the (Alt) key and then pressing the highlighted letter.) The Find Next button highlights the next virus in the list, and Info displays information about the highlighted virus. (This is the same information that is displayed if you select a virus from the list.) The Print option prints the list of viruses on the printer.

If you know the name of a virus and you want to see if MSAV has it in its list, you can type it into the box below the list. If it is found, it will be highlighted in the virus list window.

To exit the virus list window, press (Esc) or select the OK button.

Using VSAFE

VSAFE is an installed command that monitors your system for suspicious activity.

While MSAV is effective at finding viral infections, it only finds those that are present when it is run. However, DOS version 6 also includes a program called VSAFE that monitors your system at all times, watching for any action that may indicate that a viral infection is taking place. VSAFE is an installed command. Once installed, it monitors the activity that takes place in your computer and reports any suspicious activity.

To install VSAFE, execute VSAFE from the command line. VSAFE supports several options, but most are used only by system integrators and require specialized technical knowledge beyond the scope of this book. However, a few will be examined later in this section.

When VSAFE detects an action that might indicate that a virus is attempting to infect your system, it will display a window that allows you to choose a course of action. The course of action will vary depending upon the type of potential trouble detected. A sample warning window is shown here:

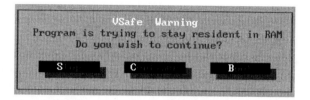

In general, you can stop the activity that might be causing your system to become infected or damaged by selecting Stop. You can ignore the potential problem by selecting Continue. You will want to select this option when you know that the activity that causes VSAFE to react is normal and desired by you. Finally, if you are completely unsure about the error, you can reload DOS by selecting Boot.

NOTE: If you are using Windows, execute Windows before installing VSAFE.

Once you have installed VSAFE, you can alter its function by setting or clearing various options using the VSAFE control panel. To activate the control panel, press Alt-V. You will see a window that contains eight options. These options are

1:	Warn if fixed disk is about to be formatted
2:	Warn if a memory-resident program is installing
3:	Prevent a program from writing to the disk
4:	Check program files before they are executed
5:	Check all disks for boot sector contamination
6:	Warn if fixed disk boot sector is being altered
7:	Warn if a floppy disk boot sector is being altered
8:	Warn if a program file is being altered

By default, options 1, 4, 5, and 6 are on. You can turn an option on or off when the control panel is displayed by pressing its corresponding

14

key. For example, to turn on option 2, press **2**. Each time you press the key, the option is turned on or off.

If you want to remove VSAFE from memory, press Alt-U while the control panel is displayed. You can also remove VSAFE from memory by executing it using the /U option. To close the control panel, press Esc.

CAUTION: At this point you may be thinking that it is a good idea to turn on all the VSAFE options. However, depending upon how you use your system, you may not be able to do this. For example, most application programs maintain data files which are frequently changed or updated. If this is the case with your computer, you will not be able to turn on option 3, which prevents the disk from being written to.

Putting VSAFE in Your AUTOEXEC.BAT File

Since VSAFE is an installed command, you will probably want to have it executed automatically from your AUTOEXEC.BAT file each time your computer is turned on. If you find its default settings acceptable (as most users will), then simply include VSAFE without any options. However, if you want to turn on additional warnings or turn off any of those set by default, you can use this form of VSAFE,

VSAFE /n /n /n ...

where n is the number of the warning (as shown previously). To turn the warning on, follow the number with a **+**. To turn it off, follow it with a **–**. For example, the following executes VSAFE with warnings 3, 4, 5, and 6 on. Remember, by default, VSAFE has warnings 1, 4, 5, and 6 on, so this command turns off number 1 and turns on number 3:

VSAFE /1– /3+

REMEMBER: For most users, VSAFE's default warnings are adequate.

Final Thoughts on Virus Protection

Protecting your computer from viral infection is an important, but not a cost-free endeavor. As you may have guessed by reading this chapter, using the highest level of virus protection provided by DOS also makes your computer more cumbersome to use. For example, turning on all options to VSAFE makes your computer practically unusable for several normal, day-to-day tasks! Therefore, you must balance the level of virus protection you use against the threat level that you feel viruses pose to your system. If you work by yourself, install only name-brand software on your system, and don't put strange diskettes into your system, then your risk from a virus is quite low. However, if you work in a large office, often use strange diskettes, or if your computer is frequently used by others, then the chance of viral infection is greatly increased. The best protection against viral attacks is common sense combined with prudent use of MSAV and VSAFE.

Summary

In this chapter you learned

+ What a virus is and how it attacks your system

+ How to check your system for viruses using MSAV

+ How to monitor your system for possible virus attacks using VSAFE

In the next chapter you will learn how to manage your disks.

14

P A R T

4

MANAGING YOUR
COMPUTER

CHAPTER

15

FLOPPY DISK MANAGEMENT

Aside from the invention of the microprocessor that makes personal computers possible, no device has contributed as much to the development and success of the microcomputer as the floppy disk drive. The reasons for this are threefold. First, floppy disk drives are inexpensive compared to fixed disks (although fixed disks are cheaper in terms of bytes of storage per dollar). In the early days of microcomputers, a fixed disk could easily cost several thousand dollars, while a floppy drive might sell for just a few hundred.

Second, compared to the only other cheap method of data storage—cassette tape—floppy disks are fast. Finally, the floppy disk gives users an easy and inexpensive way to share programs and transfer files. (Also, software developers found floppy diskettes the perfect medium on which to sell their programs.) For these reasons, the floppy disk has earned a lasting place in the world of computing.

How the floppy disk is used depends upon whether it is the main disk of the system or only a companion to a fixed disk. In most fixed-disk systems the floppy disk is not the main disk drive. In fact, in most such systems, the floppy is used for only two purposes: to back up information on the fixed disk for offsite storage and as a transfer medium for data and programs. While most new computers today come with at least one fixed and one floppy disk it is still possible to purchase floppy-only systems. Also, a great many older computers do not contain a fixed disk. In floppy-based systems the floppy drive performs not only those functions that it performs in a fixed-disk system, but also provides the main storage device for the computer. In this chapter we will concentrate primarily on the floppy disk as it is used in floppy-only systems. Its use as a backup for the fixed disk is covered in Chapter 16.

Balancing DOS and Applications on Your Work Disk

It is difficult to balance DOS and your application programs when running DOS from a floppy-based system. As you know, DOS is a very large system. In fact, it is so large that you cannot even fit all of DOS on a single floppy disk. Thus, if you are running DOS using only floppy disks, DOS may be spread among two or more diskettes. The size problem is further compounded by your application programs because, typically, you will want at least part of DOS available on your application work diskettes.

Fortunately, there is a solution to this problem. When running your applications you generally need access to only a small part of DOS. Thus, when you create your work disks, you can carefully select only those parts of DOS that you will actually need. In this way, you can reduce the amount of disk space allocated to DOS.

In this section you will learn which files are best eliminated and in which situations to eliminate them from your DOS work disks. (Remember, don't delete files on your master DOS diskettes or backups.) To begin, let's first see which files you can't eliminate.

TIP: When experimenting with removing unneeded files, first make a copy of your master DOS disk. Then erase one file at a time and try to restart your computer after each erasure. If your computer fails to start properly, you will know that the last file erased is needed by DOS. If this happens, restore that file and continue the process until you have removed all unnecessary files.

Which DOS Files Are Needed

If a disk is not going to be used to load DOS, then no part of DOS is required on that disk. However, any disk capable of loading DOS must contain the DOS system. This includes the hidden files MSDOS.SYS and IO.SYS. The file COMMAND.COM must also be present. If you are using the Shell (discussed in Part 5), then all files with the filename of DOSSHELL must also be present. Your needs and how you use your computer determine which DOS files you include beyond these. For example, if you frequently sort a file using SORT, then SORT.EXE should be on your disk.

Other files you cannot delete from a floppy disk that will be used to load DOS are CONFIG.SYS and AUTOEXEC.BAT, since these files contain important configuration information. If your CONFIG.SYS file loads any device drivers, such as RAMDRIVE.SYS, they must be present on the disk. In short, any file required to start or configure your computer must be on any floppy disk that will be used to load DOS.

REMEMBER: Files that are needed to load or configure DOS must be on the disk that you use to load DOS.

Removing Foreign-Language Files

If you speak English and use your computer in the United States or another English-speaking country, you can eliminate the following files, which are used to support foreign languages and countries:

- ✦ 4201.CPI
- ✦ 4208.CPI
- ✦ 5202.CPI
- ✦ COUNTRY.SYS
- ✦ DISPLAY.SYS
- ✦ EGA.CPI
- ✦ GRAFTABL.COM
- ✦ KEYB.COM
- ✦ KEYBOARD.SYS
- ✦ LCD.CPI
- ✦ NLSFUNC.EXE
- ✦ PRINTER.SYS

If you live in a country other than the United States, you might still be able to eliminate all but COUNTRY.SYS. (See the section in Chapter 13 on "International Configurations.")

Removing Device Drivers

You can remove any device drivers you don't use including the following:

- ✦ ANSI.SYS
- ✦ DRIVER.SYS
- ✦ EMM386.EXE
- ✦ HIMEM.SYS
- ✦ RAMDRIVE.SYS

✦   SMARTDRV.SYS

Removing Formatting and DOS Transfer Commands

On a work disk, you will probably not need any of the commands that are used to create new disks or install DOS. You will usually perform such tasks with your DOS disk rather than an application work disk. If this is the case, you can erase the following files:

✦   FDISK.EXE

✦   FORMAT.COM

✦   SYS.COM

Programmer-Related Commands

Unless you are a programmer, you can remove the following files:

✦   EXE2BIN.EXE

✦   DEBUG.EXE

✦   QBASIC.EXE

✦   QBASIC.HLP

✦   QBASIC.INI

CAUTION: If you intend to use DOS's editor, EDIT, you will need to have QBASIC.EXE on your disk. (EDIT uses QBASIC's editor.)

Also, you can probably remove any files that have the extension .BAS unless your applications are written in the BASIC language. (If you're not sure, check with a knowledgeable person.)

Fixed-Disk Commands

If you don't have a fixed disk, you can erase the following commands:

✦ BACKUP.EXE

✦ FASTOPEN.EXE

✦ RESTORE.EXE

Seldom-Used Commands

It is often useful to remove commands you seldom (or never) use. For example, you will probably never use the following commands:

✦ APPEND.EXE

✦ ASSIGN.COM

✦ ATTRIB.EXE

✦ JOIN.EXE

✦ SETVER.EXE

✦ SUBST.EXE

✦ TREE.COM

If you have your own text editor, you can remove EDIT.COM and EDIT.HLP. If you are using a version of DOS prior to 5, then remove EDLIN.EXE (the old DOS editor) if you don't use it.

If you have DOS version 5 or later and do not use the Shell, you can remove DOSSHELL.*. You also can remove DOSSWAP.EXE, which is used by the Shell.

In general, remove any command that you do not use on a daily basis. Just list the directory of your disk and erase those commands that you seldom use.

TIP: If you have a dual floppy system, the best way to balance the needs of DOS and those of your application is to let the diskette in drive A hold DOS while you use the one in drive B to hold your application programs and files.

Floppy Disks and Subdirectories

Because of the limited storage on a floppy diskette, extensive subdirectories are seldom used because it is easier (or necessary) to simply keep logically separate applications on separate diskettes. However, this is not meant to discourage you from creating and using subdirectories on your floppies. If you do use subdirectories on floppies, be aware of two performance issues.

Using subdirectories on a floppy disk can substantially affect performance.

First, each additional level of subdirectories increases the access time to the files in those subdirectories. On fixed disks this extra time is not much of an issue because they are so much faster than floppy drives. However, on floppies this additional access time can become annoying. So use heavily nested subdirectories only when you can justify them.

Second, each subdirectory uses disk space to hold its directory entries. Because space on a floppy is already limited, an unwarranted number of subdirectories could seriously decrease the amount of information that you could store on the disk.

Backing Up Floppy Disks

You must back up the floppy disks that contain your application programs and data on a regular basis. To put it bluntly, not making copies of important data is negligence of the highest order. If you lose important data, you have no one to blame but yourself.

Sources of Data Loss

Before discussing the backup routine, let's look at the four ways that valuable data can be destroyed.

Computer Failure

There are four causes of data loss: computer failure, medium failure, software errors, and human error.

The least common way that important information can be destroyed on a diskette is through computer failure. Few machine errors will destroy a file. But if a file is being written when a hardware failure occurs, the file could be damaged or destroyed. The most common causes of hardware failures are static electricity, overheating, line current transients, and physical abuse. Age is not as significant a factor in hardware failures as it once was because the integrated circuits now used to construct the computer have a very long mean time to failure.

It is very difficult to guard against machine errors except by trying to maintain a clean environment and a steady source of power. If power transients are a problem in your area, you might want to invest in a surge protector.

Medium Failure

The next least frequent source of data loss is physical destruction of the magnetic medium of the floppy disk. This can result from negligence on the part of the user or from a poorly manufactured diskette that simply disintegrates. Fortunately, with care, floppy diskettes tend to last a long time. However, any diskette that has been in heavy daily service for more than a year is a good candidate for replacement.

Software Errors

Programmers are not perfect—hence your application programs could contain one or more errors capable of destroying information. For the end user it is sometimes difficult to distinguish between software and hardware errors. However, if data is consistently lost when you perform the same sequence of actions, software is likely the culprit.

Often you can work with the developers of your application software to get these errors fixed. If not, you must find different, more reliable programs to use.

Human Error

Computers are some of the most reliable devices in use. People are not! The accidental erasing of important data is epidemic. So is accidentally reformatting a diskette! Frankly, there is no way to guard against it—it

15

is simply too easy to erase a file or reformat a diskette. As you know from reading Chapter 12, if you catch an accidental erasure immediately, you can often recover your file(s) using UNDELETE. However, human nature being what it is, accidents are usually not discovered in time.

The Backup Routine

Your only protection against having the data on a diskette destroyed is the *backup routine*. As you will come to understand, it is not enough just to make copies of important diskettes. *When* to make them, *how many* to maintain, and how to *recover* from a loss are also crucial.

> A backup routine is a procedure that you follow to ensure that important data is not lost.

Many data processing managers recommend the *rotating triad* method of backup. With this method, you have three backup diskettes for every work disk. You use the first, called the *daily backup*, to back up the work disk on a daily basis or even after a shorter period, such as every two hours, if your data is volatile. The daily disk substitutes for the work disk should failure occur. (Actually, a copy of it should be used, but we will discuss recovery shortly.)

The next disk in the triad is the *weekly backup*. Every Friday at 5 p.m., the contents of the daily disk are copied to the weekly disk. Thus, if both the master work disk and the daily disk are destroyed, the weekly disk can be used as a fairly close starting point.

At the end of each month, the weekly backup is retired and put in a safe place. A new copy of the daily disk is made and becomes the next month's weekly backup. The retired monthly backup completes the triad. In this way, if an error is not discovered for some time and has already corrupted the daily and weekly disks, the monthly backup can be used.

Because the nearest backup is potentially one month out of date, some managers employ the *snapshot* method in addition to the rotating triad. With this method, four diskettes are created for each work disk and are labeled One through Four. Every Wednesday, a copy of the daily disk is placed on one of the snapshot diskettes, beginning with One the first week, Two the second week, and so on. After Four has been used, the process cycles back to One. In this way an error will not perpetuate itself through all the diskettes.

Backing Up a Disk

The best way to back up a diskette is by using DISKCOPY. Using COPY or even XCOPY is not as good because it permits human error—you could forget to copy a file or two.

Recovering Data

If you have to go to a backup diskette, use it only to make a copy—then use the copy. If a hardware or software problem has caused the loss of a file, it could happen again. Never risk the destruction of a backup diskette. Be sure to write-protect the disk before putting it in the computer.

Remember also to restore all files even if only one is lost because many application programs use two or more files that work together. If these files are out of synchronization, you could be heading for even more trouble.

Mailing Diskettes

To close this chapter, a few words about how to mail or ship floppy disks are in order. The best way to mail a diskette is in a diskette mailer. If none is available, place the diskette between two strong pieces of cardboard and put it in a large envelope. Be sure to write on the package, in large letters, that a floppy diskette is enclosed and should not be bent or exposed to magnetic fields.

Summary

In this chapter you learned these things:

+ How to free space on your DOS work diskette
+ The effects of subdirectories on floppy disks
+ How to maintain a backup routine
+ How to mail a diskette

In the next chapter you will learn how to manage and back up your fixed disk.

CHAPTER

16

MANAGING YOUR FIXED DISK

With storage capabilities in excess of 300 megabytes, the fixed disk is a system resource that demands attention. In fact, most users will not consider buying a computer without a fixed disk because its extra storage and speed are generally judged worth the extra expense. In this chapter you will learn some valuable techniques to help you manage this important device.

How Fixed and Floppy Disks Differ

The most fundamental difference between fixed and floppy disks is that the fixed disk, unlike the floppy, is not removable from the drive. It is not removable for two main reasons. First, the read/write head is mounted very close to the surface of the disk and is quite delicate. Second, even if the drive head were retracted to a safe position, the fixed disk is very easily harmed by dust, so just opening its case is a bad idea.

From the aspect of performance, the fixed disk runs much faster than a floppy and stores from 10 to 200 times as much information. It is the increased storage, however, that really distinguishes how fixed disks tend to be used. Unlike floppies, a fixed disk tends to have a complex directory structure that holds a wide range of information and application programs. In a way, a floppy disk is like a single-family dwelling, while a fixed disk is like a high-rise condominium.

Backing Up Your Fixed Disk Using BACKUP

NOTE: If you use DOS version 6, this section does not apply to you. Instead, skip ahead to "Backing Up Using MSBACKUP."

The BACKUP command is not part of DOS 6.

Making and maintaining copies of the information on your fixed disk is seldom as easy as it is with floppy disks because of the amount of information usually found on the fixed disk. Unless you have some sort of tape backup system attached to your computer, you cannot copy an entire fixed disk the way you can copy an entire floppy. Instead, you will need to copy the information on the fixed disk to several floppy diskettes. The trouble is that often even one directory on a fixed disk will contain more information than will fit on a single floppy. With only the copying commands you have learned so far, there is no easy and trouble-free way to back up a hard disk. Instead, you must use DOS's external BACKUP command.

16

The BACKUP command has several forms and numerous options. In this book we will examine the most common forms. All the examples use drive A as the floppy drive receiving the information, though you may substitute drive B if you wish. Drive C is assumed to be the fixed disk. You should substitute a different drive letter if necessary. BACKUP has the general form,

BACKUP *source target options*

where *source* specifies the drive, path, and file names to be copied to *target*.

The number of diskettes that you will need to back up the entire contents of your disk is directly related to the amount of information on your fixed disk. Sometimes this number can be quite large. To compute the number of diskettes that you will need, run CHKDSK to find the total storage size, in bytes, of the fixed disk and the amount of free storage. Subtract the amount of free storage from the total storage and then divide this number by the storage size of the floppy drive that you will be using for backups. Rounding this number upward tells you the number of diskettes required. This formula in mathematical notation is

number of diskettes = (total–free)/size of floppy

You must number your backup diskettes because you will have to insert them in order. The exact order in which the diskettes are written is very important because a large file may be spread across two or more diskettes.

If you are going to back up only part of the disk, you can roughly compute the number of diskettes by determining the amount of space taken up by the files you are going to copy and then dividing this number by the storage capacity of your floppy drive.

REMEMBER: You must number your floppy disks so that you can use them to restore your fixed disk in the order in which they are created.

Backing Up an Entire Drive

The most important and by far most common backup scenario is backing up the entire contents of a fixed disk. This is the safest way to ensure that all the data on the disk is copied. To back up the entire contents of the fixed disk, use the following form of BACKUP:

    BACKUP C:*.* A: /S

BACKUP will automatically format the diskettes for you, but you will save time if you use preformatted ones. (BACKUP uses FORMAT to format the diskettes, so this command must be available for BACKUP's use.)

The path \ ensures that the backup will begin with the root directory, and the /S option specifies that all subdirectories will be copied. As the backup procedure begins, you will see this message:

```
Insert backup diskette 01 in drive A:

Warning!  Files in the target drive
A:\ root directory will be erased
Press any key to continue . . .
```

As BACKUP continues, you will be prompted to insert additional diskettes until all the information on C has been backed up.

NOTE: If your fixed disk is very full, the backup procedure will take a fairly long time—possibly an hour or more. Be prepared for this.

If you have more than one fixed disk drive, repeat the backup command using the next drive specifier.

Backing Up Portions of the Fixed Disk

In situations where several people use the same computer, it may make more sense for each user to back up his or her own directories rather than the entire disk. For example, assume that the directory structure shown below exists on a fixed disk:

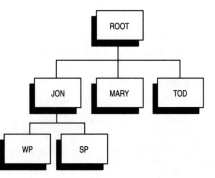

The command that Jon will use to back up his workspace, including the JON directory and its two subdirectories, is

BACKUP C:\JON*.* A: /S

In general, you specify a path to the directory where you wish to start the backup.

If you leave off the /S, then only the contents of the directory explicitly specified are copied. For example, the command,

BACKUP C:\JON*.* A:

copies only the contents of the JON directory and not its subdirectories WP and SP.

Adding Files to Backup Diskettes

The forms of the BACKUP command shown so far erase any previously existing contents of the diskettes. However, suppose that you perform a complete fixed-disk backup only once a week, and you have simply added three files while leaving the others unchanged. How can you add these files to the backup diskettes without having to recopy the entire fixed disk? The answer is to use BACKUP's /A (add) option. When you specify this option, the target diskettes are not overwritten—rather, the specified files are added to them. For example, to add the file FORMLET.WP to backup diskettes for Jon, enter

BACKUP C:\JON\WP\FORMLET.WP A: /A

When this command begins execution, you will see the following:

```
Insert last backup diskette in drive A:
Press any key to continue . . .
```

As is implied by this message, new files are added to the last diskette used by the previous backup.

TIP: Adding new or modified files is a good way to keep your backups current without going through the time-consuming process of a full backup.

Backing Up Files Modified on or After a Specified Date

You can back up only those files that have been changed on or after a specified date by using the /D: option. For example, the following command copies those files that have been changed on or after 7-10-93:

BACKUP C:*.* A: /D:7-10-93

The format of the date is determined by the country specified with the COUNTRY command in the CONFIG.SYS file, or as mm-dd-yy (standard U.S. format) if no other country is specified.

Keep in mind that use of the /D: option does not prevent the target diskette(s) from being overwritten. To add new files with dates after a certain date, also add the /A option to the command line. For example, the following command will add any new files modified after 7-10-93 to the target diskette(s):

BACKUP C:*.* A: /D:7-10-93 /A

Backing Up Files Modified on or After a Specified Time

You can tell BACKUP to copy only those files with times equal to or later than a specified time on a specified date by using the /T: option along with the /D: option. For example, the following command only backs up those files created after 12:00 noon on 7-10-93:

BACKUP C:*.* A: /D:7-10-93 /T:12:00

Again, the format for the date and time will vary in countries other than the United States. Remember, the existing set of backup diskettes will be overwritten.

Backing Up Only Files That Have Changed

By using the /M option, you can tell BACKUP to copy only those files that have changed since the last backup. As you will recall from an earlier chapter, all files have an associated archive attribute that can be either on or off. If the archive attribute is on, it indicates that the file has been modified. The BACKUP command automatically turns off the archive attribute. Therefore, only files that have been changed will actually be copied. For example, the following command backs up only the modified files of the fixed disk:

BACKUP C:*.* A: /M /S

Adding a Log File

A log file contains a record of each file copied.

With the /L: option, you can have a record of the time and date of the backup, the path and file names of each file backed up, and the number of the diskette that each file is on. You can specify a file name for the log file. If none is specified, BACKUP.LOG is used and is placed in the root directory of both the source and target. If the specified file exists, information is appended to the end. If it does not exist, the file is created. For example, the following command writes to the file called MYLOG:

BACKUP C:*.* A: /S /L:MYLOG

This command uses the default BACKUP.LOG file:

    BACKUP C:*.* A: /S /L

The first line of the log file contains the date and time of the backup. Each subsequent line lists the diskette number and file name. The first few lines will look something like this:

```
1-12-93   10:30:37

001   \AUTOEXEC.BAT
001   \ANSI.SYS
001   \ASSIGN.COM
```

The log file provides a record of which backup diskette any specific file is on. This can speed up the process of restoring a file, as you will shortly see.

If for some reason you want to have BACKUP automatically format the target diskettes to a size other than the capacity of the floppy drive being used for the backup, you can use the /F option. One reason you might want to do this is so that you can restore a fixed disk on a computer that uses different capacity diskettes. The /F option takes this form:

    /F:*size*

where *size* must be one of the sizes from the following table:

Size	Capacity	Applicable Diskette Size
160	160K	5 1/4-inch single-sided
180	180K	5 1/4-inch single-sided
320	320K	5 1/4-inch double-sided
360	360K	5 1/4-inch double-sided
720	720K	3 1/2-inch double-sided
1200	1.22MB	3 1/2-inch double-sided
1440	1.44MB	3 1/2-inch double-sided
2880	2.88MB	3 1/2-inch double-sided

If you are just backing up your fixed disk for your own use on your own computer, you won't ever need to use the /F option.

The BACKUP options are shown in Table 16-1.

Backing Up Floppies with BACKUP

You can use BACKUP to back up the contents of a floppy disk, although this is rarely done because DISKCOPY is clearly superior. However, you can specify any target and any source drive that you desire (except that they cannot be the same drive) as arguments to BACKUP.

Restoring Files

If a file is lost on your fixed disk, you can restore it from the backups that you made with BACKUP by using the RESTORE command. Assuming that you are restoring to a fixed disk, the general form of the RESTORE command is

RESTORE *bkdrive: target options*

where *bkdrive* is the drive that will hold the diskettes created by BACKUP, and *target* denotes the drive, path, and file name specifiers that tell where information will be written to the fixed disk.

Option	Meaning
/A	Add files instead of overwriting the backup diskettes
/D:	Copy files with dates on or after the specified date
/F:	Specify capacity of target diskettes
/L:	Create a log file
/M	Copy only those files that have been created or changed since the last backup
/S	Back up all subdirectories starting with the specified path
/T:	Copy files with times equal to or later than the one specified on the given date

BACKUP Options Table 16-1.

REMEMBER: RESTORE only restores files created by BACKUP.

During the restoration process, you will be prompted to insert one or more of the backup diskettes beginning with diskette number 1. When you restore the entire fixed disk, all backup diskettes will be read in order. If only certain files are being restored, RESTORE will search through the backup diskettes until it finds them. The RESTORE prompt tells you which diskette to insert next and waits until you press a key. The first prompt will look like this:

```
Insert backup diskette 01 in drive A:
Press any key to continue . . .
```

Keep in mind that restoring a file means overwriting any existing file with the same name, so use the RESTORE command carefully.

Restoring the Entire Fixed Disk

To restore all the files on the fixed disk, you must have backup diskettes containing all these files. That is, you must have recently used a BACKUP command similar to the following:

BACKUP C:*.* A: /S

With the diskettes that hold the backed up information, you should use the following form of the RESTORE command to restore all of the files:

RESTORE A: C:*.* /S

The /S option tells RESTORE to restore all files and subdirectories. Notice that you specify the path name for where the files will be placed on the fixed disk, not from where they are stored on the backup diskettes.

In general, there are only two occasions when you will completely restore a disk. The first, and most unfortunate, is when a hardware error destroys your fixed disk and a new disk is put in the system. In this case you must reload all your files. If you have been following a proper backup procedure (such as the one described later in this chapter), the disruption should be minimal. However, if the fixed disk crashes and your backups are either out of date or nonexistent, you are probably in for a very painful experience.

The other time that you will want to fully recover a fixed disk is when you are bringing up another system that is intended to have the same function as the first.

Restoring Individual Files

To restore individual files, you must specify the complete path and file names. RESTORE accepts wildcards, so it is possible to restore groups of files. For example, to restore the files LETTER.ONE, LETTER.TWO, and FORMLET.ONE found in the JON\WP directory, use the following commands:

```
RESTORE  A:  C:\JON\WP\LETTER.*
RESTORE  A:  C:\JON\WP\FORMLET.ONE
```

Restoring Files by Date and Time

RESTORE can restore files modified on or *before* a certain date when you add the /B: option. Alternately, the /A: option allows you to restore files that have been modified on or *after* the specified date. For example, the following commands restore all files changed before or on 3-3-92, and after 3-3-91 (a period of one year):

```
RESTORE  A:  C:\*.*  /S  /B:3-3-92  /A:3-3-91
```

In like fashion you can use /L: to restore those files modified *at or later* than a certain time on a given date, and /E: to restore all files modified *at or prior* to the specified time on a given date. For example, the following commands restore all files modified on 2-28-91 after 12:00 noon but earlier than 5:01 that afternoon:

```
RESTORE  A:  C:\*.*  /S  /D:2-28-91  /L:12:00  /E:17:00
```

NOTE: The time is specified using a 24-hour clock when using RESTORE.

Restoring Modified Files

The /M option lets you restore only those files that have been modified or deleted from the fixed disk since the last backup was made. For example, the following command restores all files in the WP directory that have been changed:

    RESTORE A: C:\JON\WP*.* /M

The RESTORE command simply checks the archive attribute of each file and restores those that have it turned on.

Similarly, you can use the /N option to restore only those files that have been deleted from the fixed disk.

Prompted Restoration

If you specify the /P option, RESTORE will prompt you whenever a file on the fixed disk has been changed since it was last backed up.

Special Considerations When Using RESTORE

RESTORE cannot be used with backup files created using DOS 6. RESTORE is only for files created using version 5 of DOS or earlier.

RESTORE does not restore the files IO.SYS and MSDOS.SYS. You should use the SYS command to restore these system files.

You must always start with diskette number 1 to recover a file unless you have created a log file during backup that will tell you the number of the diskette that the file is on.

Files stored on backup diskettes are not the same as standard DOS files. Don't try to use the COPY command to restore files.

You must always restore files into the same directory from which they came.

If you want to restore only those files that do not exist on the target disk, use the /N option.

To see the backup files that match the file specifier in the RESTORE command, use the /D option.

The RESTORE options are summarized in Table 16-2.

Backing Up Using MSBACKUP

MSBACKUP is available only in DOS version 6.

If you are using DOS version 6 (or later), you will not use BACKUP and RESTORE to back up your fixed disk. (In fact, BACKUP will not even be on your disk, and RESTORE will be present only to recover files backed up using an older version of DOS.) Instead, you will use MSBACKUP to back up your fixed disk and to restore files. Although MSBACKUP provides the same essential features as BACKUP and RESTORE, it operates in a much different manner and is a substantial improvement. Also, MSBACKUP is fundamentally easier to operate and provides visual feedback about what it is doing.

Option	Meaning
/A	Restore all files modified on or after the specified date
/B	Restore all files modified on or before the specified date
/D	Display backup files that match file specifier
/E	Restore all files modified at or earlier than the specified time on a given date
/L	Restore all files modified at or later than the specified time on a given date
/M	Restore all files that have been modified or deleted since the last backup
/N	Restore only those files that do not exist on the fixed disk
/P	Prompt before restoring a file
/S	Restore all subdirectories

RESTORE Options Table 16-2.

NOTE: If you need to recover files backed up using BACKUP you *must* use RESTORE no matter what version of DOS you are currently using. However, new backups made with MSBACKUP must be restored using MSBACKUP.

MSBACKUP is a window-based, menu-oriented program that fully manages the backup procedure. It performs the backup phase as well as the recovery phase. Unlike its predecessors (BACKUP and RESTORE), MSBACKUP combines the tasks of backup and recovery into one program. This makes it much easier to use.

MSBACKUP is a sophisticated program that allows substantial control over how your fixed disk is backed up. Many of MSBACKUP's options and settings require knowledge about the operation of the computer beyond that which most users have. Also, some options are highly specialized and apply only to unusual situations. Therefore, this book describes only the most common usage of MSBACKUP. However, this usage applies to about 99 percent of all backup needs. (The advanced options are used mostly by system integrators and specialists and do not apply to the general user.)

Menu and Window Selection in MSBACKUP

MSBACKUP uses windows and menus in much the same way that EDIT (the DOS editor) does. If you can use EDIT, you will have no trouble using MSBACKUP. However, since menu selection is fundamental to MSBACKUP's operation, it is reviewed here.

To select an option, first highlight it using an arrow key and then press [Enter]. To select an option using the mouse, position the mouse pointer over the option and then press the left mouse button. (This is referred to as *clicking on* an option.) You can also select an option by pressing the highlighted letter. For example, one of MSBACKUP's options is called Restore. To select it, you could simply press **R** when the menu containing it is displayed.

REMEMBER: Clicking on an object means to position the mouse pointer on the object and then press the left mouse button.

When MSBACKUP displays multiple windows, menus, or options on the screen, you can move among them by pressing the [Tab] key. Some MSBACKUP options are selected by using *check boxes*. If the box is checked, the option is active. If it is not checked, the option is not active. To change the state of a check box, first [Tab] to it and then press the [Spacebar]. Each time you press the [Spacebar], the state of the check box will change.

It is very easy to navigate in MSBACKUP, and you should have little trouble. If you need help while running MSBACKUP, simply press the [F1] key. This causes context-sensitive information to be displayed that relates directly to what you are currently doing.

Executing MSBACKUP for the First Time

The first time that you execute MSBACKUP you will need to run a compatibility test. This procedure helps MSBACKUP configure itself to best take advantage of the hardware in your computer, including the floppy disk drive used for backing up. It also confirms that reliable backups can be made. (Don't worry; MSBACKUP works with virtually all computers, including all major brands.)

MSBACKUP is an external command. To execute it, simply enter **MSBACKUP** at the prompt.

Once MSBACKUP begins executing, to run the compatibility test, follow the prompts that MSBACKUP displays on the screen. You will also need to have ready two blank floppy diskettes that are the right size for the drive that you will be using.

TIP: If you have two different types of diskette drives in your system, select the drive that has the greatest capacity for backing up your fixed disk.

If your computer system is never changed, you will only need to run the compatibility test one time. However, if you enhance or alter your computer—by adding a new type of floppy drive, for example—then you should rerun the test. (To do this, select Configure from MSBACKUP's main menu and then select Compatibility Test.)

To terminate MSBACKUP, either select the Quit option or double-click on the box in the upper-left corner of the main window. (A double-click is two presses of the left mouse button in quick succession.)

Backing Up Your Entire Drive

The most important backup procedure is backing up all the files on a drive. Backing up all files ensures that all files are protected and can be recovered. To begin, execute MSBACKUP and then select the Backup option from the main menu. (This is the default selection, so you can just press Enter.)

After selecting Backup, you will see a screen similar to that shown in Figure 16-1.

Next, activate the Backup From window, move the highlight to the drive you want to back up (if it is not already on it), and press the Spacebar. This will cause the message "All files" to be displayed. This means that the backup will copy all files.

If the method of backup displayed in Backup Type is not Full, you must select that option and change it to Full. To change the backup type when the Backup Type window is displayed, press the Spacebar until Full is selected. (You can also click on Full using the mouse.) Finally, select OK to return to the main Backup window.

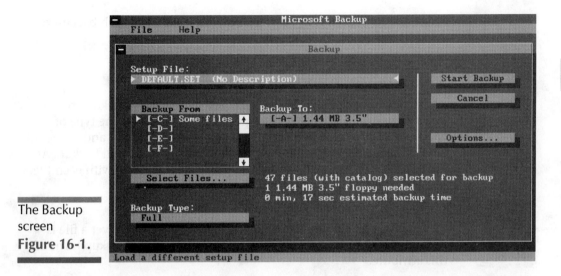

The Backup screen
Figure 16-1.

To back up all files on the specified drive, select Start Backup. This will copy all files on the Backup From drive to the drive specified in Backup To.

REMEMBER: You will need to have several blank floppy disks available to hold the files that are backed up. The exact number is displayed in the Backup window. Be sure to number each diskette because you will need to use them in sequence when restoring your fixed disk.

If you have more than one fixed drive, continue to back up files by repeating the processes just described. Just change the drive selected in the Backup From window.

Methods of Backup

As the preceding discussion hinted at, MSBACKUP allows you to back up your fixed disk in different ways. Specifically, it supports three methods of backup: Full (the default), Incremental, and Differential.

Before proceeding, it is important that you learn what each backup type does. A brief description of each follows.

Full Backup

A full backup copies all files on your disk. This type of backup ensures that all important files have been protected. This is also the type of backup that you must perform first. Both the incremental and differential backups assume that you have performed a full backup. A full backup also turns off the archive attribute associated with each file.

REMEMBER: The archive attribute is turned on whenever a file is modified or when it is first created. Performing a backup turns off this attribute.

Incremental Backup

Once a full backup has been performed, you can use an incremental backup to have MSBACKUP copy only those files that have been added or that have changed. In the process, the archive attribute is turned off. Thus, each time you perform an incremental backup only those files that are new or that have been modified since the last incremental backup will be copied. This means that in order to ensure that you have a current copy of every file, you will need to have your full backup disks and every incremental backup disk that you have created.

Differential Backup

A differential backup is similar to an incremental backup in that it only copies those files that have changed or been added. However, unlike the incremental backup, a differential backup copies all files that have been added or changed since the last *full backup*. This means that to have current versions of all files, you will need your last full backup disks and the latest differential backup. Performing a differential backup does not affect the setting of any file attributes. Specifically, it does not change the archive attribute of the files that it copies.

A Suggested Backup Strategy

Given the three different types of backups, you might wonder which you should use when. One effective and efficient method of backing up your disk is as follows: First, perform a full backup. Then, perform a differential backup periodically—every week, for example. Using the periodic differential backup takes only a little time and it ensures that all new or changed files have been copied and are in easy reach. Occasionally, start over and perform a new full backup. While other approaches are equally valid, this method requires the least amount of diskettes and minimizes the possibility of a file becoming lost.

TIP: Your backups are only as current as when they were made. Back up frequently to maintain accurate files.

Back Up Selected Files

By default, all files on a disk are copied when a full backup is performed. (Or, in the case of a differential or incremental backup, all files with their archive attribute on are copied.) However, you can select only specific directories and files to back up by using the Select Files option in the Backup window. When you do this you can select the directories and files that you want to copy.

You might want to back up only selected directories or files when the computer is used by several people and you want to back up only the portion of the disk that you use. Another reason is that you might have loaded all new software into one directory and simply want to obtain a temporary backup of these new programs before you run your usual full backup.

NOTE: Keep in mind that generally it is best to back up an entire disk rather than just selected files or directories. The ability to back up selected parts is intended to handle special situations.

To begin the file selection process, first choose the Select Files option in the Backup window. This causes a window to be displayed that lists all directories on the disk and all files in the selected directory. This window is titled Select Backup Files.

Before you can select specific files, you must select the directory that contains them. To do this, highlight the directory (or directories) in the directory list and then press the (Spacebar). Using the mouse, position the mouse pointer on the directory and press the right button (or double-click the left button). To select multiple directories, position the mouse pointer on the first directory, press and hold the right mouse button, and drag the mouse to the last directory. All directories in between will be selected.

To deselect a directory, follow the same procedure as described to select one. Any preselected directory will be deselected.

Once you have chosen the directory, you select files using the same basic approach as you did when selecting directories. First, move the highlight to the file list window by pressing (Tab), by using the arrow keys, or by clicking on it using the mouse. Then, if using the keyboard, position the highlight over the file you want and then press the (Spacebar). If using the mouse, press the right button while the pointer is on the file you want to select. Multiple files are selected in the same way that multiple directories are. To deselect a file, simply use the same process. Any preselected files will be deselected.

TIP: You can also select or deselect directories and files using the Include and Exclude buttons, respectively. To use these options, specify the path and file names when prompted. (You can use wildcards in the file names.) The specified files will then be either selected or deselected.

After you have selected the desired directories and files, select the OK button. Now, only the files you have selected will be copied by whatever type of backup you next perform. To confirm this, the message inside the Backup From window should be "Some files" instead of "All files." (If it isn't, make sure that you have correctly selected only those files that you want to back up.) To actually back up the files, select Start Backup from the main Backup menu.

Some Options When Selecting Files

Several options are available when selecting files. To set these options, select the Special option in the Select Backup Files window. The first option allows you to back up only those files that have dates within a certain range. To do this, first check the Apply Date Range box (Tab to it and then press the Spacebar, or click on it using the mouse). Next, Tab to the From date and enter the starting date. Then, Tab to the To date and enter the ending date. After doing this, only files with dates between those two dates will be copied.

Other options allow you to exclude copy-protected files, read-only files, system files, and hidden files. While these options apply mostly to specialized situations, you may want to explore them on your own.

Catalogs

When MSBACKUP backs up your drive, it creates a special file called a *catalog* that contains a list of the files that have been backed up. Catalog files make restoring files faster and easier. In general, MSBACKUP handles catalog files automatically, so you don't usually need to worry about them. However, just so you know, all catalog filenames are eight characters long and are encoded like this (from left to right):

Character	Meaning
1	First drive in catalog
2	Last drive in catalog
3	Last digit of year
4, 5	Month
6, 7	Day of month
8	Letter of backup when more than one is made on a given day

All catalog files will have one of the following extensions, which indicate the type of backup performed:

FUL	Full
INC	Incremental
DIF	Differential

For example, the following catalog file contains the file names for drives C, D, and E; was made in the year 1993 on the 28 of February; and was the second backup of that day. It was also a full backup.

CE30228B.FUL

Restoring Files Using MSBACKUP

To restore files from backup disks, execute MSBACKUP and then select Restore from the main menu. The screen will look similar to that in Figure 16-2. By default, the most recent catalog file is used. If this is not the catalog that you want to use, you can select one using the Catalog option. If either the Restore From drive is wrong or the Restore To drive is wrong, change it by selecting the appropriate option. (Generally, you restore from the same diskette drive that you backed up to, and restore to the same place that the files were originally from.) Next, you need to select the files to restore. To restore all files, first select the proper drive

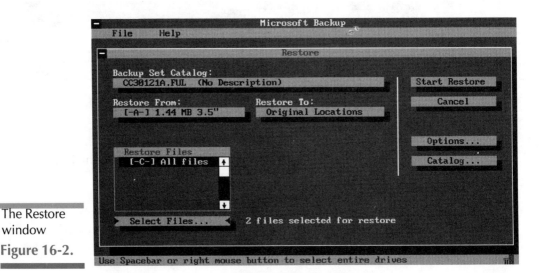

The Restore window

Figure 16-2.

in the Restore Files window and then press the (Spacebar). This causes the message "All files" to be displayed. However, if you want to restore only selected files, activate the Select Files option and select those files. (Files are selected using the same procedure described when backing up selected files.)

Once you have selected the proper drives and files, select Start Restore to begin restoring files.

Restore has several options which you might want to explore on your own. Generally, its default mode of operation is suitable for most file recovery situations.

REMEMBER: When restoring files created using a version of DOS prior to 6 you must use RESTORE and not MSBACKUP.

Backup Routine for Fixed Disks

Whether you use BACKUP or MSBACKUP, the basic philosophy for backing up the fixed disk is the same. You should use the rotating triad method of backup; that is, you should maintain daily, weekly, and monthly backup diskettes. (The rotating triad backup method was discussed in Chapter 15 relative to floppy disks, and it also applies to the fixed disk.)

Because backing up a fixed disk that contains a lot of information is a lengthy process, after an initial backup, only those files that have changed are copied to the daily backup disks. You then perform a full backup procedure at the end of the week. This will save you time and still ensure protection of the files.

Because the nearest backup is potentially one month out of date, you should use the snapshot method of backup (also described in Chapter 15) in addition to the rotating triad. In this way an error will not perpetuate itself through all the diskettes.

TIP: Your backup diskettes are typically your only protection against data loss. If you lose or misplace these diskettes, you cannot recover your files. Be sure to keep backup disks in a safe place.

Who Is Responsible?

Someone must be in charge of backing up a fixed disk if the system is used by many people. This may sound simple, but the failure to assign this task to a trusted individual is a major cause of backup diskettes being woefully out of date. When no single person is responsible, everyone assumes that someone else is doing the backups. If you are a manager, make sure that someone's job description includes backing up the fixed disk.

Using FASTOPEN

The external FASTOPEN command allows DOS to quickly access files that are several levels of subdirectories deep. For somewhat technical reasons, it normally takes DOS a lot longer to reach a file with a long path name than to reach one in the root. However, FASTOPEN allows DOS to remember the location of a file and therefore makes accessing that file much faster. The general form of FASTOPEN is

FASTOPEN *drive-specifier=num*

where *drive-specifier* is the name of the drive to which the FASTOPEN command applies. You can use FASTOPEN to provide fast access to the files on only one drive in the system. The optional *num* argument specifies the number of files and directories that FASTOPEN can remember and must be between 10 and 999. If *num* is not present, the default is 48. There can be no spaces between the drive specifier, the equal sign, and the number.

For example, the following command gives fast access to the files on drive C and allows 48 files and/or directories to have fast access:

FASTOPEN C:

16

FASTOPEN will display this message:

```
FASTOPEN installed
```

The following command allows the last 50 files and/or directories to be remembered.

FASTOPEN C:=50

TIP: You will usually want to use FASTOPEN's default setting for the number of files or directories. For technical reasons, making the number too large could actually increase rather than decrease access time. If you make it too small, you will not receive any benefit from it.

FASTOPEN installs itself the first time it is invoked, which means that you can execute it only once. For this reason, you should put it in an AUTOEXEC.BAT file.

If you have expanded memory, you can have FASTOPEN use this memory by specifying the /X option. (This will leave more room for your application programs to run in normal memory.)

Defragmenting Your Disk

As you learned earlier in this book, DOS does not necessarily save a file in consecutive disk sectors. Instead, it uses the first available sectors. When the disk is newly formatted, the first available sectors are often also consecutive sectors. However, as the disk is used and old files are erased and new files are stored, gaps of available sectors develop between files. These gaps are then reused by DOS when a new file is stored. Thus, when DOS stores a file on a well-used disk, most likely that file is stored in nonconsecutive sectors. Over time this causes many files to be scattered throughout the disk. This is called *fragmentation*. When a disk is fragmented, it takes longer for the drive to read the file. This, in turn, slows down the performance of your computer. However, if you use DOS version 6, you can defragment your disk using the DEFRAG command.

NOTE: DEFRAG is a window- and menu-based command. You make selections the same way as described for MSBACKUP and EDIT, DOS's other two window/menu-based commands.

Disk fragmentation occurs when files are not stored in consecutive sectors on a disk.

The DEFRAG command works by rearranging your disk so that files are stored in consecutive disk sectors. This improves the performance of your disk and generally speeds up all programs that access that disk. The DEFRAG command has this general form,

DEFRAG *drive*:

where *drive* is the drive to defragment. Thus, to defragment drive C, use this command:

DEFRAG C:

Enter this command now. You will see a screen similar to that shown in Figure 16-3.

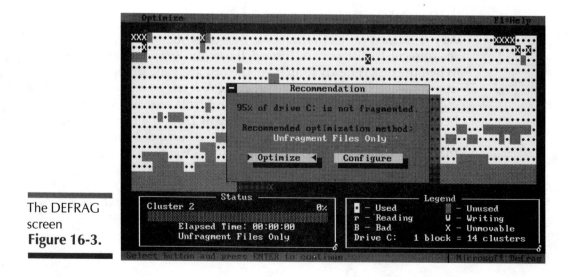

The DEFRAG screen
Figure 16-3.

The screen shows a map of the drive. The legend displayed on the screen explains the map. When DEFRAG is first executed, DEFRAG displays its opinion in its Recommendation window. If you agree with DEFRAG's opinion, you can begin the defragmentation process by choosing the Optimize option. If you want to perform a different action, choose Configure, which allows you to change various settings. (The DEFRAG options will be discussed shortly.) If DEFRAG detects that your disk does not require any optimization, it will tell you this, as well. Most of the time you will want to defragment the disk as suggested by DEFRAG.

To select an option inside the Recommendation window, first highlight the option using the ⬅ and ➡ keys and then press ⏎Enter. You can also select an option by clicking on it with the mouse.

NOTE: The defragmenting process will take several minutes. (It can take as long as an hour.) Therefore, only execute this command when you won't need your computer for awhile. A good time to defragment a drive is over your lunch hour, for example.

If you do not want to use DEFRAG's recommendation, select Configure inside DEFRAG's Recommendation window. This causes the Optimize main menu to appear, as shown in Figure 16-4.

Using this menu, you can begin the optimization, select a different drive to optimize, select the optimization method, change the way the files are arranged on the disk, obtain an expanded legend of the disk map, display DEFRAG's copyright message, and terminate DEFRAG. Each of these options is described here.

To make a selection from the Optimize menu, position the highlight over the desired item using the ⬆ or ⬇ key and then press ⏎Enter. Or, if you have a mouse, click on the desired item.

TIP: When the Optimize menu is displayed, you can also select an option by pressing the highlighted letter associated with each item. For example, to terminate DEFRAG, you can press **X** when the menu is shown.

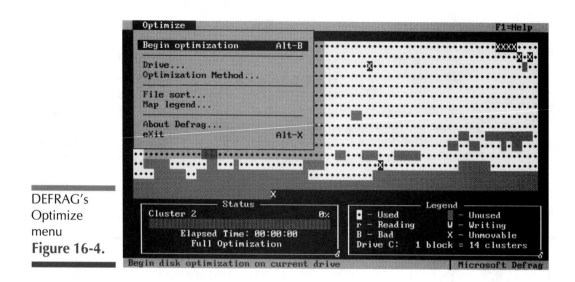

DEFRAG's
Optimize
menu
Figure 16-4.

To begin disk optimization, select Begin optimization.

To change the drive being optimized, select Drive. You will see the drive selection menu. To switch drives, select the desired drive from this menu.

There are two ways that DEFRAG is optimized: Full Optimization and Unfragment Files Only. To choose between them, select Optimization Method. You will see the window shown in Figure 16-5.

Using Full Optimization produces the best results and greatest increase in disk performance. It defragments all files, moves all subdirectories to the start of the disk (this makes access time faster), and moves all free space to the end of the disk. Use this optimization when your disk is highly fragmented.

The Select
Optimization
Method
window
Figure 16-5.

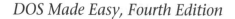

Unfragment Files Only does precisely that. It only defragments files; it does not rearrange the disk in any other way. This takes much less time than full optimization, but does not increase the performance of your disk as much. However, in cases where your disk is only slightly fragmented, this is the best choice.

To switch between Full Optimization and Unfragment Files Only, press the (Spacebar). Each time you press the (Spacebar), the option selected will change. You can also use the mouse to select an optimization by clicking on the appropriate selection.

While DEFRAG optimizes your disk, it can sort the file list in each directory on the disk. By default, DEFRAG does not sort directories. However, you can change this by selecting File Sort from the Optimize menu. You will see the window shown in Figure 16-6. This allows you to sort each directory by name, extension, time and date, and size. You can also sort the directory in ascending or descending order.

You select a new sort criterion or sort order by pressing the (Spacebar) or using the mouse to click on the option. To move between Sort Criterion and Sort Order, press the (Tab) key. When done, either press (Enter) or click on the OK box with the mouse. You can also choose Cancel if you change your mind.

To see an extended description of the symbols used by DEFRAG's disk map, choose Map legend from the Optimize menu.

The File Sort window
Figure 16-6.

```
 ┌─────────────────────────────────┐
 │▬        File Sort               │
 ├─────────────────────────────────┤
 │   Select the order to sort files│
 │      within each directory.     │
 │   ┌─ Sort Criterion ─────────┐  │
 │   │  ◉  Unsorted             │  │
 │   │  ○  Name                 │  │
 │   │  ○  Extension            │  │
 │   │  ○  Date & Time          │  │
 │   │  ○  Size                 │  │
 │   └──────────────────────────┘  │
 │   ┌─ Sort Order ─────────────┐  │
 │   │  ○  Ascending            │  │
 │   │  ○  Descending           │  │
 │   └──────────────────────────┘  │
 │   ► OK ◄       Cancel           │
 └─────────────────────────────────┘
```

About Defrag displays copyright information about DEFRAG.

Exit terminates DEFRAG and returns to the DOS prompt.

You can obtain help information about DEFRAG at any time by pressing the F1 function key.

In general, you will not want to use DEFRAG on a daily basis. Instead, use it every so often, as your computer usage dictates. For most users, once a month is sufficient.

 TIP: If you frequently create and erase files on your computer, use temporary files, or alter the purpose to which your computer is put, then you will want to run DEFRAG more frequently. Also, if file accesses seem to be slowing down, try running DEFRAG.

Loading Applications to the Fixed Disk

Remember, if an application comes with an installation program, be sure to use it.

No hard and fast rules apply to every situation involving loading applications to the fixed disk. However, some general guidelines will help you make the right decisions. We will examine these here.

Application Subdirectories

The first and most important rule is that each separate application should be loaded into its own directory. Do not put all applications into the root directory. If you do this, not only will the root directory become unmanageable, you will eventually run out of directory entries. It is also not wise to place all applications into one general-purpose applications directory because, again, that directory will become unmanageable.

For example, imagine that you have three applications: a spreadsheet, a word processor, and an inventory package. You should create three subdirectories, with descriptive names such as SPSHT, WP, and INVENT, and place the files associated with each application area into their respective directories.

Sometimes you will add an application that is really a subsystem of an already existing application. For example, if you add a spelling checker to the word processor, it does not make sense to create a new subdirectory off the root for it. Instead, you can simply add it to the WP directory because it is dependent upon the word processor. (In some special situations it might be a good idea to place it in a subdirectory of WP, but this is not commonly the case.) In general, when one application depends on another, put the dependent one in the directory of the application on which it depends or in a subdirectory of that application.

User Subdirectories

If several different users will be using an application once it is loaded, it is best to create a subdirectory for each user off the application area so that each user's files will be separate. Further, because one user may use two or more applications, it is doubly important that individual subdirectories be created off the application directory and not the root. In this way each user can have a directory bearing his or her name in each application area. For example, if Jon does both word processing and spreadsheet analysis, then the proper directory structure will look like the one shown here:

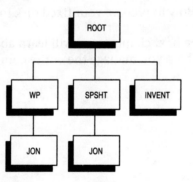

Preparing the Fixed Disk for Shipment

It is very important that the fixed disk be properly prepared for travel prior to moving it. This requires that the read/write head be retracted to a position that is not over the magnetic medium of the disk. Most modern fixed disks retract the head automatically, but some require that you give a command that retracts the head. Failure to retract the head could result in the read/write head contacting the disk, causing damage and loss of data. When the read/write head contacts the disk, it is called a *head crash*.

If you must manually retract the head (sometimes called *parking*), the exact method of doing so is determined by the type of computer that you have. Consult your owner's manual for details.

Summary

In this chapter you learned how to manage the fixed disk, including

✦ How to back up the fixed disk using BACKUP

✦ How to restore data using RESTORE

✦ How to back up and restore data using MSBACKUP

✦ How to use the fixed-disk backup routine

✦ How to use FASTOPEN

✦ How to defragment your fixed disk to improve its operation

✦ How to load applications onto a fixed disk

✦ How to prepare your fixed disk for shipment

In the next chapter, you will learn about some advanced commands that help you manage the entire computer system.

C H A P T E R

DOS DOS DOS DOS DOS DOS DOS DOS DOS

≈MADE EASY≈

17

ADVANCED COMMANDS AND MISCELLANEOUS TOPICS

In this chapter we will cover topics and commands that you will not need on a daily basis. However, you may find some of them useful in special situations. They are discussed briefly just so you know they exist. Also presented is a short guide to system maintenance.

FDISK

Before the fixed disk can be formatted, it must be partitioned. A *partition* is a portion of the fixed disk that can be either part or all of the disk. You can partition the fixed disk so that it will act as two or more drives or so that it can be used with two or more different operating systems. Generally, the FDISK command is used when a fixed disk is first brought into service or if you want to change the size of its partitions. Either way, whatever is on the disk is lost.

The FDISK command lets you do these four things:

✦ Create a partition

✦ Set an active partition (from which DOS loads)

✦ Delete a partition

✦ Display disk information

In general, your fixed disk is partitioned and formatted by the supplier of your computer. If you need to use this command, refer to the documentation that came with your computer.

CAUTION: Use FDISK with extreme care. It can destroy the data on your fixed disk.

The SET Command

The DOS environment defines several items that determine how DOS functions.

The SET command is used to create and give a value to a name that becomes part of DOS's environment. Although this name may not be of any direct value to you, it may be used by application programs. The general form of SET is

SET *name=value*

where *name* is the string that is placed into DOS's environment with the value of *value*.

For example, the following command sets the name APPSDAT to the path \PROGRAM\APPS.

SET APPSDAT=\PROGRAM\APPS\

Once this is done, an application program that wants to know where application program data files are can check the value of APPSDAT in the DOS environment.

To remove a name from the environment, use the general form

SET *name*=

For example, the following command removes APPSDAT:

SET APPSDAT=

You can use the value of a name stored in the environment in a batch file by placing the name between percent signs. For example, the following batch file uses the value of APPSDAT to copy data files from the path specified by the value of APPSDAT into the current working directory.

REM copy the data files into the working directory
COPY %APPSDAT%*.*

When this batch command runs, it will look like this:

```
COPY \PROGRAM\APPS\*.*
```

You can see the names and values active in your system by entering SET with no parameters.

Recovering Files from a Damaged Disk

In rare cases a disk will become physically damaged in such a way that part of a file will still be readable. In such cases you can partially recover the file by using the RECOVER command.

CAUTION: The RECOVER command is only for use on physically damaged files. If you accidentally erase a file, use UNDELETE. If you accidentally format a disk, use UNFORMAT.

RECOVER may
not be included
if you are using
DOS 6.

Recovering data from physically damaged files will only be useful on
text files where a small amount of text will have to be reentered. If part
of a program file is lost, the program will simply not run or may not
run correctly. Frankly, attempting to execute a program that has pieces
of it missing will almost always lead to trouble. Therefore, from a
practical point of view, RECOVER is useful only on text files.

The general form of RECOVER is

RECOVER *file-name*

where *file-name* is the name of the file to recover, which may include a
drive specifier and a path.

For example, to recover a file named FORMLET.WP on drive C, use the
following command:

RECOVER FORMLET.WP

You can use RECOVER to recover an entire disk when it is the disk's
directory that has become damaged. When a disk's directory is
damaged, it is unreadable, so DOS cannot know which files are on the
disk. In this type of recovery operation the program files may be
recovered in a usable form, but it is best not to rely on this. To recover
an entire disk, use this form of RECOVER:

RECOVER *drive-specifier*

As RECOVER recovers the files, it does not know their names (because
the directory is unreadable), so it puts them in files using the form
FILE*num*.REC, where *num* is a number between 0000 and 9999.

TIP: Never assume that you can successfully recover a damaged file;
often there is no way to do so. It is usually better to simply go to a
backup copy. (This is why back ups are so important.) But if a file does
become damaged and you have no backup copy, you can try RECOVER.

Using the FC Command

As you learned earlier in this book, if you want to compare two files for
equality, you can do so by using the COMP command. However, DOS

17

versions 5 and later supply a stronger, more flexible version of this command called FC. It takes this general form:

FC *file1 file2*

where *file1* and *file2* are the files being compared. FC is an external command. Although the FC command is of most value to programmers, it has a few features that you might want to take advantage of.

COMP may not be included if you are using DOS 6.

For most people, there are two principal advantages to using FC over COMP. First, it can compare files that are of different sizes. Although different-sized files are implicitly different, sometimes you may want to know if one file is actually just a minor variation of another or a completely different version. Therefore, using FC you can see how much files which differ in size actually differ in content. For example, you may have two files (on different disks), both called INVOICE, but differing in size by 12 bytes. Using FC you can determine if these files are simply slightly different versions of each other or if they are completely different files.

The second advantage is that FC can *resynchronize* itself when an error occurs. Resynchronization is the process by which FC attempts to find comparisons between the two files after a mismatch has occurred. For example, given these two files:

File 1	File 2
A	A
B	B
C <- mismatch ->	D
D	E
E	F
F	

Resynchronization lets FC continue to compare files that differ only slightly.

using COMP, once the mismatch between the third characters (C and D) has been flagged, all other comparisons in the file will be flagged as mismatched. However, FC will resynchronize beginning with the two Es and show only the C and D as mismatched.

The value of resynchronization is that it allows FC to provide a more accurate report of the differences between two files. This can be very valuable in a number of situations. For example, you might have two versions of the same inventory file that differ only in the fact that one has an extra entry somewhere in the middle. Using COMP, after the mismatch (caused by the extra entry) occurs, everything else in the two files will be reported as mismatching. However, FC will resynchronize, and more accurately report only the first mismatch.

In general, only text files can be resynchronized. By default, FC compares all files that have extensions of .COM, .OBJ, .EXE, .SYS, .LIB, or .BIN, as binary files and no resynchronization will occur. However, by specifying the /L option, these files can be compared as if they were text files, in which case, these program and program-related files will be compared using resynchronization.

FC displays mismatches in text files like this. First, it displays the first file name. Then, it displays those lines in which the mismatch occurs. This process continues until the end of the shortest file is reached. For example, the output of an FC on the two files shown above looks like this:

```
Comparing files TEST and TEST1
***** TEST
B
C
D
***** TEST1
B
D
*****
```

Mismatches when comparing binary files use this sort of display:

offset x y

Here, *offset* is the relative position of the mismatched bytes in the files, *x* is the value of the byte in the first file and *y* is the value in the same position in the second file. The output is in hexadecimal.

When comparing text files, you can tell FC to ignore case differences by using the /C option. To display the line numbers of mismatches, use the /N option.

You can cause text files to be compared as binary by specifying the /B option.

FC has some other options that are most useful to programmers and system integrators and are not discussed here. (You may want to explore these options on your own.)

Frankly, for most file comparison situations, the COMP command is just fine. But, if you have one of the special needs described above, or if your version of DOS does not include the COMP command, feel free to use FC.

Using DBLSPACE to Increase Disk Space

Disk compression increases disk space, but has significant side effects. Use disk compression with extreme caution.

Disk space is often at a premium. It seems that no matter how large your fixed disk is, you can always use more space. In the past, to increase your disk space, you had to either buy an additional fixed disk or replace your existing drive with one that had larger capacity. However, if you are using DOS 6, then you can increase the effective size of your hard disk using a special technique called *disk compression*.

Disk compression is the process by which information on your disk is encoded in a special way so that it takes up less disk space than it does in its non-encoded form. When disk compression is used, a special device driver automatically converts the data between its compressed form and its regular form so that as far as you (and your application programs) are concerned, the data will appear normal. Using disk compression, you can increase the storage capacity of your fixed disk by a factor of 2 or more.

Disk compression is not all gain without pain. When disk compression is used, the data on your disk is altered and may not be read without the special disk compression device driver. Therefore, if, for some reason, you need to access the information on the disk and you don't have access to the compression driver, you won't be able to read the files. Disk compression will also slow down your system slightly. In addition, some application programs may not be able to use compressed data if they bypass DOS and perform low level disk accesses. Therefore, you may not want to use disk compression before you discuss the matter with a computer professional to see if it will be compatible with the way you use your system.

CAUTION: Once you compress a drive, you cannot decompress it! Therefore, do not use disk compression until you fully understand all of its ramifications. It is best to discuss using disk compression with a knowledgeable person first.

The command that compresses your fixed drive is called DBLSPACE. To compress your fixed disk, simply run DBLSPACE. After passing through a series of safety checks, you begin disk compression by choosing either Express or Custom Setup. Unless you are a very knowledgeable computer user, choose Express Setup. (Because it requires specialized knowledge, Custom Setup is not discussed here. Refer to your DOS manual for details.) The Express Setup causes DBLSPACE to compress your disk, install the necessary DEVICE command in your CONFIG.SYS file to load the compression driver, and then restart your system. After the process is complete, your disk will have more room on it.

REMEMBER: Disk compression will create more disk space but may cause your disk to be incompatible with some software. Be sure to use DBLSPACE only after thoroughly considering the consequences. If you are new to DOS, do not use this command until you fully understand what you are doing.

Using MEMMAKER to Free Memory

Memory optimization is also discussed in Chapter 13.

If you use DOS version 6, then you can optimize your system's use of memory by running the MEMMAKER command. This command automatically determines which device drivers and installed commands or programs can be run in the upper memory area. In this way, it frees memory for your application programs. MEMMAKER only optimizes your memory if your computer uses an 80386 or an 80486 processor.

CAUTION: MEMMAKER may perform alterations to your system that are incompatible with your existing software. You may want to consult a computer specialist before using this command.

To use MEMMAKER, simply execute it and then, when prompted, choose Express Setup. (If you are a very experienced user, you can choose Custom Setup. But, if you are knowledgeable enough to use Custom Setup, you probably don't need MEMMAKER to optimize your system!) MEMMAKER then optimizes your system and, in the process, may make changes to your CONFIG.SYS and AUTOEXEC.BAT files. Once the optimizations have been made it then restarts your computer so that the changes can take effect. You will then be asked if everything seems OK. If it does, answer Yes; if not, answer No. If you answer No, MEMMAKER will attempt to fix the problem. (Generally, you won't have any trouble.)

NOTE: If your computer "locks up" when it attempts to restart after MEMMAKER has been used, just turn your system off and then on again. MEMMAKER will then fix itself. Some of your programs may be incompatible with MEMMAKER's optimizations, so be patient if you encounter trouble.

If you cannot get MEMMAKER to work correctly or are for some reason unhappy with its optimizations, you can return your system to its original configuration by entering this command:

    MEMMAKER /UNDO

Therefore, if you do encounter trouble and all else fails, simply return your system to its previous configuration.

Frankly, if you are happy with the way your computer is working and have not run out of memory while using any of your application programs, then there is no reason to use MEMMAKER.

Using POWER to Conserve Battery Power

POWER relates mostly to laptop and other battery powered computers.

If you have a battery-powered computer, such as a laptop, then battery life is important to you. If you are using DOS 6, you can use the POWER command and device driver to help conserve battery power. The POWER device driver automatically manages your computer's devices so that minimum power is used. To use POWER, first put this line in your CONFIG.SYS file and then restart your computer:

DEVICE=C:\DOS\POWER.EXE

Once the POWER.EXE device driver has been installed, power conservation will be in effect. To see the status of power conservation, enter the command POWER at the prompt. You will see a display similar to this:

```
Power Management Status
-----------------------
Setting = ADV: REG
CPU: idle 71% of time.
```

Of course, the power setting and the CPU idle time may be different.

You can control the way power is conserved by using the ADV: option. This option has these three forms: ADV:MAX, ADV:REG, and ADV:MIN. These correspond to maximum conservation, normal conservation (the default), and minimal conservation. For example, this POWER command sets power conservation to its maximum:

POWER ADV:MAX

While maximum power conservation may seem attractive, it may cause inconvenience or poor performance. (The exact effects will vary with your software and computer.) For the most part, the default conservation level provides the best power conservation. However, if you encounter problems, try the ADV:MIN setting.

To turn off power conservation, use this command:

POWER OFF

The POWER device driver is most effective when your computer conforms to the Advanced Power Management specification. (This is a hardware configuration that you cannot change.) However, even if it doesn't you will still get some savings in power by using the POWER device driver.

NOTE: The default setting of POWER is generally the best for normal use. However, be sure to check the manuals that come with your computer. It is possible that a different setting will be advised.

Using HELP to Obtain Online Help

If you have DOS 6, you can obtain information about a command by using the HELP command. You can execute HELP in one of the following two ways:

DOS 5 also contains the HELP command, but it is very limited.

> HELP
> HELP *command*

Here, *command* is the command that you want help about. If you execute HELP without a command, a list of commands is displayed from which you may select the one that you want information about.

The HELP program is a window/menu-based system that is operated in the same way as other window/menu-based DOS commands. It will work with either the keyboard or the mouse and its use is self-explanatory and largely intuitive.

NOTE: Although the information supplied by HELP is very useful, it should not and cannot substitute for a good working knowledge of DOS.

For a short description of each DOS command, you can use the FASTHELP command. (This command is only available with DOS 6.) You can use one of these forms:

FASTHELP
FASTHELP *command*

When you use the first, you receive a synopsis of each command. When you specify a command, you receive information specifically about that command.

Maintaining Your System

A computer is much like an automobile. With proper care and attention, it will run for several trouble-free years. But if you neglect the maintenance, it will be plagued with troubles. A computer system requires two types of care: physical maintenance of the computer and maintenance of the software.

Maintaining the Hardware

The golden rule of maintaining the computer's hardware is to keep it clean. Dust is the computer's worst enemy. It can build up on the circuits inside the computer, causing them to overheat by reducing their normal heat-dissipation capabilities. Further, dust and dirt on diskettes reduces the life of both the diskettes and the disk drive read/write heads.

Though it may be hard to believe, static electricity is a major cause of computer failure. Walking across a carpet on a dry winter day can cause your body to develop a charge of several thousand volts. If you touch the wrong part of the computer, this voltage could flow into the circuits and literally blow their insides apart! If static electricity is a problem in your environment, you can either use antistatic sprays on the carpet or invest in a grounded metal strip that you always touch first before touching the computer.

Along the same lines as static electricity is lightning. If lightning strikes very near the computer, enough of the charge can be picked up by the circuits to destroy them. You cannot prevent lightning, but you can minimize the risk by unplugging the computer from power and/or by using surge suppressors. The wires that carry power act like a large antenna, which can pick up the lightning charge. If your computer is unplugged, there is much less chance of damage.

Finally, don't put liquids on top of the computer. Although this seems like a simple statement, nonusers, unfamiliar with computers, often will put coffee cups or soft drink cans on top of the system. Obviously, a spill can cause significant damage.

Maintaining the Software

The most important thing that you can do to protect the software in the system is to maintain a rigid backup schedule. The average system usually has several years of information stored in it, and the dollar value of this information is often far greater than the cost of the computer. It is a resource to be protected.

In large (or even small) offices it is important to restrict access to any computer that contains important information. Though deliberate destruction of information is rare, it can happen. Most of the time, however, the damage is done by someone literally not knowing what they are doing—the "bull in a china shop syndrome." Every employee must have a clear understanding that the information in the computer is a valued asset. Being "invisible" does not reduce its importance.

Application programs are often improved by their developers and you will want to take advantage of these new versions. To avoid trouble, you must switch to the new version correctly. First, never destroy an old version of the program! Sometimes, though rarely, the new version will have an unknown problem that prevents it from being used. If you have destroyed the old version, you will have no way to run the application. Second, always follow the installation instructions that come with the new version. Unless specifically told otherwise, if you run the application from a fixed disk, make sure that all the old programs are replaced by the new ones. Mixing different versions of the programs that make up an application can cause serious trouble.

 ## Summary

In this chapter you learned some advanced DOS commands and various miscellaneous topics, including

- ◆ The FDISK command
- ◆ Using the SET command
- ◆ Recovering files from a damaged disk
- ◆ Using the FC command
- ◆ Using DBLSPACE to increase disk space
- ◆ Using MEMMAKER to optimize memory
- ◆ Using POWER to conserve power
- ◆ Using HELP
- ◆ Maintaining your system

In the next chapter we will begin our exploration of the DOS Shell, DOS's window-driven interface.

PART

5

USING THE
DOS SHELL

CHAPTER

18

AN INTRODUCTION TO THE DOS SHELL

This chapter introduces the DOS Shell. The Shell is a menu-driven interface to DOS that provides an alternative to the command prompt. It also contains a few features that the command prompt does not have. It is called a shell because, conceptually, it encloses DOS. It effectively masks the low-level functioning of DOS and can make DOS easier to use. The DOS Shell is quite powerful and contains many features. The purpose of this chapter is to get you acquainted with several essential concepts and procedures so that you can begin using it. Don't worry if some things are a bit confusing. As you progress, they will begin to make sense.

The Shell provides a menu-driven way to run DOS.

It is important to understand that most things you know about running DOS from the command prompt apply to the Shell as well. You will simply be learning a different, and sometimes easier, way of doing things.

You should read this part of this book even if you intend to use the command prompt for most of your work. The Shell allows you to perform certain operations that are not possible from the command prompt. Therefore, if you ever need to use one of these operations, you will be able to do so using the Shell.

NOTE: The Shell is only available in DOS version 5 or later. Version 4 did include a limited Shell, but it was not widely used and is not discussed here. Earlier versions of DOS contained only the command prompt.

Activating the Shell

To activate the Shell, enter **DOSSHELL.** Do this now.

What If Things Look Different?

It is possible that the figures in this part of the book will differ slightly from what you see on your computer screen. The main cause of differences is the fact that the Shell allows you to arrange the layout of the screen several different ways. The arrangement used in this book reflects the default layout. However, it is possible that your layout has been changed if your computer is used by other people. You will learn how to return your screen to its default configuration shortly.

REMEMBER: The way your computer is used will differ from the one used to produce the figures in this book. This means that the directory structure and file names will differ.

Text Versus Graphics

The Shell can be configured to run in two different modes: text and graphics. If your computer has a monochrome video adapter, then the Shell will be configured for text mode. Otherwise, it will be configured for graphics mode operation. The differences between these two modes are slight, but the graphics mode version does present a more visually appealing display. The example screens in this book are shown in graphics mode.

The Shell: An Overview

When the Shell begins execution, you will see a screen that looks like the one shown in Figure 18-1.

The Shell consists of these parts:

✦ Title bar

✦ Menu bar

✦ Disk drive window

✦ Directory Tree window

✦ File list window

✦ Main group window

✦ Status bar

You will learn to use these parts of the Shell to run DOS, execute your application programs, and manage your system. If this is your first experience with the Shell, then its screen might seem a little intimidating and confusing. Don't worry, very soon, you will be navigating the Shell like a pro.

NOTE: If your screen is not organized like one shown in Figure 18-1, do this: Hold down the Alt key and press V once. Release the Alt key. Next, press the F key one time. Now, the layout of your screen should look like that shown in Figure 18-1.

Title bar

Menu bar

Disk drive
window

Directory
tree window

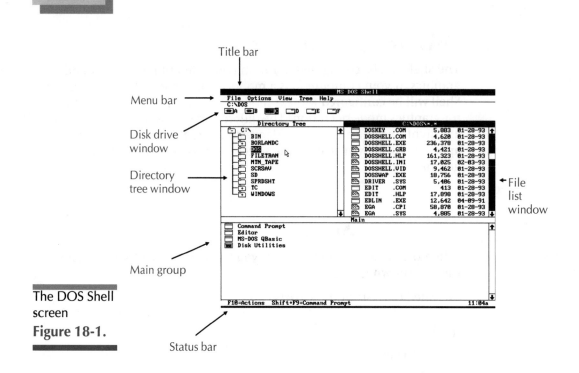

Main group

The DOS Shell
screen
Figure 18-1.

← File
list
window

Status bar

At the top of the screen is the Shell's title bar. The next line down
contains the Shell's menu bar. The *menu bar* provides a means of
selecting various operations that pertain to the Shell. As you learn more
about the Shell, you will see that menus play a key role in its operation.

In the disk drive window, the currently active drive is highlighted. This
is the drive that is the focus of DOS.

The Directory Tree window shows a list of all the directories on your disk.

To the right of the Directory Tree window is the file list window. It
shows the names and various other bits of information about the files
on your disk.

The Main group window contains a list of options associated with the
Main group. Groups are used to organize related programs and
activities. It is possible to add or delete items to or from the Main
group, so your screen may show a different list of options.

Finally, on the bottom of the screen is the status bar. The *status bar*
displays helpful hints related to what you are currently doing, as well as

displaying the time. As you can see, there are two reminders. First, that pressing F10 activates the menu bar. Second, that pressing the Shift key at the same time you press F9 activates the DOS command prompt. (How to return to the command prompt is discussed at the end of this chapter.)

Now that you have had a short tour of the Shell, it's time for you to see how to use it.

Making a Menu Selection

18

The operation of the Shell is based on menus. While some DOS commands that you have studied earlier in this book, such as EDIT, have used menus in a limited fashion, the Shell is completely run by them. Therefore, before you can do much else, you need to know how to make a menu selection. The Shell supports both the keyboard and the mouse as input devices. You can completely run the Shell using the keyboard alone, but the mouse makes a handy addition. This section explores how to make a menu selection using either device. Although you have used menus when you learned about other menu-based commands, the Shell is so dependent upon them that a complete discussion of menus is warranted.

NOTE: This section discusses making a menu selection from the Shell's menu bar. However, the selection process is the same for other menus that you will encounter when using the Shell.

Menu Selection Using the Keyboard

Before you can make a menu selection using the keyboard, you must activate the menu bar. As the status line suggests, to activate the menu bar, press the F10 key. Try this now. As you can see, the File option is highlighted. You can move the highlight about using the ← and → keys. To select an option, press Enter when the highlight is over the desired object. To deactivate the menu bar, press F10 a second time. The F10 key acts as a toggle, alternately activating and deactivating the menu bar each time it is pressed. (The Alt key may be used as an alternative to the F10 key.)

To activate the menu bar, press F10.

Let's try an example. Activate the menu bar, position the highlight over the Help option, and press Enter. Your screen will look like that shown in Figure 18-2. By selecting the Help item, you cause a list of options associated with Help to be displayed. This is called a *drop-down menu*. Each of the menu bar items has a drop-down menu associated with it. Don't worry about what this drop-down menu contains. We will come back to it shortly.

A drop-down menu presents a list of options associated with a menu bar selection.

To make a selection from a drop-down menu, use the ↑ and ↓ keys to position the highlight on the item you want and then press Enter. Try moving the highlight at this time, but don't press Enter.

Once a drop-down menu has been displayed, you can use the ← and → keys to display the drop-down menus associated with the other menu bar options. Try pressing the ← key a few times. Notice how the menus change. Return to the Help drop-down menu now.

To deactivate a drop-down menu, press F10 (or Alt). Since we don't actually want to make a selection from the menu, press F10 at this time. This causes the drop-down menu to go away, but the menu bar is still active. To deactivate the menu bar, press F10 a second time. Additionally, when a drop-down menu is present, you can cancel the menu bar by pressing Esc.

Help
drop-down
menu
Figure 18-2.

```
 Help
┌─────────────────────┐
│ Index               │
│ Keyboard            │
│ Shell Basics        │
│ Commands            │
│ Procedures          │
│ Using Help          │
├─────────────────────┤
│ About Shell         │
└─────────────────────┘
```

TIP: The (Esc) key is the Shell's "emergency stop" key. Pressing it will very often cancel whatever you are doing. It cannot, however, cancel a command once it has begun execution.

18

Deactivate the menu bar at this time and then reactivate it by pressing (F10). Look closely at the options in the menu bar. Notice that the first letter of each is underscored. Once the menu is activated, you can make a selection from a menu by pressing the key that is underscored in the item of your choice. For example, press (H). This causes Help to be selected and its drop-down menu to be displayed. Notice that each item in the drop-down menu also contains underscored letters for easy selection. In the terminology of DOS, the underscored letters are called *hot keys*.

Hot keys provide a shortcut for making menu selections.

Although most hot keys are the first letter in an item's name, sometimes they are not. If a menu contains two options starting with the same letter, then clearly one of them must use a different hot key. Just look for the underscored letter; that is that item's hot key. The main advantage of using hot keys is that they allow you to make faster menu selections using the keyboard.

At this time deactivate the menu bar.

Menu Selection Using the Mouse

Using the mouse to select a menu item is somewhat easier than using the keyboard because you don't have to first activate the menu bar. Instead, the menu bar is activated automatically during the selection process. To select a menu bar option, move the mouse pointer to the item you want and click the left button one time. The mouse pointer will either be a small arrow or a solid box depending upon what sort of video adapter your system has. The right button of the mouse is not used by the Shell. (However, it is possible that you will have application programs that do use it.) To try making a selection using the mouse, move the mouse pointer to the Help entry and press the left button one time. As you can see, the menu bar is activated, the Help entry is selected, and its drop-down menu is displayed, all by a single click of the mouse.

To make a selection from a drop-down menu, simply position the mouse pointer over the desired entry and press the left mouse button. However, do not try this now.

To deactivate the menu bar using the mouse, move the mouse pointer to a part of the screen that does not contain any menus and press the left mouse button. Do this now. In general, until you have actually made a selection from a menu, you can change what you are doing by moving the mouse to some other part of the screen and single-clicking.

TIP: You can intermix keyboard and mouse commands. The Shell doesn't care which you use.

Moving About the Shell

In addition to the Shell's menu bar there are four other areas in which activity can occur. These are the disk drive window, the Directory Tree window, the file list window, and the Main group window. However, before one of these windows can become the focus of your commands, it must be activated. When a window is activated, its title is highlighted. (The disk drive window highlights the letter of the current drive when it is activated. It has no title bar.) The way to activate a window differs depending upon whether you are using the keyboard or the mouse.

To move from one window to the next in the Shell, press the Tab key.

When using the keyboard, you change the active window by pressing the Tab key. Try pressing the Tab key a few times now. Notice that the highlight moves from one window to the next. The window that contains the highlight is active and will be the focus of any input that you give.

To activate a window using the mouse, position the mouse pointer in the window you want to activate and press the left button one time.

Try this now. One small exception to this method is when activating the disk drive window. This window will only become active when you click on one of the drive symbols. For now, only click on the drive whose letter is currently highlighted.

Making a Selection from the Main Group

Making a selection from the Main group is similar to making a selection from a drop-down menu. To see how, activate the Main group window now. To make a selection from a group using the keyboard, use the ⬆ and ⬇ keys to position the highlight on the item you want and then press Enter. For example, move the highlight to the Disk Utilities option and press Enter. This causes the options associated with the Disk Utilities entry to be displayed.

To deactivate the Disk Utilities subgroup, either select the Main entry or press the Esc key. Either way, the Main group is once again displayed. Press the Esc key at this time.

If you have a mouse, you can select an option from the Main group by double-clicking on the desired item. Remember, a double-click is two presses of the mouse button in quick succession. You must be careful not to move the mouse between the two clicks. (If the mouse is moved between the first and second click, no command is activated.) To try this, make sure that the mouse is positioned over the Disk Utilities entry and double-click. As you can see, this activates the Disk Utilities group. (If it didn't work the first time, try it again. It can take a couple of tries to learn the art of double-clicking.) Keep in mind that only items in the Main group (or one of its subgroups) require a double-click. Other types of menus allow selections with just a single-click.

Although we will come back to the subject of groups later, a brief discussion is in order now. The Shell provides the Main group. The Main group may contain two types of items: programs and subgroups. By default, it contains one subgroup, which is the one you just activated: the Disk Utilities group. You make selections from a subgroup in just the same way as you do from the Main group. As you will learn later in this book, it is possible to define your own subgroups. Therefore, if your Main group looks different from the one shown in the figures, don't be concerned.

Before continuing, press ⌜Tab⌟ until the disk drive window is once again active.

Using the Online Help System

One feature of the Shell that you will want to make extensive use of is its online context-sensitive help system. In general, a help system provides information about a program. You have used one help system already because the command-line interface provides one (accessed through either the HELP or FASTHELP commands). It provides information about the command prompt. In the case of the Shell, the help system provides information about the Shell. What makes the Shell's help system even more valuable is that it is context sensitive. This means that it will give you information about whatever it is that you are doing at the time. Once the help system is activated, you may also request information about other topics if you wish. Keep in mind that, in general, the information displayed by the help system is intended to act as a reminder. It cannot be substituted for a good working knowledge of DOS.

Since the help system is especially useful when you first begin using the Shell, now is a good time to discuss it.

To activate the help system, either press ⌜F1⌟ or select the Help entry in the menu bar. When you activate the help system using the Help menu bar option, you are presented with a drop-down menu of topics from which you can select your area of interest. However, when you activate the help system by pressing ⌜F1⌟, you receive information that relates to what you are currently doing. For example, highlight the File menu bar entry and then press ⌜F1⌟. As you can see, a small window appears that tells you about the File option. Your screen will be similar to the one shown in Figure 18-3. (The specific help text may be slightly different.) All help windows are organized in a way similar to the one shown in this example.

At the bottom of the window is a list of the command buttons that relate to the help system. The first is the Close button. Selecting this command tells DOS that you are done with the help system, and the window is removed. (You can also press ⌜Esc⌟ to exit the help system.) To the right of Close is the Back option. This button allows you to go back to a previously displayed help screen. Next is Keys. Selecting it causes

```
                              MS-DOS Shell
  File  Options  View  Tree  Help
  C:\DOS
  ⊟A   ⊟B   ■C   ⊟D   ⊟E   ⊟F
                          MS-DOS Shell Help
  ┌──────────────────────────────────────────────────────────────┐
  │                          File Menu                          ↑│↑
  │ You can use the commands on this menu to carry out actions on files│█│
  │ and directories, or to quit MS-DOS Shell. To carry out an action on│█│
  │ one or more files or a directory, select the files or the directory│█│
  │ before you choose the command.                              │█│
  │                            —•—                              │█│
  │                                                             │█│
  │                                                             │█│
  │                                                             │█│
  │                                                             │█│
  │                                                             │█│
  │                                                             │█│
  │                                                            ↓│█│
  │                                                             │ │↓
  │  ( Close )    ( Back )    ( Keys )    ( Index )    ( Help )  │↑│
  └──────────────────────────────────────────────────────────────┘
  □  MS-DOS QBasic
  ▦  Disk Utilities
                                                              │ │
                                                              │↓│
  F10=Actions  Shift+F9=Command Prompt                      11:04a
```

Help window for the File menu bar option **Figure 18-3.**

help about using the keyboard to be displayed. After selecting this option, you can return to the original help screen by selecting Back. The Index button presents a list of help topics from which you can select. After selecting a topic, information about it will be shown. As with the Keys option, you can return to the previous window by selecting Back. The final button is Help, which gives you information about the help system. To move the highlight to the command button you want, use the [Tab] key. To execute the selected command, press the [Enter] key. You can also execute a command by clicking on a button using the mouse.

Deactivate the help window at this time by pressing [Esc] or by selecting Close.

REMEMBER: Pressing [F1] activates the Shell's context-sensitive help system. Selecting the Help menu bar option lets you obtain help about a topic of your choosing.

Understanding the Shell's Windows

In the preceding section, you saw what was called the help window, but there was not much discussion of the window itself. As you use more of the Shell you will see that its interface is based upon windows, so it is important to know more about them. A *window* is a portion of the screen that is dedicated to one specific task. If you think of the screen as a desk, then you can think of a window as a piece of paper on that desk. For example, if you activate the help window again you can see that it overlays a portion of the screen. This is like laying one piece of paper over another. When you deactivate the help window, what was previously on the screen is restored. This process of overlaying and restoring is common to all windows used by the Shell. There can be many windows on the screen at the same time, but only one will be active at any one time.

All windows contain the elements shown in Figure 18-4.

If the information contained in a window exceeds its height, then the window will include a scroll bar. All scroll bars work the same no matter what the window is used for. The components of the scroll bar are shown in Figure 18-5. A scroll bar is used to move text through the window so that you can see all of it. To use the scroll bar you must have a mouse.

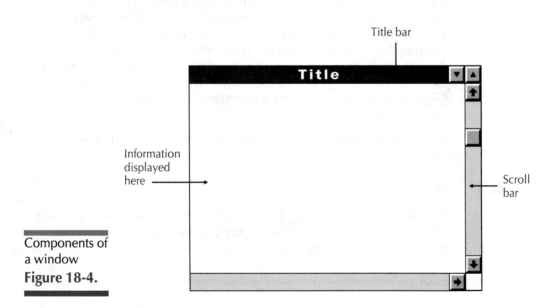

Components of
a window
Figure 18-4.

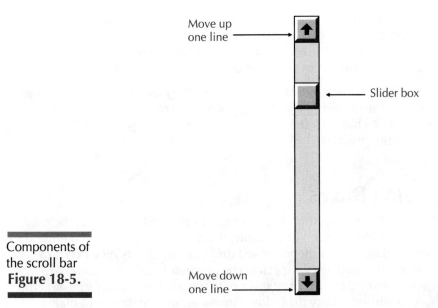

Move up
one line ————→

Slider box

Components of
the scroll bar
Figure 18-5.

Move down
one line ————→

To move the text in the screen down one line, position the mouse
pointer over the down arrow at the bottom of the scroll bar and
single-click. To move the text up one line, click on the up arrow at the
top of the bar. To move down one full window, click anywhere on the
scroll bar that is below the slider box. To move up one full window,
click on the scroll bar anywhere above the slider box.

*A scroll bar
is used to
move text
through a
window.*

If you wish to move several lines up or down quickly, position the
mouse pointer on the arrow you desire and press and hold the left
mouse button. The text inside the window will scroll smoothly until
you release the button or reach the end.

If you have a mouse, you can try a scroll bar by using the one that is
(almost certainly) on the right side of the file list window. (In rare
situations, you might not have enough files in this window to generate
a scroll bar.) Notice that the slider box moves up or down in the
direction of the scroll. Its position in the scroll bar is in the same
proportion to the total text as the position of the text currently in view.
For example, when the slider box is in the middle of its range, the text
on the screen is in the middle of the total text.

You can use the mouse to *drag* the slider box to a new position. To do this, position the mouse on the slider box and press and hold the left button down. Next, move the mouse and the box will follow. The text on the screen will be moved by the same amount. You should try this now.

If you don't have a mouse, you can use the ⬆ and ⬇ keys to scroll the text one line or the [Pg Up] and [Pg Dn] keys to scroll the text one window full. Also, to move to the top of the text, press the [Home] key. To move to the end, press the [End] key.

Dialog Boxes

Not all information that you will need to give to the Shell can be entered using menus. For example, it would be very clumsy to enter the time or date using a menu. When information of this type needs to entered, the Shell uses a special type of window called a *dialog box*. Dialog boxes allow input that is not easily accomplished using a menu. As you will see, many drop-down menu options make use of dialog boxes. If a pull-down menu item is followed by three periods, it means that selecting this item will cause a dialog box to be displayed. Although dialog boxes were introduced when discussing some commands earlier in this book, they will be examined in detail here.

A dialog box is a special type of window that allows different types of input from the user.

To see an example of a dialog box, activate the menu bar and select the Options entry. Next, select the File Display Options item. Your screen will look like the one shown in Figure 18-6.

Dialog boxes consist of one or more of the following items:

✦ Command buttons

✦ Check boxes

✦ Input boxes

✦ List boxes

✦ Radio buttons

When a dialog box is active, one of these items will be selected and highlighted. The highlighted item is the focus of input. You can move from one item to the next by pressing the [Tab] key or by clicking on the desired item using the mouse. Let's look closely at what each of these items does.

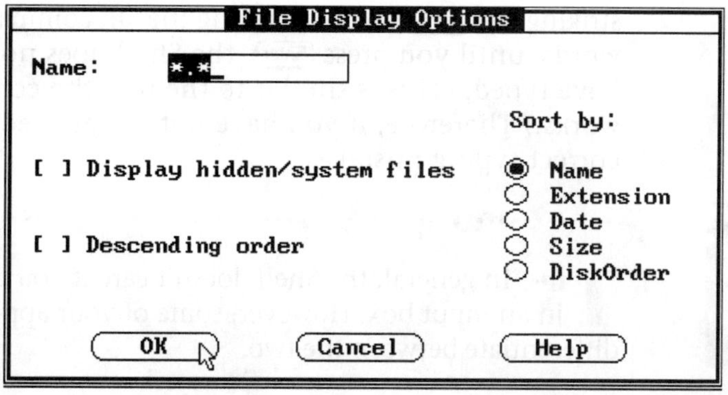

```
┌─────────────────File Display Options──────────────────┐
│┌───────────────────────────────────────────────────── │
││ Name:     * . *_                                      │
││                                                       │
││                                     Sort by:          │
││                                                       │
││ [ ] Display hidden/system files    ◉ Name             │
││                                     ○ Extension        │
││                                     ○ Date             │
││ [ ] Descending order                ○ Size             │
││                                     ○ DiskOrder        │
││                                                       │
││   (    OK    )    ( Cancel )      ( Help )            │
│└───────────────────────────────────────────────────── │
└───────────────────────────────────────────────────────┘
```

Sample
dialog box

Figure 18-6.

18

Command buttons display possible courses of action that relate to the dialog box. You saw an example of these in the help window. Selecting a command button causes that course of action to be performed immediately. Almost all dialog boxes have at least two command buttons, OK and Cancel. Most will also have Help. To activate a button using the keyboard, first select the command buttons by pressing [Tab]. Next, use the arrow keys to select the button you want and then press [Enter]. If you have a mouse, simply click on the appropriate button.

A check box looks something like this:

   [X] *option*

Here, *option* is some option that can be enabled or disabled. When the box has an X in it, that option is selected. If the box is empty, the option is not selected. To change the state of a check box, [Tab] to the box and then press the [Spacebar]. The [Spacebar] acts as a toggle; each time you press it the state of the box changes. You can also change the state of a check box by clicking on it with the mouse.

An input box allows you to enter text, such as the time or date. To activate the input box either press [Tab] until the box is active or click on it using the mouse. Once the input box has been selected, enter text using the keyboard and press [Enter] when done. Or, press [Tab] to move to another dialog box option.

When using an input box it is important to understand that the Shell does not have any idea of what you are typing until you enter it by striking the (Enter) key (or selecting the OK command button). In other words, until you press (Enter), the Shell does not know what you have typed. (This is similar to the way the command prompt works.) Therefore, if you have not yet pressed (Enter), you can correct typing mistakes.

TIP: In general, the Shell doesn't care if you use upper- or lowercase in an input box. However, some of your applications may differentiate between the two.

A list box presents a list of items from which you can choose. (A list box is similar to a drop-down menu.) To activate the list box, either press (Tab) until the box is active or click on it using the mouse. Once activated, select the item you want by moving the highlight to the appropriate item using the arrow keys and then press (Enter). Or, double-click on the item using the mouse.

Radio buttons are a list of mutually exclusive options that take this general form:

() option 1
(•) option 2
.

.

.
() option *n*

Radio buttons are a list of mutually exclusive options.

To activate the radio buttons, (Tab) to them and then use the arrow keys to change the selection, or click on the desired selection using the mouse. The circle containing the dot is the item that is selected. One and only one radio button can be selected at any given time.

Before moving on, you might want to try changing some of the information in the File Display Options dialog box. However, be sure to end by selecting the Cancel command button. At this stage, you do not want to alter anything controlled by this window. Selecting Cancel means that none of your changes will actually take effect.

Now that you have seen what constitutes the Shell and how it works, you can move on to the remaining chapters in this section that describe how to use it to run DOS.

18

 # Returning to the Command Prompt

There are two ways you can leave the Shell and return to the command prompt. First, you can press [Shift]-[F9] (or choose the Command Prompt option in the Main group—the effect is the same). The screen will clear and the command prompt will be displayed. Using this method, the Shell actually stays resident in memory waiting for you to come back to it. If you activate the command prompt using this method, then you can return to the Shell by entering the EXIT command. The advantage to deactivating the Shell in this way is that you can return to it very quickly, and it will be exactly as you left it. The disadvantage is that by remaining in memory, it uses memory that could otherwise be used by applications you run from the command prompt.

The second way to activate the command prompt is to press [F3] or [Alt]-[F4], or to select the Exit option in the File menu. This causes the Shell to be terminated (and, thus, removed from memory) and the command prompt reactivated. If you use this method, then to reactivate the Shell, you must execute the DOSSHELL command again. This method also gives application programs you run from the command prompt access to all available memory.

TIP: If you plan to leave the Shell for a short time, exit by pressing [Shift]-[F9]. If you are leaving the Shell for a longer period, it is best to do so by pressing [F3] (or [Alt]-[F4]).

Summary

In this chapter you learned how to:

✦ Start the Shell

✦ Activate the menu bar and make a selection

✦ Move between the Shell's windows

✦ Make a selection from the Main group

✦ Use the help system

✦ Use the Shell's windows

✦ Use dialog boxes

✦ Return to the command prompt

In the next chapter you will learn about the Shell's File Manager.

CHAPTER

19

FILE MANAGER BASICS

Although the preceding chapter made little distinction between the two, the Shell is composed of two major components. The first component manages the files on your disks. The second manages your programs. For the sake of discussion, the part of the Shell that works with your files will be called the File Manager, and the part that works with programs is called the Program Manager.

In the Shell, the File Manager manages your files, and the Program Manager manages your programs.

In general terms, the File Manager manages the information on your disks. The Program Manager helps you organize programs.

The File Manager is accessed through a system of three related windows: the disk drive window, the Directory Tree window, and the file list window. The Program Manager includes the Main group window and all subgroups. This chapter introduces the File Manager. The Program Manager is discussed in a later chapter.

Selecting the DOS Directory

Before starting, it is necessary that you select the DOS directory so that you can follow along with the examples. To select a directory, first activate the Directory Tree window. Next, highlight the desired directory by using the arrow keys or by single-clicking on it using the mouse. When selecting a directory, there is no need to press Enter. Highlighting it is all that is necessary.

If DOS was installed on your computer using the normal installation procedure, you should see a directory in the Directory Tree window called DOS. (You may have to scroll the Directory Tree window to find it.) You should select that directory now. Your screen will look similar to that shown in Figure 19-1.

If you don't see a DOS directory, you will need to ask the person in charge of your computer where the DOS files are stored and select that directory.

If you are running DOS from a floppy disk, just leave your startup disk in drive A. What you see will still be similar to (though not the same as) that shown in subsequent examples.

REMEMBER: To follow along with the examples in this section, select the DOS directory before proceeding.

The Directory Listing

Once a directory has been selected, the files that are contained within that directory are displayed in the file list window. The entry for each file contains four elements. First is the filename followed by the file's

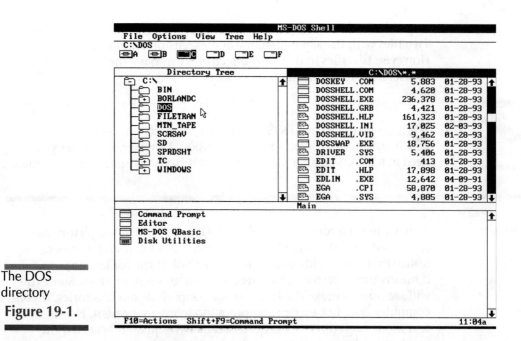

The DOS
directory
Figure 19-1.

extension. Next comes the length of the file in bytes. Finally, the
creation date of the file is shown.

NOTE: Unlike a command-prompt directory listing, the time of a
file's creation is not shown in the file list window. (This is because
of space limitations.)

If the Shell is running in graphics mode, a fifth element is included in
the directory listing for each file: a small rectangular icon at the start of
each filename, which tells you whether or not a file is a program file.
(In computerese, an *icon* is a small symbol that represents something.)
If the icon shows a computer screen, the file contains a program. If it
shows a piece of paper with a corner turned over, the file does not
contain a program. In text mode, no icons are shown.

When a file is selected, its file name is highlighted in graphics mode. In
text mode, a small triangle is put in front of the file name.

As you know, all files listed in the same directory have unique names. Two files with the same filename and extension will not be allowed. However, two files in different directories can have the same names. (Of course, their full path names will differ.)

REMEMBER: When DOS displays the file names, it puts spaces between the filename and its extension. However, whenever you need to tell DOS about a file, you must not have any spaces in the name.

Notice the Directory Tree window in Figure 19-1. Each directory has associated with it a small icon that looks like a file folder. Further, notice that some folders contain a + symbol. If the folder contains a +, it means that directory contains one or more subdirectories. Soon you will see how to make the File Manager display all subdirectories. If your computer does not support graphics, no icons are present. However, in text mode each directory is preceded by two square brackets. If the brackets enclose a +, then that directory has one or more subdirectories.

A Shell Error Message

Earlier in this book, you learned how DOS reports errors and what type of responses you can give to an error. However, errors are reported a little differently when using the Shell. Therefore, let's take a brief look at one now.

To begin, an error message must be generated. To do this, open the drive door on drive A. Next, select the A drive using the disk drive window. Because the drive door is open, DOS will not be able to read the diskette's directory, and it will generate the error window shown in Figure 19-2. Notice that there are two options shown in the error dialog window. They are

1. Try to read this disk again.
2. Do not try to read disk again.

Since there is no disk in drive A, select the second option. Next, log back into drive C, if you have a fixed disk, and select the DOS directory

A Shell error
window
Figure 19-2.

```
┌──────────────────[ WARNING! ]──────────────────┐
│  Drive not ready.                               │
│ ┌─────────────────────────────────────────────┐│
│ │ 1. Try to read this disk again.             ││
│ └─────────────────────────────────────────────┘│
│   2. Do not try to read disk again.            │
│    ┌──────────┐   ┌──────────┐   ┌──────────┐  │
│    │    OK    │   │  Cancel  │   │   Help   │  │
│    └──────────┘   └──────────┘   └──────────┘  │
└─────────────────────────────────────────────────┘
```

again. If you are working from a floppy disk, close the drive door and
log back into drive A.

As you know, errors can occur for a variety of reasons. Some errors, like
the one we just generated on purpose, can be fixed by changing
something. For example, you could insert a diskette and then select the
first option. For these types of errors, you will generally want to change
whatever is wrong and then try the operation again. However, there are
some types of errors that cannot be rectified at the time. For example,
suppose you try to log into a broken disk drive. For this type of error,
select the second option and do not retry the operation. The Shell can
generate other types of error messages. In general you will handle them
in the same way. Just remember that the Shell reports errors a little
differently than the command prompt does.

Formatting Diskettes

To follow along with the examples you will need a blank formatted
diskette. Although you know how to format diskettes using the
command prompt, you use a different procedure when using the Shell.
To see how to format a diskette using the Shell, let's make one now.

To format a disk, first activate the Main group window and select the
Disk Utilities option. Then, select Format. You will see the Format
dialog window. It will look like the one shown in Figure 19-3. By
default, the Format option formats the disk in drive A. (You can change
it to drive B if you like, by changing the A: to B:.) The formatting
option ultimately uses the FORMAT command, but the way you enter
the information is a little different.

To start formatting, press (Enter). The screen will clear, and you will be told
to insert the blank diskette into drive A and press (Enter). For now, remove
any diskette that might be in drive A, put in the blank diskette you are
going to format, and then press (Enter). (You *must* press (Enter); clicking the

Format dialog
box
Figure 19-3.

```
┌─────────────────────────[ Format ]─────────────────────────┐
│  Enter the drive to format.                                 │
│                                                             │
│  Parameters . . .   │a:│                                  │ │
│                                                             │
│     ( OK )            ( Cancel )           ( Help )         │
└─────────────────────────────────────────────────────────────┘
```

mouse has no effect at this point.) After FORMAT has finished, you will be prompted to format another. Since you need only one diskette, respond by pressing **N**, which terminates the FORMAT command.

When FORMAT terminates, the following message appears:

```
Press any key to return to MS-DOS Shell
```

To return to the Shell, press any key. This causes the Disk Utilities group to be displayed once again. To return to the Main group, select the Main option.

Starting a Program

Since running your application programs is the point of having a computer in the first place, a good way to start using the Shell is by executing a program. It is very easy to run a program using the File Manager. The general process is to first highlight the program you want to run in the file list window and then press ⏎Enter. Or, using a mouse, simply double-click on the program you want to execute. To see an example of this, we will execute a DOS external command. If DOS has been installed in the normal way, then about two-thirds down in the file list window you will see the file CHKDSK.EXE. This is the file that contains the CHKDSK command. To execute this command, position the highlight on this command and press ⏎Enter. If you have a mouse, you can double-click on CHKDSK.EXE to execute it.

NOTE: Be sure that you are logged into drive C and that the DOS directory has been selected. (If you are running DOS from a floppy, make sure that a DOS diskette is in drive A, and log into drive A.)

Execute CHKDSK.EXE at this time. The screen will clear, the disk drive will be accessed, and the CHKDSK command is executed. After the information is displayed, you will be told to press a key to return to the Shell. Press a key now. The screen will again clear, and the Shell will be reactivated.

When working with files in the file list window it is important to understand that there is a difference between selecting a file and executing a file. When you select a file by moving the highlight to it or by clicking on it with the mouse, you are telling the Shell that you are interested in this file and that you may want to do something with it in the future. However, the file itself is not directly affected. On the other hand, when you press Enter or double-click on a file, you are doing something with the file now—you are executing it. The distinction may seem blurred at this point, but as you learn more about how the File Manager operates, the difference between selecting a file and executing a file will become clearer.

Before continuing, let's execute another of DOS's commands. Using either the scroll bar or the Pg Up and Pg Dn keys, locate and highlight the file MEM.EXE. Recall that this is the DOS command that displays information about the memory in your system. Execute it now. Again, your screen will clear and information will be displayed about the memory in your computer. Press any key to return to the Shell.

19

A Closer Look at the File Manager Menu Bar

As you know, the File Manager menu bar has five options: File, Options, View, Tree, and Help. Each of these options displays a drop-down menu when selected. The following sections present an overview of what each option does.

NOTE: Sometimes an option in a drop-down menu is not available or applicable to what you are currently doing. When an option is not available for use, it is shown in low-intensity and cannot be selected.

The File Option

Most of the File options relate to a file that you have selected in the file list window. So, to follow along, activate the file list window and move the highlight to the file called DOSSHELL.HLP.

Select the File option now. Your screen will look similar to the one shown in Figure 19-4. The File option allows you to perform several operations that relate to files.

The first option is Open, which starts running the program highlighted in the file list window. Selecting this option accomplishes the same thing as starting a program using the file list window. This option is only meaningful for program files. You cannot run a non-program file. If the Open command is shown in low-intensity, it means that you forgot to highlight the DOSSHELL.HLP file.

The next option, Run, is similar to Open except that it allows you to specify certain options required by some programs when you execute them. In essence, the Run option lets you run programs in the same way as you do from the command prompt.

If you have a printer, you can use the Print option to print the contents of a text file. If the Print option is shown as not available, you must first install the PRINT command.

The Associate option is used to link one file to another.

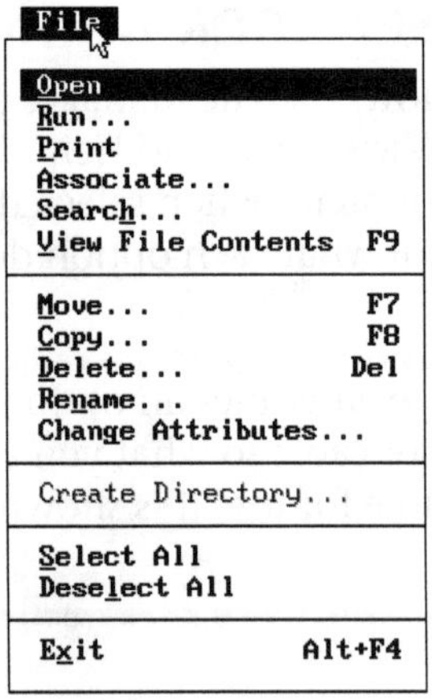

The File options
Figure 19-4.

Search lets you search your disk for a specific file (or set of files). If the file is found, then it is displayed.

View File Contents lets you see the contents of a file. This is most useful with text files. Program files with the extension .EXE or .COM contain codes that only the computer can read, so viewing one of these is of little value (except to programmers). Also, some types of data files cannot be read because the information in them is in a special form.

The Move option lets you move a file from one place to another. In general, you can move a file between disks or between directories. When you move a file, it is erased from its original position after being copied to its new place.

Copy is like Move except that the original file is not erased.

Delete lets you remove (erase) a file from a disk. It also lets you remove a subdirectory.

The Rename option allows you to change the name of a file or a subdirectory.

Change Attributes is used to change one or more of a file's attributes. Recall that the file attributes are archive, read-only, system, and hidden.

The Create Directory option allows you to create a new subdirectory.

Select All selects all the files in the current directory.

Deselect All deselects all the files in the current directory.

The Exit option removes the Shell and activates the command-prompt interface.

Options

Press the ↵ key to activate the Options menu. This entry allows you to change the way various parts of the Shell operate.

The first option is Confirmation. This option lets you control whether various safety check windows are displayed when you delete or replace a file or use the mouse for certain operations.

The next option is File Display Options. It is used to change the way the files are displayed in the file list window.

The Select Across Directories option allows you to select files in more than one directory.

The Show Information option displays information about the current disk and directory.

The Enable Task Swapper option allows you to activate the Shell's Task Manager. The Task Manager will be discussed in the next chapter.

The Display option lets you change the resolution of your screen so that either more or fewer lines of text are displayed within the Shell's windows.

Colors lets you change the colors displayed by the Shell.

The View Option

Press the ⏎ key to activate the View menu. The options associated with View let you change how the Shell arranges the screen.

The first option is Single File List. Selecting this option causes the Program Manager to be removed from the screen, and the extra room is allocated to the Directory Tree and file list windows.

Selecting the Dual File Lists option splits the screen horizontally and lets you display the contents of two separate directories and/or drives at the same time. In this arrangement, the Program Manager is also removed from the screen.

Selecting the All Files option causes the directory structure of the disk to be ignored and all files on the logged-in disk to be displayed.

The Program/File Lists option causes the screen to be configured in its default arrangement, with both the File Manager and the Program Manager present.

Selecting the Program List option causes the Directory Tree and file list windows to be removed and the extra space allocated to the Program Manager.

The Repaint Screen option redisplays the screen. Some types of programs may cause the Shell's screen to be overwritten. If this happens, simply select this option. The Refresh option repaints the screen and updates the Shell's file information.

The Tree Option

Press the ⏎ key to activate the Tree option. The options associated with Tree let you control how a disk's directory is displayed in the Directory Tree window.

The Expand One Level option causes the next level of subdirectories contained within the currently selected directory to be displayed in the Directory Tree window.

Expand Branch causes all levels of subdirectories contained within the currently selected directory to be displayed in the Directory Tree window.

The Expand All option causes all subdirectories to be shown in the Directory Tree window.

Collapse Branch causes any subdirectories of the highlighted directory to be removed from the screen. This is the opposite of Expand Branch.

The Help Option

Press the ⏎ key to activate the Help option. This option lets you access the help system.

The Index option displays an index of help topics.

The Keyboard option explains various keys that have a special meaning for DOS.

Shell Basics displays information about the basic operation of the Shell.

The Commands option displays information about the Shell commands.

Procedures discusses how to perform various common operations.

The Using Help option teaches you how to use the help system.

Selecting About Shell causes the DOS version number to be displayed.

Using the Menu Bar's Hot Keys

As you worked through the preceding sections relating to the various menus, you probably noticed that several of the menu options had keys (or key combinations) listed to the right of the menu item. These keys are the hot keys that, when pressed, immediately activate the item that they are associated with, without having to first activate the menu. For example, activate the File menu now. Notice that the Move option can also be directly activated by pressing the F7 key. You will want to make mental notes of these hot keys, because after you have learned them, they will make running the Shell easier and faster. Keep in mind that sometimes an option will have a hot key that activates it even though one is not shown alongside of it in the menu.

In some cases, instead of a single key, a key combination is shown to the right of the menu option. A *key combination* is created when two keys are pressed at the same time. For example, the hot key that exits the Shell is Alt-F4. To create this key combination, press the Alt and F4 keys at the same time. (Or, if easier for you, press and hold the Alt key and then press the F4, finally releasing both keys at the same time.) As you will see, key combinations are used quite frequently when running the Shell.

Viewing a File

Now that you have seen the various elements of the File Manager, let's begin putting them to work. To begin, if it is not already selected, select the file DOSSHELL.HLP. Remember, to select a file, activate the file list window, move the highlight to the file, or move the mouse pointer to the desired file name and click on it. When a file is selected, it is highlighted in graphics mode, or a small triangle is put in front of its name in text mode.

To view the file, activate the menu bar and select File. From the menu, select View File Contents. This causes the contents of DOSSHELL.HLP to be displayed. DOSSHELL.HLP is the file that contains the Shell's help information. You will see the screen shown in Figure 19-5. You can use the ↑ and ↓ keys to scroll the contents of the file up or down one line. You can use the Pg Up and Pg Dn keys to view the entire contents of the file a screen full at a time. Also, pressing Enter is the same as pressing Pg Dn.

If you press F9 while using the View File Contents utility, the display will show the contents of a file in a format that is used by

```
┌──────────────────────── MS-DOS Shell - DOSSHELL.HLP ──────────────────────┐
│  Display  View  Help                                                       │
│ ─────────────────────────────────────────────────────────────────────────│
│ [     To view file's content use PgUp or PgDn or ↑ or ↓.                 ] │
│                                                                            │
│ Help For MS-DOS Shell for MS-DOS 6                                          │
│ ─────────────────────────────────                                          │
│                                                                            │
│ ↑I↑@                                                            ▷           │
│ MS-DOS Shell Help Index                                                    │
│                                                                            │
│ To see a topic:                                                            │
│                                                                            │
│  - Double-click the topic.                                                 │
│                                                                            │
│ Or                                                                         │
│                                                                            │
│  - Press TAB to select the topic you want, and then press ENTER.           │
│                                                                            │
│ KEYBOARD HELP                                                              │
│ ─────────────                                                              │
│                                                                            │
│    " General MS-DOS Shell Keys "~K101~                                     │
│    " Movement Keys "~K102~                                                 │
│    " Help Keys "~K109~                                                     │
│    " Active Task List Keys "~K103~                                         │
│    " Program List Keys "~K104~                                             │
│    " File List Keys "~K105~                                                │
│    " File Selection Keys "~K106~                                           │
│    " Directory Tree Keys "~K107~                                           │
│    " Drive Selection Keys "~K108~                                          │
│                                                                            │
│ COMMANDS HELP                                                              │
│ ─────────────                                                              │
│                                                                            │
│ File List Menus                                                            │
│ ─────────────────────────────────────────────────────────────────────────│
│  ←┘=PageDown  Esc=Cancel  F9=Hex/ASCII                         11:09a       │
└────────────────────────────────────────────────────────────────────────────┘
```

The View File
Contents utility
Figure 19-5.

programmers. Each letter in the file will be shown using its internal
machine representation in hexadecimal format. (*Hexadecimal* is a
number system based on 16 instead of 10.) Unless you are a
programmer, you will probably not use this version of the View File
utility. However, feel free to try it at this time. The ⏺F9⏺ key is a toggle
that switches between the two displays each time it is pressed.

The View File Contents window has three items in its menu bar:
Display, View, and Help. The Display option's drop-down menu
contains two items: ASCII and Hex. Selecting ASCII causes the file to be
displayed normally. Selecting Hex causes the file to be shown using the
hexadecimal notation discussed in the preceding paragraph. Essentially,
the Display menu is simply an alternative to the ⏺F9⏺ key. The View
option has two entries in its drop-down menu. You can redisplay the
screen by selecting Repaint Screen. The second option, called Restore
View, causes the Shell to be redisplayed. The Help option is the same
here as it is in the Shell.

Press ⏺Esc⏺ to cancel the View File utility.

Copying and Moving Files

It is easy to copy or move a file using the Shell. However, the procedure differs depending upon whether you use the keyboard or the mouse. Both are examined here.

Copying and Moving a File Using the Keyboard

The general procedure for copying a file using the keyboard is to first select a file in the file list window. Next, activate the File option and select Copy. You will then be prompted for the destination. Before going into too many details, let's try an example.

Select the file called CHKDSK.EXE. Next, activate the menu bar and select File. From the drop-down menu select Copy. You will see a screen similar to that in Figure 19-6. Notice that the name of the file you selected (in this case CHKDSK.EXE) is on the From line, and the cursor is blinking on the To line. If you are using a fixed disk, the To line will contain C:\DOS. If you are running DOS from a floppy, the To line will display A:\. These are the default path names. However, you can specify any path name you like. For this example, if you have a fixed disk, change the To line so that it is as shown here:

    C:\DOS\CD.EXE

If you are running DOS from a floppy, change the To line so that it is like the one shown here:

    A:\CD.EXE

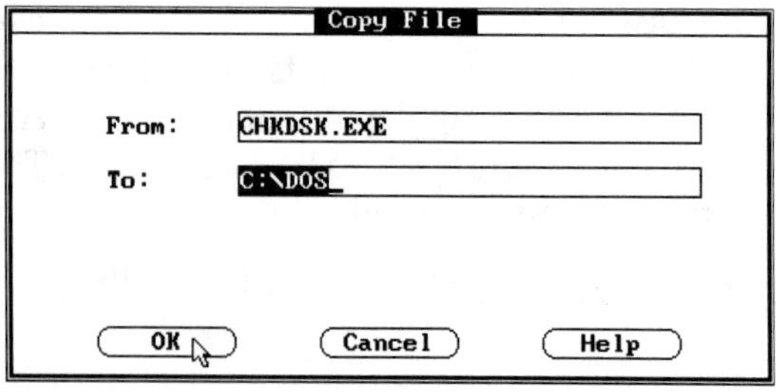

The Copy window
Figure 19-6.

```
┌────────────────────── Copy File ──────────────────────┐
│                                                        │
│                                                        │
│   From:   ┌CHKDSK.EXE─────────────────────────────┐    │
│           └──────────────────────────────────────┘     │
│   To:     ┌C:\DOS────────────────────────────────┐     │
│           └──────────────────────────────────────┘     │
│                                                        │
│     ( OK )        ( Cancel )        ( Help )           │
└────────────────────────────────────────────────────────┘
```

After you have entered the file name correctly, press Enter to begin the copying process. When the process has completed, you will see a directory entry for CD.EXE directly above the one for CHKDSK.EXE. Notice that the only difference between the two entries is the names. Everything else is the same.

You can specify any drive and directory when using the Copy option. Simply enter it on the To line.

A small variation on copying a file is moving a file. When you move a file, it is deleted from its original location and moved to the new location you specify. If you want to move a file, use the Move option in the File drop-down menu.

Copying and Moving a File Using the Mouse

You can use the mouse to copy a file from one disk to another or from one directory to another on the same disk, by *dragging* the file from one disk or directory to another. In order to follow along, if you are a fixed disk user, make sure your formatted diskette is in drive A. If you are running DOS from floppies, then your formatted diskette should be in drive B.

To copy a file using the mouse, first position the mouse pointer on the file you want to copy. Next, press and hold the Ctrl key. Then, press and hold the left mouse button. A small icon will appear. Now, while continuing to press the left mouse button and the Ctrl key, drag the icon to the new directory or drive that you want to copy the file to. When the icon is at the desired location, release the mouse button and then the Ctrl key, and the file will be copied.

To see how this actually works, let's try an example. Move the mouse pointer to the file you just created, called CD.EXE. Press the Ctrl key and then press and hold the left mouse button. Next, if you are using a fixed disk, drag the icon to the A drive in the disk drive window. (If you are using floppies, drag the icon to drive B, instead.) Once the icon is on the proper drive, release the mouse button and the Ctrl key. You will see the confirmation dialog box shown in Figure 19-7. In its default configuration, the Shell double checks every copy or move operation performed using the mouse. The reason for this is that it is easy to accidentally release the mouse button at the wrong spot when dragging the icon to a new location. If you have, indeed, positioned the icon at

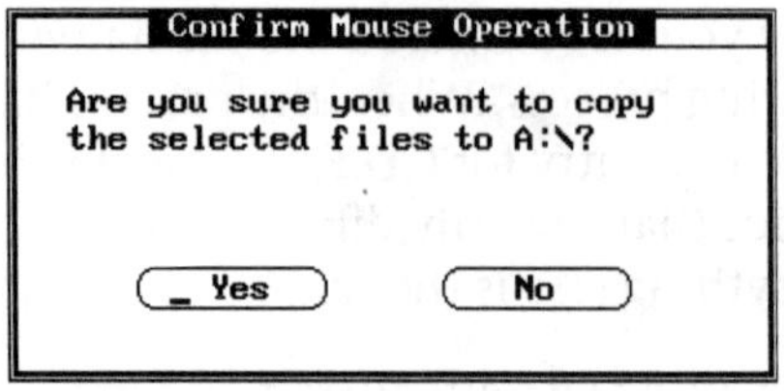

Mouse operation confirmation window

Figure 19-7.

```
┌───────────────────────────────────┐
│      Confirm Mouse Operation      │
├───────────────────────────────────┤
│  Are you sure you want to copy    │
│  the selected files to A:\?       │
│                                   │
│   ┌───────────┐   ┌───────────┐   │
│   │ _ Yes     │   │   No      │   │
│   └───────────┘   └───────────┘   │
└───────────────────────────────────┘
```

Dragging is a mouse technique that moves an object from one place to another on the screen.

the correct location, then select Yes to copy the file. Otherwise, select No and try again.

As stated, you can use the mouse to copy a file to another directory on the same disk. To do this, drag the file to a directory in the Directory Tree menu.

Moving a file uses a procedure almost identical to the copying procedure. The only difference is that you do not press the ⌈Ctrl⌉ key. If you are moving a file to another directory on the same drive, just drag the file to the new directory. (You don't need to press any key.) However, if you are moving the file to a new drive, hold down the ⌈Alt⌉ key and then drag the file to the new drive. On your own, try moving the CD.EXE file to drive A (or B, whichever applies) and then copying it back.

TIP: You might want to practice moving and copying files using the mouse before proceeding. It can take a little practice to become proficient at it.

Erasing Files

It is a simple matter to remove a file from a disk by using the File Manager. To begin, let's erase the file CD.EXE that we created in the previous section. First, highlight the CD.EXE file in the file list window. Next, activate the menu bar and select File. From the drop-down menu, select the Delete option. You will then be shown a safety check window that will look like the one in Figure 19-8. Erasing a file can be a one-way operation; you might not be able to bring it back once it's gone. For this reason, DOS gives you a second chance to change your mind before

File deletion
safety check
window
Figure 19-8.

```
┌─────────────────────────────────────┐
│      Delete File Confirmation        │
├─────────────────────────────────────┤
│                                      │
│   Delete C:\DOS\CD.EXE?              │
│                                      │
│  ( Yes )    (  No  )   ( Cancel )    │
│                                      │
└─────────────────────────────────────┘
```

erasing the file. Since you do, in fact, want to erase the file, select the
first option.

Renaming a File

19

If you have been following along with the examples, then you will have
copied CD.EXE to a previously blank disk. Make sure that this disk is in
drive A at this time.

You can change the name of a file by first selecting that file in the file
list window and then selecting the Rename option in the File menu.
You will then be prompted for the new name of the file. To try this,
let's rename the copy of CD.EXE you put on the diskette to TEST.EXE.

First, select drive A using the drive specifier window. Next, select
CD.EXE in the file list window. Activate the menu bar and choose File.
Next, select Rename. You will then be prompted for the new name for
CD.EXE in the Rename window. Enter **TEST.EXE** and press Enter. You
will see that the name change takes place.

To change the name back to CD.EXE, repeat the procedure.

If you are running DOS from the fixed disk, select drive C at this time
and activate the DOS directory. If you are using floppies, put your DOS
disk back in drive A now.

REMEMBER: When you rename a file, you must give a name that is
not already used by another file in the same directory.

Changing the Way Files Are Displayed

You can change what files are displayed in the file list window and the order in which they are displayed using the Options entry. Select Options at this time. The second entry in the pull-down menu is File Display Options. Select it at this time. You will see the File Display Options dialog box, as shown in Figure 19-9.

The File Display Options dialog box gives you four ways to control how files are displayed in the file list window. The first is the Name field, which is used to specify the name of the file or files you want to see displayed. By default, the name is *.*, which tells DOS to display all files. The second item is the Sort by radio buttons. Using these buttons, you can change the way files are ordered in the file list window. The third and fourth items in the File Display Options dialog box are two check boxes. The first allows some files that are not normally shown to be displayed. The second causes the directory to be shown in descending order. Let's take a closer look at these options now.

Looking for Specific Files

Until now, the Shell has displayed the entire contents of the current directory in the file list window. However, you can use the Name option to find a specific file by entering its name. You can use this method to quickly determine whether a file is in the directory. For example, enter **SORT.EXE** and press Enter. The file list window will clear and then only the file SORT.EXE will be displayed. To have the entire directory displayed again, reactivate the File Display Options dialog box and enter *.* at the Name field.

File Display
Options
dialog box
Figure 19-9.

```
╔═══════════════ File Display Options ════════════════╗
║  Name:      *.*                                      ║
║                                      Sort by:        ║
║                                      ◉ Name          ║
║  [ ] Display hidden/system files     ○ Extension     ║
║                                      ○ Date          ║
║  [ ] Descending order                ○ Size          ║
║                                      ○ DiskOrder      ║
║                                                      ║
║    (   OK   )      ( Cancel )        (  Help )        ║
╚══════════════════════════════════════════════════════╝
```

When you specify a file name, DOS attempts to find a file in the current directory that matches that name. If you specify a file that is not in the directory, you will see this message:

```
No files match file specifier.
```

If you think that the file you requested is really in the directory, you may have made a typing error. If, after a second try, DOS still reports the file as nonexistent, try listing the entire directory; you may have forgotten the file's name or its exact spelling.

You can use wildcard characters when you specify the name to cause groups of files to be displayed. In fact, any wildcard file name that you can use at the command prompt can be used in the Name field. For example, assume that you want to list the names of all the files on a disk that share the .EXE extension. To do this, enter the following at the Name field of the File Display Options window:

```
*.EXE
```

This causes DOS to display all files with an .EXE extension. You might want to try some examples on your own. (Be sure to return the Name field to *.* before moving on.)

Changing the Sorting Order

Reselect the File Display Options entry in the Options menu. Activate the Sort by radio buttons. (Press the [Tab] key three times.) By default, the directory is sorted by the file names. However, you can also have the directory sorted by extension, date, or size. You can also request that the contents of the directory not be sorted, which is accomplished by choosing the DiskOrder entry.

To see the effects of changing the sorting method, choose to sort by extension and press [Enter]. The directory will then look similar to that shown in Figure 19-10.

You might want to try the other sorting methods on your own. However, before moving on, reset the Sort by option to Name.

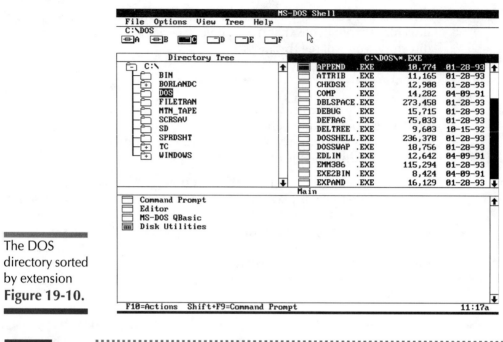

The DOS
directory sorted
by extension
Figure 19-10.

TIP: Sorting by date helps you locate the most recently created or
modified files. They will be the last files displayed.

Displaying Hidden and System Files

By default, hidden and system files will not display in the file list
window. However, you can cause these files to be displayed by
activating the Display hidden/system files check box. Frankly, unless
you are directed to do so by some application program you are using,
there is probably no reason to activate this option.

Display the Directory in Descending Order

By default, the directory is shown in the file list window in ascending
sorted order. You can reverse this by selecting the Descending order

check box. If you try this, be sure to deactivate it before moving on. If you forget, your screen will not look like the ones shown in this book.

Displaying Information About a File

Select the DOSSHELL.HLP file in the file list window at this time. Now, activate the menu bar and choose Options. From the Options menu select Show Information. You will see the Show Information window, which will be similar to the one shown in Figure 19-11.

This window displays information about the selected file, the current directory, and the logged-in disk. We will come back to this window later in the book, but one important thing for you to know is that the number of selected files will be shown under the Selected heading. This can be useful when you are unsure about how many files have been selected—especially prior to a deletion operation.

Press Esc to exit the Show Information window at this time.

Arranging the Screen

As you learned earlier in this chapter, you can have the Shell display the directory one of five ways using the View menu bar option. To conclude this chapter, let's experiment with some different screen arrangements. Activate the View drop-down menu at this time.

19

```
┌──────────────────────────────┐
│      Show Information         │
├──────────────────────────────┤
│ File                          │
│   Name  : DOSSHELL.HLP        │
│   Attr  : ...a                │
│ Selected        B      C      │
│   Number:       0      1      │
│   Size  :        161,323      │
│ Directory                     │
│   Name  : DOS                 │
│   Size  :      4,827,948      │
│   Files :            157      │
│ Disk                          │
│   Name  : CDISK               │
│   Size  :     33,454,080      │
│   Avail :      5,902,336      │
│   Files :          1,100      │
│   Dirs  :             45      │
│  (  Close  )    (  Help  )    │
└──────────────────────────────┘
```

Show
Information
window
Figure 19-11.

One very useful screen variation is activated by the Dual File Lists option. This option splits the screen and allows you to display the contents of two different directories or disks at the same time. Choose this option now. Your screen will look like the one shown in Figure 19-12. Once the screen is split, you can change which directory or disk (or both) either directory window is displaying. You might want to try this now. (Remember: use the Tab key to move among the various windows.) You might find this option useful when you are copying files between directories or disks.

Another useful screen arrangement is created by selecting the All Files option. This causes the entire contents of the disk to be displayed, bypassing the directory structure of the disk. Try this option now. Notice that information about the file currently highlighted is shown. As you move the highlight about, the information changes to reflect the new file. Notice further that the directory that contains the file is displayed.

Two directory structures displayed simultaneously using the Dual File Lists option **Figure 19-12.**

The All Files option is particularly useful when you forget what directory a file is in. To find the file, activate the All Files option. Next, using the File Display Options selection in the Options menu, change the file name specifier to that of the file you want to find. If the file is on the disk, its name will appear in the file list window. To try this, activate the File Display Options option and enter **CHKDSK.EXE** for the file specifier. As you can see, it will be found.

On your own, you should try the other screen arrangement options. However, before moving on, be sure to return the screen to its default configuration by selecting the Program/File Lists option.

Summary

In this chapter you learned

✦ What the File Manager is

✦ How directories are displayed in the Shell

✦ How the Shell displays error messages

✦ How to format a diskette using the Shell

✦ How to start a program

✦ About the various menu bar options

✦ How to view a text file

✦ How to copy files

✦ How to erase and rename files

✦ About changing the directory display

✦ About arranging the screen

In the next chapter we will take a look at some of the File Manager's more advanced features, including creating and managing directories, changing file attributes, and copying files across directories. You will also learn about one of the Shell's most exciting features: the Task Switcher.

CHAPTER

ADVANCED FILE MANAGER FEATURES

Now that you know your way around the File Manager and can perform many of the most common operations, it is time to unlock some of the system's more advanced features. Even though many of these features are quite powerful, you will be pleased to know that they are not difficult to learn and master.

For the examples in this chapter you will need a blank, formatted diskette. Put the blank diskette in drive A and log into the A drive at this time.

Creating Directories

You learned how to create and manage directories, and the theory behind them, earlier in this book when using the command prompt. Here, you will learn about them using the Shell.

In this section, we will create on the disk in drive A the directory structure shown in Figure 20-1. This is the same directory structure that was created when you learned about directories in Chapter 6. As you will see, the process you use to create directories from the Shell differs greatly from that used at the command prompt.

NOTE: Be sure that you are logged into drive A before continuing.

When working with directories, the Shell differs greatly from the command prompt.

To begin, activate the menu bar and select File. From the File menu, select Create Directory. You will see the Create Directory window shown in Figure 20-2.

The prompt will be at the line that says "New directory name." Enter **WP** and press (Enter). Here, WP is short for word processing, which is too long to be a directory name. In the Directory Tree window you will see that the WP directory has been added off the root of drive A.

To create the FORMLET directory under the WP directory, first select the WP directory in the Directory Tree window. Next, activate the menu bar and select File. From the File drop-down menu select Create Directory. When prompted for the directory name enter **FORMLET** and press (Enter). After the operation completes, you will see this directory tree displayed:

```
A:\
 └─WP
     └─FORMLET
```

In general, when you use the Shell to create a subdirectory you must first select the directory that you want the subdirectory to be under. That is why when you created the FORMLET directory under WP, you

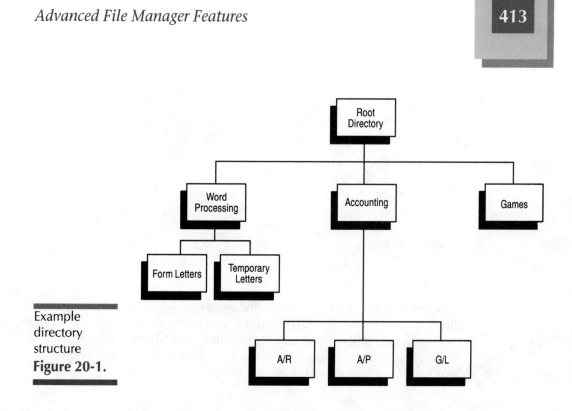

Example
directory
structure
Figure 20-1.

first had to select the WP directory. Put a different way, the directory you specify in the Create Directory window will always be created under the directory currently selected in the Directory Tree window.

Creating the Rest of the Subdirectories

Let's create the rest of the subdirectories that we will need. First, select the WP directory and then activate the Create Directory option. Enter **TEMP** for the name and press (Enter).

```
┌─────────────────Create Directory─────────────────┐
│                                                   │
│   Parent name: A:\                                │
│                                                   │
│   New directory name. .   [_____]         │
│                                                   │
│                                                   │
│                                                   │
│    ( OK ▷ )      ( Cancel )      ( Help )          │
└───────────────────────────────────────────────────┘
```

Create
Directory
window
Figure 20-2.

20

Next, select the root directory and then create the ACCOUNTS directory. With the root still selected, create the GAMES directory. The tree in the Directory Tree window should now look like this:

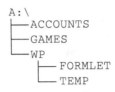

```
A:\
   ├──ACCOUNTS
   ├──GAMES
   └──WP
         ├── FORMLET
         └── TEMP
```

Now, let's fill in the ACCOUNTS subdirectories. Select the ACCOUNTS directory in the Directory Tree window and then create the AR (accounts receivable), AP (accounts payable), and GL (general ledger) subdirectories at this time. When you have finished, your screen should look similar to that shown in Figure 20-3.

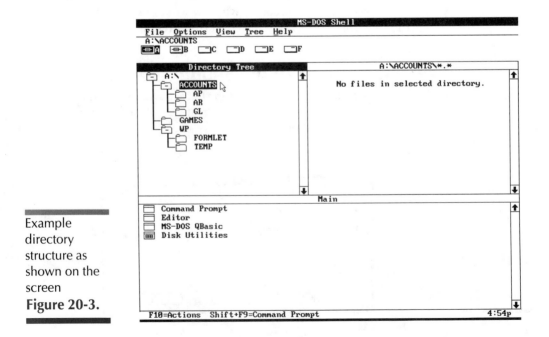

Example directory structure as shown on the screen
Figure 20-3.

Removing a Directory

Now that you have learned to create a subdirectory, it is time to learn how to delete one. To remove a directory, first select the directory you want to remove and then use the Delete option in the File menu. You can only remove a directory if it is empty and has no subdirectories.

Switch to the GL directory at this time. Since it is empty, remove it now. You will see a confirmation window, which gives you a second chance to not delete the directory. Go ahead and delete the directory at this time. You will see that GL no longer appears in the Directory Tree window. Before continuing, recreate the GL directory.

If you try to remove a directory that either contains files or has its own subdirectories, you will be notified that you cannot delete the directory. If you do, indeed, want to remove that directory, you must erase all files in it and remove all subdirectories first.

20

Using the Tree Menu Bar Option

Before moving on to actually using the directories that you just created, you need to learn how to use the options in the Tree drop-down menu. At this time, activate the Tree option. As mentioned in Chapter 19, this menu affects how the directory of a disk is displayed in the Directory Tree window. In this section, each entry in the menu is examined in detail.

As shown in Figure 20-3, the directory structure of the disk in drive A is fully *expanded*. This means that all subdirectories are displayed. However, sometimes you will not want to see all subdirectories of a directory. For example, very complex directories are overwhelming when fully displayed. When this is the case, you can collapse a branch using the Collapse Branch option. When you *collapse a branch*, it means that all subdirectories under the selected directory are no longer displayed. To see how this works, select the WP directory. Next, activate the Tree menu and select Collapse Branch. As you will see, the directories FORMLET and TEMP are no longer displayed.

REMEMBER: When you collapse a branch, only those subdirectories of the directory currently highlighted are affected. All other subdirectories that were displayed are still displayed.

It is important to understand that collapsing a branch does not imply that the directories have been removed from the disk. They are still very much there. It is just that they are no longer displayed in the Directory Tree window. To redisplay these directories, select the WP directory and reactivate the Tree menu. This time select Expand Branch. This causes the subdirectories of WP to be displayed again.

The Collapse Branch option causes all subdirectories of the selected directory to be removed from the screen. The Expand Branch option causes all subdirectories of the selected directory to be displayed.

At this time, select the root directory and then activate the Tree option and select Collapse Branch. This causes all directories, except the root, to be removed from the screen. Now, reactivate the Tree option and select Expand One Level. Now, the Directory window will look like this:

The Expand One Level option causes just the next level of subdirectories to be displayed, not the entire branch.

To see all directories, use the Expand All option. Try this now.

If you have a mouse, you can control how directories are displayed by clicking on the file-folder icons associated with each directory. If the icon has a + in it, there is at least one other layer of subdirectories associated with the directory, but it is not currently displayed. If you click on the folder, another level of directories is shown. If the folder contains nothing, then no more subdirectories are present. If you click on a folder that contains a –, then the entire branch is collapsed.

You can also use special hot keys to expand and collapse directories. First, move the highlight to the directory you want to affect. Then, to expand one level, press the ⊞ key. To collapse a branch, press ⊟. To expand a branch, press *****. Finally, to expand all branches, use Ctrl-*****

Replacing a File

The Shell warns you before you replace one file with another by the same name. To see an example, copy CHKDSK.EXE from the DOS directory of drive C into the root directory of drive A. Then, repeat the procedure. (If you are using only floppy drives, copy CHKDSK.EXE from your DOS work disk.) This time, before the copy commences, you will see a confirmation window similar to the one shown in Figure 20-4. Whenever you attempt to copy a file to a destination that already has a file by that name you will see this window. Since it is easy to accidentally replace a file that you did not mean to replace, confirmation windows act as safety checks which help prevent mistakes.

At this time, press (Enter) so that the copy process can proceed.

TIP: The warning before replacing provides a margin of safety when using the Shell. However, you should not rely on this warning as a substitute for caution when working with important files.

20

Changing a File's Attributes

As you know from earlier in this book, all files have these four attributes associated with them, which you can examine and/or modify:

✦ Hidden

✦ System

✦ Read-only

✦ Archive

Confirmation
window
displayed when
replacing a file
Figure 20-4.

```
┌───────────────┤ Replace File Confirmation ├───────────────┐
│                                                            │
│  Replace File:                                             │
│    A:\CHKDSK.EXE                                           │
│    01-28-93  (12,908 bytes)                                │
│                                                            │
│  With File:                                                │
│    C:\DOS\CHKDSK.EXE                                       │
│    01-28-93  (12,908 bytes)                                │
│                                                            │
│   ⟨  Yes  ⟩      ⟨   No   ⟩      ⟨ Cancel ⟩                │
│                                                            │
└────────────────────────────────────────────────────────────┘
```

With the Shell, you can change a file's attribute using the Change Attributes option in the File menu. To see an example, switch to the root directory of drive A and select CHKDSK.EXE at this time. Next, activate the menu bar, select File, and then select Change Attributes. Your screen will look like that in Figure 20-5. To change an attribute, first press the Tab key until the list of attributes is highlighted. Next, using the arrow keys, position the highlight on the attribute you want to change and press the Spacebar. The Spacebar works as a toggle. Each time you press it, it changes the state of the highlighted attribute. When an attribute is on, it has a small diamond just to the left of it. You can also toggle the state of an attribute by clicking on it using the mouse.

For now, since there is no reason to change any attribute, exit the dialog box by selecting Cancel or by pressing Esc.

Associating Files

You can associate a program file with a group of other files that share a common extension. For example, a word processing program can be associated with all files that have the extension .WP. After this association has been made, each time you select a .WP file the word processor is automatically executed and you can begin editing the file.

As you know from preceding chapters, you cannot execute non-program files. If you try to do so by highlighting one in the file list window and pressing Enter or by double-clicking, the Shell will beep at you and do nothing else. However, when a non-program file is associated with a program, you can "execute" the file. When you do this, the program associated with that file is actually executed, and the file you selected is then used by that program.

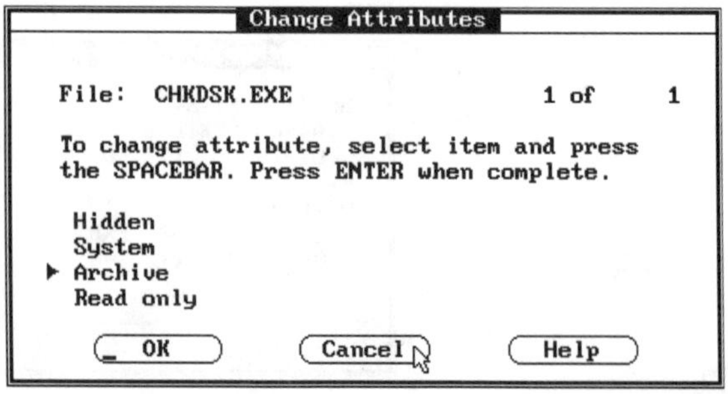

Change Attributes dialog box
Figure 20-5.

To see an example of associated files, return to the DOS directory on drive C if you have a fixed disk, or put the DOS disk in drive A if you are running DOS from a floppy. Next, find the file EDIT.COM in the file name window and highlight it. Now activate the File menu and select Associate. You will see an Associate File window that looks similar to that shown in Figure 20-6. You will be prompted for the extensions of the files you want to associate with the editor. At this time enter **HLP** (with no period before the *H*) and press ⌷Enter⌷. Now, EDIT is associated with any file that ends in HLP.

To see how the association works, activate the file list window, move the highlight to DOSSHELL.HLP, and press ⌷Enter⌷. (Or double-click on it using the mouse.) The screen will clear and you will see the DOS editor screen. As you can see, the DOS editor has been activated and DOSSHELL.HLP has been automatically loaded into the editor. (DOSSHELL.HLP is the file that contains the help information used by the Shell's help system.)

Exit EDIT at this time. (To do this, press the ⌷Alt⌷ key to activate the editor's menu bar. Select the File entry and select the Exit option. This causes the Shell to return.)

To disassociate a set of files from a program, select the program file and then activate the Associate option. When prompted for the extensions, you will see the current associations. Simply remove the one you no longer want. Try this now by removing HLP from EDIT's association list.

How you will use the Associate option or whether you will use it at all depends upon what you are going to be using the computer for. For example, in addition to word processing, another area that lends itself to associated files is a spreadsheet program. You could associate the

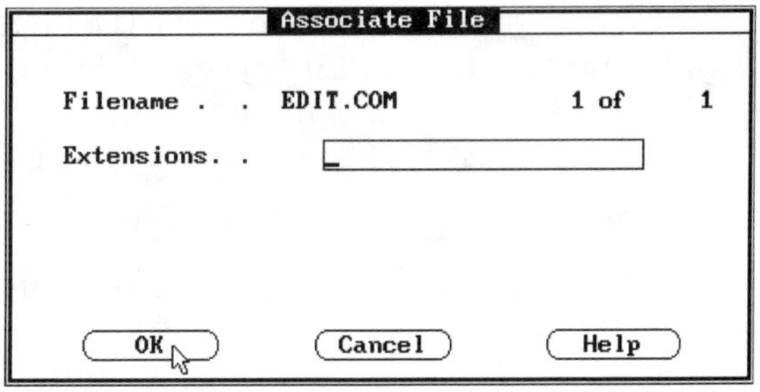

20

Associate File window

Figure 20-6.

spreadsheet with its files. However, associated files may not make much sense if you use the computer primarily for an accounts payable program, for example.

 # Working with Groups of Files

So far, using the file list window, you have been able to select and work with only one file at a time. However, it is possible to work with two or more at the same time. In this section, you will learn how to work with groups of files.

Selecting Multiple Files

Before you can work with a group of files, you need to know how to select them. As you know, by default only one file in the file list window can be highlighted at any one time. However, in this section you will learn how to highlight multiple files. The method by which this feat is accomplished varies between the keyboard and the mouse. Both variations are examined here.

To select multiple files using the keyboard, first activate the file list window. Next, press Shift-F8. After doing this you will see the word "ADD" just to the left of the time at the bottom of the screen. Now, to select a file press the Spacebar. To add another file, move the highlight and press the Spacebar again. The Spacebar acts as a toggle. Therefore, if you accidentally select a file you don't want, simply move the highlight to it and press the Spacebar a second time. When you have selected all the files you want, press Shift-F8 a second time.

If you want to select a range of adjacent files, follow this procedure: First, press Shift-F8 and then move the highlight to the first file. Next, press and hold down the Shift key while you use the ↓ key to move the highlight to the last file in the list. All files between the two ends will be selected. Press Shift-F8 to stop selecting files.

You can use Shift-Pg Up and Shift-Pg Dn to select an entire window full of files.

To select multiple files using the mouse, press the Ctrl key and then click on the files you want. To select a range, click on the first file. Next, hold down the Shift key and click on the last file.

Selecting and Deselecting All Files

Sometimes you will want to perform a file operation on all of the files in a directory. The easiest way to select them all is to use the Select All option in the File menu or press Ctrl-/. Try this now. As you can see, all the files are selected.

To deselect all files use the Deselect All option in the File menu or press Ctrl-\. Deselect all files at this time.

One good use for the Deselect All option is when you are working with a directory containing many files and you are not sure which have been selected. By using Deselect All you can be sure that no files are selected.

Now that you know how to select multiple files, it's time to see why they are useful.

20

Copying Groups of Files

When using the command prompt, you copy a group of files by using the DOS wildcard characters. However, this approach cannot be used with the Shell. Instead, to copy more than one file at a time, first select all the files you want to copy. Next, activate the Copy option in the File menu and specify the destination. All the specified files will be copied. For example, assuming that you have a fixed disk, put the directories disk created in the first part of this chapter into drive A and log into the DOS directory of drive C. Next, select a few small files and then activate the Copy command. For the destination, simply specify **A:** and press Enter. This causes the selected files to be copied into the root directory of the disk in drive A.

You can also move multiple files in the same way. Simply select those you want to move and activate the Move command.

Deleting Groups of Files

To erase a group of files using the Shell, first select the files that you want to erase. Then, use the Delete option in the File menu to erase them. When you do this, all selected files will be erased. However, you will be prompted by the Delete confirmation window for each file individually.

As you continue to use DOS you will find more instances in which working with groups of files can make things easier.

Eliminating the Confirmation Windows

As you have seen in the examples, whenever you delete a file or replace a file in a copy operation, a confirmation window is displayed which gives you a chance to change your mind. A confirmation window is also displayed each time you copy or move a file using the mouse. Once you become experienced with DOS and its Shell, these extra steps can become tedious. For this reason, the Shell lets you disable the confirmation windows using the Confirmation selection in the Options menu. Select this option now. As you can see, there are three options in this window:

> Confirm on Delete
> Confirm on Replace
> Confirm on Mouse Operation

By default, all confirmation windows are on. If you deselect the Confirm on Delete option, then no confirmation window will be displayed when you delete a file or a directory. Deselecting Confirm on Replace means that there will be no safety check when you copy a file to a destination that already has a file by the same name. Deselecting Confirm on Mouse Operation prevents the confirmation window from appearing when using the mouse.

As long as you know what you are doing, there is no harm in deactivating these safety check windows. However, you might want to leave them active just to avoid making a disastrous error.

CAUTION: The confirmation windows are one of the Shell's safety features that should only be eliminated after careful consideration.

Selecting Files Across Directories

By default, when you change directories, any files selected in the previous directory are automatically deselected. However, you can change this by selecting the Select Across Directories option in the Options menu. When this option is activated, files that you have selected stay selected until you explicitly turn them off. The principal advantage to this is that it allows you to perform operations on files in different directories at the same time.

A Closer Look at the Show Information Window

To begin, select CHKDSK.EXE in the file list window. Then, activate the Show Information option in the Options menu. We took a brief look at the Show Information window in the previous chapter. Let's explore it more thoroughly now.

20

The Show Information window is divided into four main sections: File, Selected, Directory, and Disk. The File section displays the name of the currently selected file (if any) and shows that file's attributes. When the hidden attribute is on, an "h" is displayed. When the read-only attribute is set, an "r" is shown. When the archive attribute is on, an "a" is displayed. When the system attribute is on, an "s" is displayed.

The Selected section tells you which disk drives are active and how many files (if any) are currently selected. It also tells you the size of those files.

The Directory section shows you the name of the directory, the amount of space the files in that directory take up, and the number of files contained in the directory.

The Disk section reports the name of the disk, the capacity of the disk, and the number of bytes not currently in use. It also displays the number of files and directories on the disk.

Using the Task Manager

DOS versions 5 and later include an important new feature not found in any earlier versions of DOS: the Task Manager. After activating the Task Manager you can rapidly switch between different programs without having to first terminate one program to execute the next. Instead, the Task Manager simply pauses one program while you run another. For example, without the Task Manager, if you are using your

Task is essentially another word for program.

word processor, but want to do a quick calculation using your spreadsheet program, you need to terminate the word processor and then execute the spreadsheet. However, with the Task Manager, you can simply switch between the two programs without having to end either. As you can imagine, this is quite an increase in efficiency.

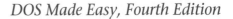

NOTE: You may have heard about multitasking operating systems like OS/2 or Windows. In these operating systems, it is possible to actually run more than one program simultaneously. However, this is not the case with DOS—even using the Task Manager. DOS suspends execution of one program while you run another. Although DOS does not actually concurrently execute programs, the Task Manager still makes it much easier for you to switch between your application programs.

To activate the Task Manager, activate the menu bar and choose Options. Next, select Enable Task Swapper. The Swapper is the part of the Task Manager that allows you to switch between programs. After doing so, your screen will look like the one shown in Figure 20-7.

```
╔══════════════════════════ MS-DOS Shell ══════════════════════════╗
  File   Options   View   Tree   Help
 ┌─────┐
 │C:\DOS│
 └─────┘
 ┌─┐A  ┌─┐B  ███C  ┌─┐D  ┌─┐E  ┌─┐F

┌──────── Directory Tree ────────┐  ┌────────── C:\DOS\*.* ──────────┐
 ┌─┐ C:\                    ↑        DOSKEY   .COM     5,883  01-28-93 ↑
 │─┌┐ BIN                            DOSSHELL .COM     4,620  01-28-93
 │ ┌┐ BORLANDC                       DOSSHELL .EXE   236,378  01-28-93
 │ ┌┐ DOS                            DOSSHELL .GRB     4,421  01-28-93
 │ ┌┐ FILETRAN                       DOSSHELL .HLP   161,323  01-28-93
 │ ┌┐ MTN_TAPE                       DOSSHELL .INI    17,025  02-03-93
 │ ┌┐ SCRSAV                         DOSSHELL .VID     9,462  01-28-93
 │ ┌┐ SD                             DOSSWAP  .EXE    18,756  01-28-93
 │ ┌┐ SPRDSHT                        DRIVER   .SYS     5,406  01-28-93
 │ ┌┐ TC                             EDIT     .COM       413  01-28-93
 │ ┌┐ WINDOWS                        EDIT     .HLP    17,898  01-28-93
 │                                   EDLIN    .EXE    12,642  04-09-91
 │                                   EGA      .CPI    58,870  01-28-93
 │                          ↓        EGA      .SYS     4,885  01-28-93 ↓

┌──────────── Main ──────────────┐  ┌───────── Active Task List ─────┐
   Command Prompt           ↑                                        ↑
   Editor
   MS-DOS QBasic
   Disk Utilities



                            ↓                                        ↓
 F10=Actions   Shift+F9=Command Prompt                          2:40p
```

The Shell after activating the Task Manager

Figure 20-7.

Notice that a new window has been added. The new window, although blank now, is used to hold a list of active tasks in the system. We will come back to it in a moment.

Starting a Task

After the Swapper is activated, to start a task, simply execute a program in the normal way. For example, highlight the file LABEL.EXE in the file list window and execute it. This is the DOS command that gives a disk a label. Your screen will clear, and you will see the current disk label, the serial number and the following prompt:

```
Volume label (11 characters, ENTER for none)?
```

Don't enter anything at this prompt. The only reason that we are using LABEL.EXE is that it will continue to execute in the computer until it receives a response. This gives us a way to illustrate the Task Manager. (Had we used something like VER, it would have terminated before you would have had time to explore the Task Manager.)

As you can see, starting a task is just the same as starting a program. The only difference is how DOS treats it.

Switching Between Tasks

There are now two active tasks in your computer: LABEL.EXE and the Shell. To switch between tasks, press and hold the [Alt] key and then press [Tab]. (Continue to press the [Alt] key.) The screen will clear and you will see the following line:

```
MS-DOS Shell
```

While still holding down the [Alt] key, press the [Tab] key a second time. This time the line changes to "LABEL.EXE." Press the [Tab] key again, and "MS-DOS Shell" is displayed. Each time you press the [Alt]-[Tab] combination, the Task Switcher displays the next task in the list of active tasks. At this point the "MS-DOS SHELL" task should be displayed. (If it isn't, press [Tab] again.) Now, to select a task, simply stop pressing the [Alt] key. This will cause the Shell to return to the screen.

When the Shell returns, you will see that LABEL.EXE is in the Active Task List window. When you are in the Shell, you can activate a task listed in the Active Task List window in just the same way that you execute a program from the file list window. First highlight it and press ⌈Enter⌉, or double-click on it using the mouse. Try this now by activating LABEL.EXE again. As you will see, the screen clears and LABEL's prompt is once again displayed on the screen.

Let's add another task. To do this, press ⌈Alt⌉-⌈Tab⌉ once to return to the Shell. This time, execute CHKDSK.EXE. However, before it has a chance to terminate, press ⌈Alt⌉-⌈Tab⌉ again. This time you will find that there are three tasks that you can switch between by pressing ⌈Alt⌉-⌈Tab⌉. Try pressing ⌈Tab⌉ a few times now. When you are ready, select the SHELL. Now, you will find two items listed in the Active Task List window: LABEL.EXE and CHKDSK.EXE. This time, select CHKDSK.EXE. As you will see, the CHKDSK command resumes execution at the point at which you left it.

When CHKDSK finishes, the Shell is resumed, and CHKDSK.EXE is no longer shown in the Active Task List window because it has terminated.

There are several other ways you can switch between tasks, which make task switching easier. You can return directly to the Shell without having to select it from the list of tasks by pressing ⌈Ctrl⌉-⌈Esc⌉. Pressing ⌈Alt⌉-⌈Esc⌉ activates the next application task. Pressing ⌈Shift⌉-⌈Alt⌉-⌈Esc⌉ activates the previous application task. Pressing ⌈Shift⌉-⌈Alt⌉-⌈Tab⌉ moves through the tasks in a backwards direction. When you are in the Shell, pressing ⌈Alt⌉-⌈Tab⌉ activates the previous task. Finally, you can activate several applications at the same time without leaving the Shell by holding down the ⌈Shift⌉ key when you start each program. You will simply see their names added to the Active Task List window.

REMEMBER: Once the Task Manager is active, to start a task, simply run a program in the normal manner. To switch between tasks, press ⌈Alt⌉-⌈Tab⌉. To return directly to the Shell, press ⌈Ctrl⌉-⌈Esc⌉.

Terminating a Task

By far, the best way to terminate a task is to let it end normally. This is what happened to CHKDSK in the preceding example. Since LABEL.EXE is still active in the system, let's terminate it, too. First, activate it by pressing  or selecting it in the Active Task List. Now, press (Enter) and then **N** (if necessary). This leaves the volume label unchanged. You will then see the keypress prompt. Press another key, and the Shell will be reactivated and LABEL.EXE will no longer be in the Active Task List. If you press (Alt)-(Tab) now, DOS will simply beep at you since there are no other tasks to switch to.

Once in a while, for various reasons, a program might not be able to terminate normally. If this happens, you can still remove that program from the computer by first highlighting it in the Active Task List window and then using the Delete option in the File menu.

Summary

In this chapter you learned about several advanced File Manager features, including:

✦ Creating subdirectories

✦ Removing a directory

✦ Replacing files

✦ Working with groups of files

✦ Changing file attributes

✦ Associating files

✦ Eliminating the confirmation windows

✦ Using the Task Manager

The next chapter wraps up the Shell with a discussion of the Program Manager.

CHAPTER

21

USING THE PROGRAM MANAGER AND MISCELLANEOUS TOPICS

This is the last chapter of the book. You have come a long way in your study of DOS. When you complete this chapter, you can definitely call yourself a knowledgeable DOS user!

In this chapter you will learn how to run programs that require additional information. You will also learn to add programs and groups to the Program

Manager. The Program Manager primarily exists to help you manage your application programs and to make it easier to run your most commonly used programs.

Executing Programs Using the Run Option

Up to now, when you have run a program from the Shell you have simply selected it from the file list window. While this is perfectly fine for some programs, many programs take certain options, and others may require that additional information be specified in order to run properly. As you know from your experience using the command prompt, each piece of extra information used by a program is called a *parameter*. One way to execute a program that uses parameters is to use the Run option in the File menu. The Run option essentially lets you execute a program in the same way as you do when using the command prompt.

The Run option allows you to run programs as you do from the command prompt.

Let's begin with an example. First, make sure that either the Directory tree or file list window is active. Now, activate the menu bar and select the File menu. (There is no need to highlight a file in the file list window.) Next, select the Run option. You will see a dialog box like the one shown in Figure 21-1. When using the Run option, you must enter the name of the command you want to execute in the Command Line input box. For example, to execute the CHKDSK command, enter **CHKDSK** in the box and press Enter. You do not need to use the .EXE extension. It won't hurt to use the extension, but it is completely unnecessary. Try this now. As you can see, the CHKDSK command is executed. Notice also that when CHKDSK terminates, you see this prompt:

```
Press any key to return to MS-DOS Shell
```

When you run a command using Run, the Shell will not return after the command terminates until you press a key. The advantage to this is

Run dialog box
Figure 21-1.

```
┌──────────────────────────[ Run ]──────────────────────────┐
│                                                            │
│  Command Line . .  ┌─────────────────────────────────────┐│
│                    │_                                    ││
│                    └─────────────────────────────────────┘│
│                                                            │
│         (    OK   )            (   Cancel  )               │
│                                                            │
└────────────────────────────────────────────────────────────┘
```

that it gives you time to read any information displayed by the program on the screen.

Although the preceding example is a valid use of Run, there is no advantage over simply selecting CHKDSK in the file list window. What makes the Run option important is that it also allows parameters to be applied to a program. To see how, if you have a fixed disk, put a formatted diskette in drive A. If you are running DOS from a floppy, put a formatted diskette in drive B. Now, reactivate the Run option and enter this command if you have a fixed disk:

CHKDSK A:

Enter this command if you use floppies:

CHKDSK B:

As you can see, CHKDSK A: causes the A drive to be tested and CHKDSK B: causes the B drive to be checked. This is just the way that the command operates when using the command prompt. In addition to any parameters required by a program, you can also use Run to supply any necessary options required by a command.

TIP: To execute a program that does not require parameters or options, just execute it from the file list window. If parameters or options are required, use the Run option.

Running a Series of Commands

Using the Run option, it is possible to string together several programs and/or DOS commands on one single command line. To do this, simply separate each command from the next using a semicolon. For example, activate the File menu and select Run. At the Command Line, enter the following:

CHKDSK ; MEM ; VER

Make sure that each semicolon has at least one space on each side of it. Now, press (Enter). As you will see, first the CHKDSK command is

21

executed, then the MEM command. Finally, the VER command executes.

When executing multiple commands using Run, remember two things. First, no command line may exceed 255 characters. Second, each semicolon must have at least one space on each side.

Using the Program Manager

The final major part of the Shell that we will explore is the Program Manager. As you know, the Program Manager is the window on the bottom of your screen that is titled Main. In this and the next few sections, you will learn how to add programs and groups to the Program Manager, how to execute programs using the Program Manager, and how to prompt for parameters. You will also learn about several options that control the way programs are executed.

Highlight the Main window of the Program Manager at this time.

Groups Versus Subgroups

The Program Manager uses a main group/subgroup approach to its organization. A group may contain both programs and subgroups. For example, by default, the Main group contains one subgroup called Disk Utilities and three programs: the Command Prompt, the Editor, and MS-DOS QBasic. In a way, groups and subgroups are similar in concept to directories and subdirectories.

In the Program Manager, any group can have a subgroup. Except where the distinction is important, the term "group" will apply to both groups and subgroups.

The theory behind the main group/subgroup method is that you can put related programs into their own group. For example, you might create a word processing group and put the word processor, spelling checker, and thesaurus programs in that group. The Program Manager lets you manage and structure your programs by allowing you to keep related programs in separate groups.

NOTE: Although conceptually similar, don't confuse subgroups with subdirectories. The subgroup in which a program appears in the Program Manager window has nothing whatsoever to do with what directory the program is in on the disk.

Adding a Program to the Main Group

If you haven't yet done so, activate the Program Manager and make sure that the Main group window is displayed.

You can add a program to a group so that you can execute it from the Program Manager window instead of having to use the File Manager. Not only can this be more convenient, saving you time and keystrokes, but it can also help ensure that the program is started correctly. Further, you can also add any DOS command, whether internal or external, to a group.

Since all of DOS's external commands are programs, let's add CHKDSK to the Main group. Activate the menu bar and select the File option. You will see a menu that has the following entries:

21

New
Open
Copy
Delete
Properties
Reorder
Run
Exit

NOTE: When the Program Manager is active, the contents of both the menu bar and the File option, specifically, are different from when the File Manager is in use. Further, there is no Tree option.

Select the New option. You will see the dialog box shown in Figure 21-2. Since you can add either a program or a subgroup to a group, this dialog box allows you to select which type of item you are adding. Since we are adding a program, select Program Item and press (Enter). You will see the dialog box shown in Figure 21-3.

Each program has five fields of information associated with it, along with one check box. The first two input boxes must be filled in. The others are optional.

The first piece of information you must enter is the title of the program, which will be displayed in the group window. For CHKDSK, enter this title: **Check the Disk**. Titles can be up to 23 characters long. The second thing you must enter is the command you want to execute. The Commands line is similar to the Command Line input box of the Run option. The command line may be up to 255 characters long. Therefore, to execute CHKDSK, enter **CHKDSK** now. Although we will come back to the other options in the dialog box later, notice that the check box labeled "Pause after exit" is checked by default. You will see the effect of this shortly. Now, either press (Enter) or select the OK command button. If you inspect the Main group, you will see that the "Check the Disk" title is present.

To verify that you did everything correctly, execute Check the Disk by highlighting it and pressing (Enter), or by double-clicking on it. As you will see, the screen will clear, and the disk is checked. After the CHKDSK command terminates, you will again see the prompt to press a key to return to the Shell. Because the Pause after exit option was turned on in the Add Program dialog box, this message is displayed.

New Program
Object dialog
box
Figure 21-2.

```
┌─────────────────[ New Program Object ]─────────────────┐
│  ┌ New ───────────────────────┐                        │
│  │  ○  Program Group          │     (━━━━ OK ━━━━)      │
│  │                            │                        │
│  │  ◉  Program Item           │     ( Cancel )         │
│  └────────────────────────────┘                        │
└────────────────────────────────────────────────────────┘
```

```
┌─────────────────────────────────────────────────────────┐
│                      Add Program                          │
├─────────────────────────────────────────────────────────┤
│  Program Title . . . . [_                              ] │
│                                                           │
│  Commands  . . . . . . [                               ] │
│                                                           │
│  Startup Directory . . [                               ] │
│                                                           │
│  Application Shortcut Key  [                        ]    │
│                                                           │
│  [X] Pause after exit      Password . .  [          ]   │
│       ( OK )    ( Cancel )    ( Help )   ( Advanced... ) │
└─────────────────────────────────────────────────────────┘
```

Add Program
dialog box
Figure 21-3.

REMEMBER: You can quickly tell whether an entry in a group is a program or a group by looking at the icon associated with it. Program icons look like blank folders and group icons look like folders that contain other folders.

Program Properties

21

As you saw in the preceding example, when you add a program to a group you must specify certain bits of information. In the language of the Shell, these pieces of information are called *properties*. In the preceding example, we only used two properties. However, the Program Manager has several others, and they are the subject of this section.

Instead of adding another program to the Main group just to illustrate the other properties that can be associated with a program, we can simply reuse the CHKDSK entry. After a program has been added to a group it is possible to modify or enhance its properties. This is accomplished using the Properties option in the File menu. We will make use of this option to explore the other properties supported by the Program Manager.

To view and/or change the properties associated with a program, first highlight the desired program in the Program Manager. Next, select the Properties option in the File menu. You will see a dialog box that is virtually identical to the Add Program box. For the example at hand, first highlight Check the Disk, and then select the Properties option in the File menu. You will see that the first two input boxes contain the information you entered when you added CHKDSK to the Main group. Let's explore the other properties in this box now.

The Startup Directory input box lets you specify a disk and/or directory that you want to switch to before the command you entered in the Commands box begins execution. This is useful when a program exists in one place and its data files in another. For example, your word processing program might be on the C drive, but you keep your files on the disk in drive A. By specifying **A:** in the Startup Directory input box, you will cause your word processor to use that disk and directory for your files. You may enter up to 63 characters in this field. Since there is no need to switch directories at this time, leave this field blank.

The Application Shortcut Key lets you specify one special key combination that, when pressed, causes the Task Switcher to automatically switch directly to that program. The key combination must be constructed using either the Alt, Ctrl, or Shift key in conjunction with a letter of the alphabet. For example, Alt-F, Ctrl-G, or Shift-W are all valid Application Shortcut Keys. If you like, you can enter a shortcut key in this box.

If you deactivate the Pause after exit option, once a program terminates (in this case CHKDSK), the Shell is immediately redisplayed. For now, simply leave this box as is.

You can give a program password protection if you like, using the Password input box. The password can be up to 20 characters long. If you add a password, each time you try to run the program, you will first be prompted for the password. Also, any time you try to change that program's properties you will be prompted for the password. If you want to try adding a password, go ahead, but just make sure that you don't forget it! (We will come back to passwords later in this chapter.)

Advanced Properties

Notice that one of the command buttons in the Program Item Properties window is labelled "Advanced." While the properties shown in the Program Item Properties window are the ones that you will use the most often, there are other properties that programs can have. To see them, select the Advanced command button now. You will see a dialog box like that in Figure 21-4.

The first item is the Help Text input box. This box lets you enter some helpful information about the program. This information can be up to

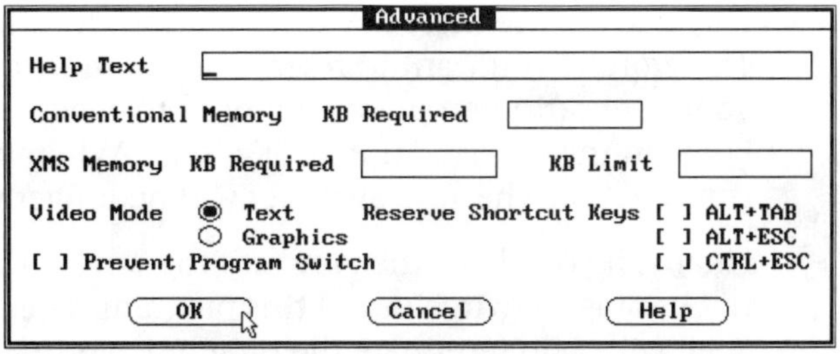

The Advanced
properties
dialog box
Figure 21-4.

255 characters long. As you enter text past the end of the window, the text will automatically be scrolled to the left. (Don't use any carriage returns when you enter the help text.) If you want, you can use this for the help information:

> The CHKDSK program checks the disk drive
> for errors. It also reports the size of
> the disk, the size of memory, and amount
> of each that is free.

When this text is displayed, the help system will automatically format it for you.

The next three input boxes have to do with the memory of your computer, and they require technical knowledge that is beyond the scope of this book. Unless your situation is very unusual, the defaults provided by DOS for these properties are just fine.

If you will be using the Task Manager, then you may need to change the setting of the Video Mode option. By default, the Program Manager assumes text mode, and this is the mode that you will want to use with CHKDSK. However, if the program uses graphics, change this option to Graphics. Keep in mind that once the Shell returns, the video mode is reset. Therefore, you define the video mode for *each program* you add to a group. (That is, this option does not permanently affect your computer's display mode. It is in effect only for the time that a program is executing.)

As you know, the Task Switcher uses the [Alt]-[Tab] key to switch between tasks, [Ctrl]-[Esc] to return directly to the Shell, and [Alt]-[Esc] to switch to the next program in the task list. However, some application programs may need to use these key combinations for their own purposes. Therefore, if you want to reserve one or more of these keys for use by your application program, you need to check the appropriate box or boxes in the Reserve Shortcut Keys list. When you reserve a key combination, the Task Switcher will no longer respond to it.

Finally, if you check the Prevent Program Switch, the Task Switcher will not be able to switch out of this program. The only way to return to the Shell will be to terminate the program. Normally, you will not want to use this option unless the instructions to one of your application programs tell you to do so.

TIP: When adding a program to a group, first try using a few advanced properties as necessary. Then, add properties only as needed. This way you don't unnecessarily impact your system.

Specifying Program Parameters Using the Program Manager

Earlier in this chapter, you learned how to use the Run command in the File Manager's File menu to specify one or more parameters when executing a program. In this section, you will see how to specify various parameters and options when running a program using the Program Manager.

Let's begin with an example. Highlight the Check the Disk entry and activate the File menu. Next, select the Properties option. Now, change the Commands input box so that it contains the following (use B: if you are running DOS from a floppy):

CHKDSK A:

Once you have made the change, press Enter or select the OK command button. Now, try selecting Check the Disk. As you will see, it checks the disk in drive A.

In this case, the Program Manager used the A: drive specifier to tell CHKDSK which disk to test, thus allowing it to check a drive other than the default. You could, in theory, create several slightly different

CHKDSK commands, each testing one of the drives in your system (that is, one for drive A, one for drive B, and so on). However, such an approach is quite inefficient and unnecessary.

A better solution to the preceding problem is to use a replaceable parameter in much the same way you did when working with batch files in the command prompt. The replaceable parameter will act as a place holder for the actual drive to be checked. To see how to add a replaceable parameter to a program in the Program Manager, let's continue with the previous example. First, highlight the Check the Disk entry. Next, activate the Properties option in the File menu. Finally, change the Commands line so that the A: is replaced by %1. Your Commands input box should contain this:

CHKDSK %1

Once you have made the change, press Enter. Now, you will see a new dialog box called Program Item Properties, as shown in Figure 21-5. This box is displayed because the %1 replaceable parameter, in this context, tells the Program Manager that you want to be prompted for additional information needed by the program when it is executed. This dialog box lets you specify how you want the dialog box associated with CHKDSK to appear.

The title of the dialog box that will prompt for the %1 may be entered in the Window Title input box. The title may not be more than 23 characters long. If you wish instructions to appear above the prompt, enter those instructions in the Program Information input box. This field may not exceed 180 characters. You can define a prompting message in the Prompt Message input box. This message may not

21

Program Item
Properties
dialog box
Figure 21-5.

```
┌────────────────────────────────────────────────────────────┐
│              ▐ Program Item Properties ▌                    │
├────────────────────────────────────────────────────────────┤
│                                                             │
│   Fill in information for % 1    prompt dialog.             │
│                                                             │
│   Window Title  . . . .   [▁_____]     │
│                                                             │
│   Program Information .   [_____]     │
│                                                             │
│   Prompt Message  . . .   [_____]     │
│                                                             │
│     Default Parameters . .    [_____]     │
│                                                             │
│         ( ─── OK ─── )      ( Cancel )      ( Help )        │
│                                                             │
└────────────────────────────────────────────────────────────┘
```

exceed 18 characters and will be displayed to the left of the input box. Finally, if you want a parameter that will be displayed as the default selection (which the user may, of course, override), specify it in the Default Parameters input box.

To see an example, enter

Which Drive?

in the Window Title box. Enter

Choose the drive you want to test.

for Program Information and

Enter Drive:

in the Prompt Message input box. Finally, enter

C:

for Default Parameters. Your dialog box should look like the one shown in Figure 21-6. Once you have entered the information correctly, press Enter (or select OK).

Now, try the Check the Disk program again. This time you will see the dialog box shown in Figure 21-7. Try entering **A:** to respond to the prompt. As you will see, this causes the disk in drive A to be tested. Let's see why.

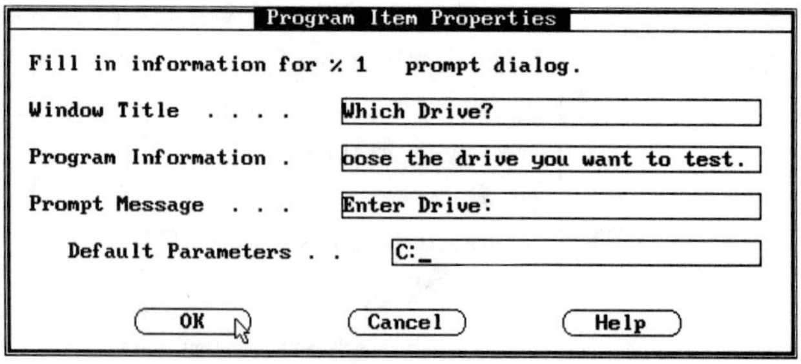

```
┌──────────────── Program Item Properties ─────────────────┐
│                                                          │
│  Fill in information for % 1   prompt dialog.            │
│                                                          │
│  Window Title  . . . .   │Which Drive?              │    │
│                                                          │
│  Program Information .   │oose the drive you want to test.│
│                                                          │
│  Prompt Message  . . .   │Enter Drive:              │    │
│                                                          │
│      Default Parameters . .  │C:_                   │    │
│                                                          │
│          ( OK )         ( Cancel )      ( Help )         │
└──────────────────────────────────────────────────────────┘
```

Information about %1
Figure 21-6.

Check the Disk
dialog box
Figure 21-7.

```
┌─────────────────────────────────────────────────────────┐
│                      ▌Which Drive?▐                       │
│   Choose the drive you want to test.                      │
│                                                           │
│   Enter Drive:      ▌C:▏                        │        │
│        ╭──────────╮      ╭──────────╮      ╭──────────╮    │
│        │    OK    │      │  Cancel  │      │   Help   │    │
│        ╰──────────╯      ╰──────────╯      ╰──────────╯    │
└─────────────────────────────────────────────────────────┘
```

When you entered **A:** in response the prompt, you caused A: to be automatically substituted for the %1. If you had simply pressed [Enter], then C:, the default, would have been substituted for the %1. The purpose of the %1 is similar to its use in a batch file. It acts as a place holder in the Commands line until you fill in the actual parameter when the program is run. You might want to try this command again at this time, seeing how it responds to different input.

REMEMBER: The %1 is a place holder that will be substituted by the information that you enter when you run the program.

21

Specifying Multiple Parameters

As is the case in batch files, you can specify more than one replaceable parameter when using the Program Manager's Run option. As you can probably guess, these parameters are called %1 through %9. Using these parameters, you can specify up to nine parameters to any program you execute using the Program Manager. In this section you will see how to use multiple replaceable parameters.

Again, let's begin with an example by adding another command to the Main group. First, activate the menu bar, select File, and then select New. Since we will be adding a program, select the Program Item. Now, in the Add Program dialog box, enter

        Copy Disk

into the Title box, and enter

DISKCOPY %1 %2

into the Commands box. Remember, DISKCOPY is the DOS command that copies two diskettes. Although this feature is already part of the Disk Utilities group, it is used here for illustration. (It will also give you insight into how the default options in the Main group were created.) Next, press Enter or select the OK command button.

You will be prompted to fill in information relating to the %1 replaceable parameter. For Window Title enter

Copy Disk

In the Program Information window, enter

This program copies a disk.

In the Prompt message, enter

Source drive

Don't enter anything in the Default Parameters box. Now, press Enter.

Next, you will see the dialog box that lets you define information about %2. For the first two input boxes use the same text as you did for the %1 dialog box. However, for Prompt Message enter the following:

Target drive

Again, leave the Default Parameters box blank, and press Enter.

Before trying the Copy Disk program, have both your work disk and a blank diskette ready. Now, execute the Copy Disk command. As you will see, you will first be prompted for the source drive. Enter **A:**. Put your work disk in drive A and (if you have two floppy drives) the blank disk in drive B. (If you have only one floppy, you will need to swap diskettes.) Next, you will be prompted for the target drive. Enter **B:**. As you can guess, the **A:** you enter for the source drive replaces %1, and the **B:** you enter for the target drive replaces %2. After you have completed the prompts, the diskette in drive A is copied to the one in drive B.

As with batch files, the replaceable parameters are replaced in the order in which you are prompted for information. Therefore, if you have an application program called MYAPP that takes four parameters, you will specify a Commands line that looks like this:

    MYAPP %1 %2 %3 %4

You will be prompted for four pieces of information when the program is run.

As a final example, one very common use for a replaceable parameter is as a place holder for a file name. For example, your word processor might require that the name of the file that you will be editing be specified when the program is executed. Therefore, if your word processor is called WDPRC, then the following is the Commands line that you should specify when adding this program to a group:

    WDPRC %1

Then, when you run the word processor, you will be prompted for the name of the file you want to edit.

21

TIP: Using replaceable parameters is a good way to generalize your program entries.

Creating a Subgroup

You will probably want to add only a few programs to the Main group. For example, if your most common task is using a spreadsheet, you will want to be able to start that spreadsheet from the Main group in order to save yourself the extra step of first selecting a subgroup before selecting the program. However, in general, you will not want to add programs to the Main group, but rather to subgroups, so that you can keep your programs organized.

To create a subgroup, first activate the Main group window, activate the File menu, and select New. Now, when the New Program Object dialog box is displayed, select Program Group. You will see the Add Group dialog box, as shown in Figure 21-8. As the dialog box suggests, the only thing that you must do is give the group a title. The title can be up to 23 characters long. For now, use "My Group." If you want, you can also enter help information about the group and a password. The help text can be up to 255 characters long, and the password can be up to 20 characters long.

Once you are done, press ⌷Enter⌷ or select the OK button. Now, you will see that My Group has been added to the Main window. Select My Group at this time. Notice that the first, and only, entry is Main. The Shell automatically makes Main an entry in any subgroup's list of items. In general, whenever you create a subgroup, the parent group's name will always be the first entry in the subgroup's menu.

Adding a Program to a Subgroup

Adding a program to a subgroup is exactly like adding a program to the Main group. First, select the subgroup that you want to add the program to, and then activate the File menu. From this menu select New to add the program.

For illustration, let's add the MEM command to the My Group group. This is an external command, so it must be on the currently logged-in disk.

If you haven't done so, select My Group at this time. Next, activate the menu bar, select the File menu, and activate the New entry. Since we are adding a program, select Program Item from the New Program Object. The Add Program dialog box will be shown. In the Title input box enter **Report System Memory**. For the Commands line, use

Add Group
dialog box
Figure 21-8.

```
┌─────────────────────[ Add Group ]──────────────────┐
│                                                     │
│  Required                                           │
│                                                     │
│    Title . . . .    ┌─────────────────────────┐     │
│                     └─────────────────────────┘     │
│  Optional                                           │
│                                                     │
│    Help Text . .    ┌─────────────────────────┐     │
│                     └─────────────────────────┘     │
│    Password   . .   ┌───────────────────┐           │
│                     └───────────────────┘           │
│                                                     │
│    ( OK )         ( Cancel )      ( Help )           │
│                                                     │
└─────────────────────────────────────────────────────┘
```

MEM

Leave the rest of the input boxes blank, and either press ⌜Enter⌟ or select the OK command button. You will see that a new program entry is in your My Group subgroup. You might want to try executing it now, just to prove that it works.

Copying Programs Between Groups

You can copy a program's entry from one group to another using the Copy command in the File menu. The general method to accomplish this is as follows: First, highlight the program that you want to copy inside its own group and then select the Copy option. Next, select the group that you want to copy the program into. Finally, press ⌜F2⌟ to actually copy the program entry.

Let's try this by copying CHKDSK from the Main group into My Group. First, activate the Main group and highlight the Check the Disk entry. Activate the File option and select Copy. Next, select My Group and press ⌜F2⌟. As you can see, the information for the CHKDSK command has been copied into the My Group group.

21

The Copy operation does not erase the original entry for the program. To perform a move operation, you must first perform a copy followed by a delete, as described in the next section.

Deleting a Program from a Group

To delete a program from a group, first highlight the program you want to remove and then activate the File option. Next, select the Delete option. You will then see a confirmation window that gives you one last chance to change your mind before the program is deleted.

 TIP: Removing a program's entry from a group does not remove it from the disk. It simply removes it from the Program Manager.

To try removing a program, let's remove the copy of the CHKDSK program from the Main group. First, activate the Main group and highlight the Check the Disk entry. Next, activate the File option and choose Delete. When the safety check window appears, choose to delete the program.

Deleting a Group

You can remove a group using the Delete option in the File menu. First, highlight the name of the group and then activate the Delete option. The group must be empty. Also, you cannot delete the Main group.

Reordering Programs Within a Group

You can change the order of items in a group using the Reorder command in the File window. The basic procedure is as follows: First, activate the group you want to reorder and then highlight the item whose position you want to change. Next, activate the File option and select the Reorder option. Now, move the highlight to the position where you want the item to be put and press ⌷Enter⌷, or double-click using the mouse. The item will be moved, and the list will reflect the new order. You might want to try this feature on your own.

Using a Password

You can restrict access to a program by giving it a password when you enter the program into a group. If you use a password, then only those people who know the password can activate the program from the Shell. (The program can still be executed using the command prompt interface, however.)

The best passwords are composed of randomly selected letters.

You can use any characters you like for a password. Be sure to remember the password because you will also need it to activate the Properties option in the File menu. That is, to alter any properties associated with a program protected by a password—such as removing the password—also requires the use of the password.

You can also control access to an entire group by giving the group a password when you define it. The password will also be needed to modify any properties associated with the group.

CAUTION: The password only controls access to a program if that program is executed from the Shell. Anyone who knows how to use the DOS command prompt interface will still be able to run the program. Therefore, at best, a password is a mild deterrent. It is not real protection. At worst, using a password may tip someone off that a sensitive program is on your computer. Quite frankly, a better approach to security is to lock up the computer when it is not in use.

The Program Manager's Run Option

In the Program Manager's File menu, the Run option performs in the same way as it does in the File menu of the File Manager.

Some More Shell Editing Keys

Before concluding this chapter, a few additional editing keys that relate to the Shell's input boxes will be discussed. To follow along, activate the File Manager, activate the menu bar, select File, and then select the Run option. Although we won't actually be running a program, this input box makes a good place to experiment.

When you enter information into an input box, there are some special keys you can use to make changing or fixing what you have entered easier. These keys are (Home), (End), (◄), (►), (Backspace), and (Del). Let's see how they work.

First, enter this into the Command Line input box:

    this is a test

Now, press the (Home) key. The cursor will move to the beginning of the line. Next, press the (End) key. This time the cursor moves to the end of the line. In general, whenever you press the (Home) key, the cursor moves to the start of an input box. Pressing the (End) key causes the cursor to move to the end of the text.

If you want to change something in the middle of what you have entered, you may use the (◄) or (►) keys to move the cursor to the point you want to change without erasing what is already there. For example, press (End) and then press the (◄) key five times. The cursor will be under the space before the **t** of "test." When you are in the middle of text, you can add characters by simply typing them. Whatever is to the right of what you enter will be moved over, making room for the new characters. To see an example, enter **small** at this time. Now, the input box contains

this is a small test

To delete a character to the left of the cursor, press the (Backspace) key. If you want to delete the character that the cursor is on, use the (Del) key.

You might want to experiment with the input box editing keys for a while. However, when you are through, be sure to exit the Run dialog box by selecting Cancel or by pressing (Esc).

Summary

In this final chapter you learned

✦ How to execute programs using the File Manager's Run option

✦ How to add programs to a group

✦ How to execute programs using the Program Manager

✦ How to use replaceable parameters when using the Shell

✦ How to create a subgroup

✦ How to copy programs between groups

✦ How to reorder a group

✦ About using passwords with programs and groups

✦ About some additional editing keys

This concludes your study of DOS. However, DOS is somewhat like a living animal because it continues to grow and change as the ways in which it is used evolve. The knowledge and understanding that you have gained about DOS will benefit you both now and in the future, because the same basic concepts can be applied to other environments and situations. In fact, you will probably be using DOS on one computer, and another operating system, such as Windows, on another computer, in the near future. You can easily generalize your knowledge of DOS, and you will have no trouble using virtually any type of system.

REMEMBER: While DOS is still fairly new to you now, in just a short while, its operation will be completely second nature.

21

APPENDIX

A

QUICK COMMAND REFERENCE

This appendix contains a short summary of all commonly used DOS commands presented in alphabetical order. (The few not covered here are used mostly by programmers and system integrators.) The purpose of this appendix is to help you quickly learn what a command does or find which command you should use for a certain operation. As such, only the most common forms and options of each command are shown. For a full discussion of each command, please refer to the book proper.

The following notational conventions will be used. Items enclosed between square brackets ([]) are optional. Except where explicitly noted otherwise, the term *path* refers to the full path name, including an optional drive specifier. The term *file-name* may include a drive specifier and/or a path name. Finally, three periods (...) indicate a variable-length list, and two periods (..) indicate a range, such as 1..10.

NOTE: Only those commands that can be executed from a command prompt or from a batch file are contained here. Shell commands, configuration commands, and device drivers are discussed in their appropriate sections inside the book.

APPEND

The external APPEND command is used to define a search path for data files that are in a directory other than the current one. APPEND is executed the first time using one of the following two forms:

>   APPEND *path1*[;*path2;...pathN*]

or

>   APPEND [/X] [/E]

The first form uses APPEND's default method of operation which applies to data files. The second form only applies when APPEND is first installed. (APPEND is an installed command.) The /X option allows DOS to search appended directories when executing a program. (This option must be specified the first time you execute APPEND.) The /E option causes the appended paths to be held in the DOS environment area. APPEND is used to allow access to data files, much as PATH is used to allow access to program files.

You can see the currently appended directories by entering the APPEND command with no arguments. The following form disassociates any appended directories:

```
APPEND ;
```

For example, the following command appends the \WP directory:

```
APPEND \WP
```

ASSIGN

The external ASSIGN command is used to redirect input/output (I/O) operations from one disk drive to another. It takes the general form:

> ASSIGN *drive1=drive2* [*drive3=drive4* ...]

For example, to reverse the assignments of drives A and B, you could use the following command:

```
ASSIGN A=B B=A
```

Now all I/O operations for A will go to B, and all I/O operations for B will be redirected to A.

You reset the drives to their original assignments by entering ASSIGN with no arguments. Remember, do not use ASSIGN with the BACKUP or PRINT commands. Also, ASSIGN may not be available if you are using DOS 6.

ATTRIB

The external ATTRIB command is used to set or examine the file attributes. It takes the general form,

> ATTRIB [+R] [–R] [+A] [–A] [+H] [–H] [+S][–S] [*file-name*] [/S]

where *file-name* is the name of the file(s) that will have its attributes set or examined. Wildcard characters are allowed. +R turns on the read-only attribute, while –R turns it off. The +A turns on the archive attribute, while –A turns it off. +S turns on the system-file attribute; –S turns it off. +H turns on the hidden-file attribute; –H turns it off. If one of these is not present, the current state of the file attributes is displayed. The /S option tells ATTRIB to process files in the current directory and any subdirectories.

A

For example, the following command turns on the read-only attribute for all .EXE files in the current directory:

```
ATTRIB +r *.EXE
```

BACKUP

The external BACKUP command is used primarily to back up the contents of a fixed disk by copying it to several floppy diskettes. Used in this way, it takes the general form:

BACKUP *source-drive[file-name] target-drive* [/A] [/D:*date*]
[/F] [/L] [/M] [/S] [/T:*time*] [/F:*size*]

The *file-name* may include wildcard characters.

The meaning of each BACKUP option is shown in the following table:

Option	Meaning
/A	Add files to existing target diskettes
/D:*date*	Copy only those files with dates the same as or later than *date*
/F:*size*	Specify capacity of target disk
/L	Create and maintain a log file
/M	Copy only those files that have been modified since the last backup
/S	Process all subdirectories
/T:*time*	Copy only those files with times equal to or later than *time* on the specified date

The /F option is used to specify the capacity of the target disk when you want it to be something other than its normal capacity. See Chapter 16 for a full description.

For example, if executed from the root directory of drive C, the following command backs up the entire fixed disk:

```
BACKUP C:*.*  A: /S
```

NOTE: BACKUP applies only to versions of DOS prior to 6. For backing up files using DOS 6, refer to the MSBACKUP command.

BREAK

The internal BREAK command tells DOS how to check for the [Ctrl]-[Break] key combination, which is used to cancel commands. It takes the general form:

BREAK [ON]

or

BREAK [OFF]

Setting BREAK on causes DOS to check more frequently for [Ctrl]-[Break]. BREAK is off by default.

Though setting BREAK to on may seem tempting, it is usually not a good idea because it slows down the execution of all commands and programs.

The following command tells DOS to check more frequently for the [Ctrl]-[Break] key combination:

```
BREAK ON
```

CALL

The CALL batch command is used to execute another batch file from within a batch file. The general form of CALL is

CALL *batch-file*

where *batch-file* is the name of the batch file that you wish to execute.

For example, the following command calls the batch file named COPYALL.BAT:

```
CALL COPYALL
```

CHCP

The internal CHCP command is used with code page switching for extended foreign language and country support. This little-used command is seldom required. Refer to your DOS manual.

CHDIR

The internal CHDIR command (CD) is used to change the current directory. The general form of the command is

CHDIR *path*

where *path* is the path name of the directory you are changing to. For example, the following command makes the \WP directory current:

```
CHDIR \WP
```

CHKDSK

The external CHKDSK command reports the status of the specified drive and repairs certain types of disk errors. It takes the general form:

CHKDSK [*drive-specifier*] [*file-name*] [/F] [/V]

If *drive-specifier* is absent, the current disk is checked. The /F option instructs CHKDSK to fix any errors that it can. The /V option displays all files and their paths. Specifying a *file-name*, which may include wildcard characters, causes CHKDSK to report the number of noncontiguous (nonadjacent) sectors used by the file(s).

For example, the following command reports the status of drive A and attempts to fix any errors:

```
CHKDSK A: /F
```

CHOICE

CHOICE is a batch file command that is available in DOS version 6. It is used to allow the user to select between two or more options. CHOICE is too complex to synopsize here. Refer to Chapter 8 for details.

CLS

The internal CLS command clears the screen of the computer's display monitor.

COMP

The external COMP command is used to compare two files. It has the general form,

COMP *first-file second-file* [/D] [/A] [/L] [/C] [/N=*num*]

COMP may not be included if you are using DOS version 6. If this is the case, refer to the FC command.

where *first-file* and *second-file* are file names that may contain wildcard characters.

For example, the following command compares the contents of the file ACCOUNTS.DAT on drive A to the file by the same name on drive B:

```
COMP A:ACCOUNTS.DAT B:ACCOUNTS.DAT
```

By default, the output of COMP is displayed in hexadecimal. To display in decimal, use the /D option. To display the results as characters, use the /A option. To display line numbers of mismatches, use /L. To have COMP ignore case differences, use /C. Using the /N=*num* option, you can have COMP compare only the first *num* lines in the file.

COPY

The internal COPY command is used to copy the contents of one file into another. It takes the general form,

COPY *source destination* [/V]

where *source* is the name of the file to be copied into *destination*. Both file names may use wildcard characters. The /V option causes COPY to

A

automatically verify that the information was copied correctly into the destination file. The /V option is not available in the Shell version of COPY.

For example, the following command copies all files that end with the extension EXE to the C drive:

```
COPY *.EXE C:
```

CTTY

The internal CTTY command is used to switch console control to a different device, such as a remote terminal. It takes the general form,

CTTY *device-name*

where *device-name* must be one of DOS's standard device names. Do not try this command unless there is actually another device attached to your computer that can control it.

DATE

The internal DATE command is used to set the date of the system. It takes the general form,

DATE [*date*]

where *date* is the current date. You must use the proper date convention for the country you live in. For the United States, it is mm-dd-yy. If you do not specify *date* on the command line, DATE reports what it thinks is the current date and waits for you to either enter the correct date or press Enter, indicating that you accept the date reported.

For example, the following command sets the date to June 26, 1993:

```
DATE 6-26-93
```

DBLSPACE

The external DBLSPACE command increases the effective storage capacity of your fixed disk by using data compression. (This command is available only with DOS version 6.) Refer to Chapter 17 for details.

CAUTION: Use DBLSPACE only after you are sure you understand its consequences. Once you have compressed your disk, it cannot be decompressed.

DEBUG

The external DEBUG command is used by programmers to help find problems in programs.

DEFRAG

The external DEFRAG command rearranges the files on your disk to eliminate fragmentation. Removing fragmentation causes access to your files to be faster and, thus, increases the overall effective speed of your applications. DEFRAG is available with DOS version 6. Because DEFRAG is a window-based, menu-driven command, refer to Chapter 16 for details.

DEL

The internal DEL command erases files from a disk. It takes the general form,

DEL *file-name* [/P]

where *file-name* is the name of the file to be erased. You can use wildcard characters in the file name to erase groups of files. ERASE is another name for DEL.

If you specify the /P option, DEL will ask for your OK before erasing a file.

For example, the following command erases all files that begin with INV from the disk in drive B.

```
DEL B:INV*.*
```

DELTREE

The external DELTREE command deletes the specified directory tree and any files in that directory tree. The specified directory and any of its subdirectories need not be empty. The general form of DELTREE is shown here,

DELTREE [/Y] *directory*

where *directory* is the top-level directory of the tree to be deleted.

By specifying the /Y option, you prevent DELTREE from prompting you before deleting the directory.

DELTREE is only available with DOS version 6.

DIR

The internal DIR command is used to list a disk's directory. It has the general form:

DIR [*file-name*] [/P] [/W] [/A:*attr*] [/O:*order*] [/S] [/B] [/L]

If a file name is present, only those files that match the file name will be displayed. Otherwise, the entire directory is listed. Wildcard characters are allowed in the file name. The /P option pauses the display every 23 lines, while the /W option causes the directory to be displayed in five columns across the screen. The /A option specifies what types of files are displayed. The *attr* codes are shown in the following table. (You may use any combination of these attributes.)

Attribute	Files Listed
a	Files with archive attribute on
–a	Files with archive attribute off
d	Directories only
–d	Files only
h	Hidden
–h	Non-hidden
r	Read-only files only
–r	Non-read-only files
s	System
–s	Non-system

The value of *order* determines how the /O command sorts the directory. The values of *order* are shown here:

Order	Sort By
d	Date and time
–d	Reverse order by date and time
e	Extension
–e	Reverse order by extension
g	Directories before files
–g	Directories after files
n	Name
–n	Reverse order by name
s	Size
–s	Reverse order by size

A

NOTE: For DOS version 6, you can also specify /O:C to display the files by order of compression ratio, if applicable to your drive.

To list all files that match *file-name* in all subdirectories, use the /S option. To list file names only, specify /B. To display output in lowercase, use /L.

For example, the following command lists only those files with the extension .BAT in lowercase:

```
DIR *.BAT /L
```

DISKCOMP

The external DISKCOMP command is used to compare two diskettes for equality. Its most common form is

DISKCOMP *first-drive second-drive*

where *first-drive* and *second-drive* are drive specifiers. For example, the following command compares the diskette in drive A with the one in drive B:

```
DISKCOMP A: B:
```

DISKCOPY

The external DISKCOPY command is used to make a copy of a diskette. Its most common form is

DISKCOPY *source destination* [/V]

where *source* and *destination* are drive specifiers. DISKCOPY cannot be used to copy the fixed disk.

To have DISKCOPY verify that the copy was made correctly, use the /V option.

For example, the following command copies the diskette in drive A to the one in drive B:

```
DISKCOPY A: B:
```

DOSKEY

The external DOSKEY command gives you greater control over the way the command-line interface works. Refer to Chapter 11 for details.

DOSSHELL

The external DOSSHELL command executes the Shell or restarts the Shell, after you leave the Shell by pressing [Alt]-[F4]. (If you leave the Shell by pressing [Shift]-[F9], use EXIT to reactivate the Shell.)

ECHO

The ECHO batch command is used to write messages to the screen and turn on or off the echoing of other batch commands. It takes this general form:

ECHO [ON] [OFF] [*message*]

For example, the following command prints the message "Backing up all files" to the screen:

```
ECHO Backing up all files
```

EDIT

The external EDIT command is the DOS screen editor. (EDIT is supplied only with DOS versions 5 and later.) See Chapter 7 for details.

EDLIN

The external EDLIN command is the old, outmoded DOS line editor.

A

ERASE

The internal ERASE command erases files from a disk. It takes the general form,

ERASE *file-name* [/P]

where *file-name* is the name of the file to be erased. You can use wildcard characters in the file name to erase groups of files. DEL is another name for ERASE.

If you specify the /P option, ERASE will ask for your OK before erasing a file.

For example, the following command erases all files that have the extension .DAT from the disk in drive B:

```
ERASE B:*.DAT
```

EXIT

This command reactivates the DOS Shell from the command-prompt interface. Use it only if you activate the command prompt by pressing
Shift - F9 .

FASTHELP

The external FASTHELP command displays a synopsis of each DOS command when entered by itself. If you use this form,

FASTHELP *command*

then you will receive a synopsis of the specified command. The summary provided by FASTHELP is not intended to substitute for a good working knowledge of DOS.

FASTHELP is only available with DOS version 6.

FASTOPEN

The external FASTOPEN command remembers the location of files that are in deeply nested subdirectories, thus providing faster access to these files. Its general form is

FASTOPEN *drive-specifier*[=*num*]

where *num* determines the number of files that DOS will remember. This number can be in the range of 10 through 999; the default is 48. FASTOPEN is an installed command; that is, you can only execute it once each time the computer is turned on.

For example, the following command causes DOS to remember the location of 48 files on the fixed disk:

```
FASTOPEN C:
```

FC

FC is an enhanced version of the COMP command. It is used to compare two files. Its simplest form is

FC *file1 file2*

Here, *file1* and *file2* are the files to be compared.

The two principal advantages to FC over COMP are that it can compare files of differing sizes, and it will resynchronize the files after a mismatch. Resynchronization enables FC to provide a more accurate picture of the differences between the files than COMP does.

This command is fairly complex. Refer to Chapter 17 for details of its operation.

FDISK

The external FDISK command is used to partition the fixed disk when it is first prepared for use. Refer to your DOS manual for information.

FIND

The external FIND command searches for occurrences of a string in a list of files. FIND is a filter that sends its output to the standard output device, which may be redirected. The general form of FIND is

FIND [/C] [/N] [/V] [/I] *"string" file-list*

where *string* is the string searched for, and *file-list* is the list of files to search. Notice that the options must precede the string.

The /C option causes FIND to display a count of the occurrences. The /N option causes the relative line number of each match to be displayed. The /V option causes FIND to display those lines that do not contain the string. The /I option causes FIND to ignore case differences.

For example, the following command searches the files REC1.DAT and REC2.DAT for the string "payroll":

```
FIND "payroll" REC1.DAT REC2.DAT
```

FOR

The FOR batch command is used to repeat a series of commands using different arguments. The FOR command takes the general form,

FOR %%*var* IN (*argument list*) DO *command*

where *var* is a single-letter variable that will take on the values of the arguments. The arguments must be separated by spaces. The FOR will repeat *command* as many times as there are arguments. Each time the FOR repeats, *var* will be replaced by an argument moving from left to right.

For example, the following command prints the files TEXT1, TEXT2, and TEXT3:

```
FOR %%F IN (TEXT1 TEXT2 TEXT3) DO PRINT %%F
```

FORMAT

The external FORMAT command is used to prepare a diskette for use. Its most common form is

FORMAT *drive-specifier*

The diskette to be formatted must be in the specified drive. Remember that formatting a disk destroys any and all preexisting data, so use the FORMAT command with care.

For example, the following command formats the disk in drive A:

```
FORMAT A:
```

FORMAT takes several options. Refer to Chapter 9 for details.

GOTO

The internal GOTO batch command is used to direct DOS to execute the commands in a batch file in a nonsequential order. Its general form is

GOTO *label*

where *label* is a label that is defined elsewhere in the batch file. When the GOTO is executed, it causes DOS to go to the specified label and begin executing commands from that point. With GOTO, you can cause execution to jump forward or backward in the file.

For example, the following command causes execution to jump to the label DONE:

```
GOTO DONE
```

GRAPHICS

The external GRAPHICS command allows graphics images to be printed on the printer using the print screen function. Its general form is

GRAPHICS [*printer*] [/R] [/B/] [/LCD]

where the name of *printer* is determined according to the following list:

Printer Type	Name
IBM Personal Graphics Printer	GRAPHICS
Wide-carriage IBM Personal Graphics Printer	GRAPHICSWIDE
IBM Proprinter	GRAPHICS
IBM PC Convertible printer	THERMAL
IBM Color printer with black ribbon	COLOR1
IBM Color printer with red, green, blue, and black ribbon	COLOR4
IBM Color printer with black, cyan, magenta, and yellow ribbon	COLOR8
Any Hewlett-Packard DeskJet printer	DESKJET
Hewlett-Packard LaserJet	LASERJET
Hewlett-Packard LaserJet II	LASERJETII
Hewlett-Packard PaintJet	PAINTJET
Hewlett-Packard QuietJet	QUIETJET
Hewlett-Packard QuietJet Plus	QUIETJETPLUS
Hewlett-Packard PCL printer	HPDEFAULT
Hewlett-Packard Rugged Writer	RUGGEDWRITER
Hewlett-Packard Rugged Wide Writer	RUGGEDWRITERWIDE
Hewlett-Packard ThinkJet	THINKJET

If no printer name is specified, the IBM Personal Graphics Printer is assumed. The Epson series of printers is quite commonly used with microcomputers and can be specified with the GRAPHICS printer name.

By default, white on the screen is printed as black on the printer, and black on the screen is printed as white. The /R option causes black to print as black and white to print as white. The background color of the screen is usually not printed, but if you have a color printer, you can print the background by specifying the /B option. Finally, the /LCD option should be specified for computers using the IBM PC Convertible Liquid Crystal Display.

For example, the following command allows graphics images to be printed using the default GRAPHICS printer:

```
GRAPHICS
```

 # HELP

The HELP command gives you information about other DOS commands. It takes this general form,

HELP [*command*]

where *command* is the command that you want information about. The information provided by HELP serves only as a reminder. It is not a substitute for a thorough understanding of DOS.

For example, this displays information about the COPY command:

```
HELP COPY
```

In DOS version 6, the HELP command activates DOS's window-based, menu-driven help facility. Earlier versions simply display information about the specified command.

If *command* is not specified, then a synopsis of each command is shown. Or, in DOS version 6, the menu-based help system is activated.

 A

IF

The IF batch command takes the general form:

IF *condition command*

If the *condition* evaluates to true, the *command* that follows the condition is executed. Otherwise, DOS skips the rest of the line and moves on to the next line (if there is one) in the batch file. (See Chapter 8.)

JOIN

The external JOIN command joins one drive to the directory of another. Thus, files on the first drive may be accessed from the joined drive as if they were in a subdirectory. JOIN takes the general form:

JOIN *joining-drive joined-drive\directory* [/D]

The *joining-drive* will appear to be in the specified directory of the *joined-drive*. The /D option is used to disconnect a join.

For example, this joins the A drive to the C drive using the directory ADRIVE:

```
JOIN A: C:\ADRIVE
```

KEYB

The external KEYB command loads keyboard information for foreign language support. Its most common form is

KEYB *keyboard-code,code-page*

where *keyboard-code* and *code-page* define the keyboard code and code-page code. (See Chapter 13 for details.) If you speak English, you will not need this command.

For example, the following command configures the keyboard for use in Germany:

```
KEYB GR,437
```

LABEL

The external LABEL command is used to create or change a disk's volume label. It has the general form:

LABEL [*drive-specifier*] [*name*]

If no *drive-specifier* is used, then the current disk is assumed. If you do not specify the volume *name* on the command line, you will be prompted for one. Disk volume labels may be up to 11 characters long. You cannot use the following characters in disk volume labels:

* ? / \ | . , ; : + = < > [ ] "

For example, the following command changes the volume label on the current disk to MYDISK:

```
LABEL MYDISK
```

LOADHIGH

The LOADHIGH (LH for short) command is used to load a program into extended memory. It has this general form,

LOADHIGH *file-name*

where *file-name* is the name of the program that you want executed in extended memory.

Before you can use LOADHIGH, several conditions must be met. Refer to Chapter 13 for details.

MEM

The external MEM command displays information about the memory in your computer.

MEMMAKER

The external MEMMAKER command is provided with DOS version 6. It is a menu-based command that organizes and optimizes any extra memory in your system. Refer to Chapter 17 for details.

A

MIRROR

MIRROR is part of DOS's error recovery system. (It is available only with DOS version 5. (Version 6 includes MIRROR's functions in the UNDELETE command.) Refer to Chapter 12 for details.

MKDIR

The internal MKDIR command (MD for short) is used to create a subdirectory. Its general form is

MKDIR *path*

where *path* specifies the complete path name to the directory. The path name may not exceed 63 characters in length.

For example, the following command creates the directory \WP\FORMS:

```
MD \WP\FORMS
```

MODE

The external MODE command is used to set the way various devices operate. MODE is a very complex command with several different forms. (Refer to its description in Chapter 13.)

MORE

The external MORE command allows you to page through a text file 23 lines at a time. It is a filter that reads standard input and writes to standard output. Its most common form is

MORE < *file-name*

where *file-name* is the file to be viewed.

You can also use MORE in conjunction with other commands, such as DIR, to provide a convenient way to page through displays that are larger than one screen. For example, the following command displays the directory 23 lines at a time:

DIR | MORE

MOVE

The external MOVE command moves a file from one disk and/or directory to another. It has this general form,

MOVE *source destination*

where *source* is the file (or files) to be moved, which may include a path specifier, and *destination* is the drive or directory that will receive the file(s). Wildcards are permitted. You can also specify a new file name if you are moving only one file.

You can also use MOVE to change the name of a directory. To do this, use this general form,

MOVE *old-dir-name new-dir-name*

where *old-dir-name* is the full path name of the directory to be renamed, and *new-dir-name* is its new name.

For example, this moves the file MYFILE from the C drive to the A drive:

```
MOVE C:MYFILE A:
```

MOVE is only available in DOS version 6.

MSAV

The external MSAV command is available only with DOS version 6. It is a window-based, menu-driven command that provides protection against computer virus infection. Refer to Chapter 14 for details.

MSBACKUP

The external MSBACKUP command backs up the fixed disk. It is a window-based, menu-driven command and is available only in DOS version 6. Refer to Chapter 16 for details.

A

NLSFUNC

The external NLSFUNC command is used by DOS to provide extended support for non-English-speaking users. You will probably never need to use it. For details, refer to your DOS manual.

PATH

The internal PATH command is used to define a search path that DOS uses to locate program files in directories other than the current one. It takes the general form,

> PATH *path*[;*path*...;*path*]

where *path* is the specified search path. You define multiple search paths by separating each path with a semicolon. There cannot be spaces in the path list.

For example, the following command defines a path to the \WP\FORMS directory:

```
PATH \WP\FORMS
```

PAUSE

The PAUSE batch command is used to temporarily stop a batch file's execution. It takes the general form:

> PAUSE [*message*]

If the *message* is present, it will be displayed. PAUSE waits until a key is pressed.

POWER

The external POWER command is used to conserve battery power when running a portable computer. Before you can use the POWER command, the POWER.EXE device driver must be installed. For the correct procedure and usage, refer to Chapter 17.

PRINT

The external PRINT command prints text files on the printer. Its most common form is

PRINT *file-name file-name ... file-name* [/T] [/C]

where *file-name* is the name of a file you want printed. The /T option cancels the PRINT command. The /C option cancels the printing of the file name that it follows.

For example, the following command prints the files LETTER1.WP and LETTER2.WP:

```
PRINT LETTER1.WP LETTER2.WP
```

PROMPT

The internal PROMPT command is used to change the DOS prompt. It takes the general form,

PROMPT *prompt*

where *prompt* is the desired prompt. The prompt string can contain one or more special format commands that allow greater flexibility. The commands are shown in the following table:

Code	Meaning
$$	Dollar sign
$b	l character
$d	System date
$e	Escape character
$g	> character
$h	A backspace
$l	< character
$n	Current drive letter
$p	Current directory path

Code	Meaning
$q	= character
$t	Current time
$v	DOS version number
$_	Carriage return-linefeed sequence

For example, one of the most popular prompts is created by the following command:

```
PROMPT $P$G
```

It displays the current directory path followed by the > symbol.

RECOVER

The external RECOVER command attempts to recover damaged files. It has the general form:

RECOVER [*drive-specifier*] [*file-name*]

RECOVER may not be included if you are using DOS 6.

If only the drive specifier is present, RECOVER attempts to recover all files on a disk. Otherwise, only the specified file is recovered. When the entire disk is recovered, RECOVER creates file names following this convention: FILE*num*.REC, where *num* is a number between 1 and 9999.

Remember, not all files can be recovered. Further, recovered program files are very likely unusable. It is best to use RECOVER only on text files—and then only as a last resort.

For example, the following command attempts to recover the file FORMLET.WP:

```
RECOVER FORMLET.WP
```

REM

The REM batch command has the general form:

REM *remark*

The *remark* can be any string from 0 to 123 characters in length. No matter what the remark contains, it will be completely ignored by DOS.

For example, the following remark is ignored:

```
REM this is a test
```

RENAME

The internal RENAME (REN for short) is used to change the name of a specified file. It takes the general form,

> RENAME *old-name new-name*

where *old-name* and *new-name* are file names.

For example, the following command changes the name of the file originally called INV.DAT to INV.OLD:

```
RENAME INV.DAT INV.OLD
```

REPLACE

The external REPLACE command replaces files on the destination disk with those by the same name on the source disk. It takes the general form:

> REPLACE *source destination* [/A] [/P] [/R] [/S] [/W] [/U]

If you specify the /S option, all files in all subdirectories will also be examined and replaced. You can use /A to add to a disk only those files that are not currently on the destination disk. This prevents existing files from being overwritten. If you need to insert a different diskette before REPLACE begins, use the /W option. This causes REPLACE to wait until you press a key before beginning. The /P option causes REPLACE to ask you before a file is replaced. The /U option only replaces files that are older than files that will replace them.

For example, the following command replaces the files on A with those by the same name found on B, including all subdirectories:

```
REPLACE B: A: /S
```

A

RESTORE

The external RESTORE command is used to restore files to the fixed disk from diskettes created using BACKUP. It takes the general form,

RESTORE *backup fixed* [/A:*date*] [/B:*date*] [/E:*time*] [/L:*time*]
[/P] [/S] [/M] [/N] [/D]

where *backup* is a drive specifier defining the drive that holds the backup diskette, and *fixed* is a drive and path specifier for the fixed disk. The options are summarized in the following table:

Option	Meaning
A:*date*	Restore all files modified on or after the specified date
B:*date*	Restore all files modified on or before the specified date
D	Display names of files to be restored
E:*time*	Restore all files modified at or earlier than the specified time on a given date
L:*time*	Restore all files modified at or later than the specified time on a given date
M	Restore all files that have been modified or deleted since the last backup
N	Restore only those files that do not exist on the fixed disk
P	Prompt before restoring a file
S	Restore all subdirectories

For example, the following command restores all files having the .DAT extension into the DATA directory, using drive A to read the backup diskettes:

```
RESTORE A: C:\DATA\*.DAT
```

RMDIR

The internal RMDIR (RD for short) is used to remove a subdirectory. It has the general form,

RMDIR *directory*

where *directory* is a complete path name to the desired directory. The specified directory must be empty. It is not possible to remove a directory that still has files in it.

For example, the following command removes the WP directory:

```
RMDIR \WP
```

SET

The internal SET command is used primarily by programmers and system integrators to put a name and its value into DOS's environment. (Refer to Chapter 17 for details.)

SETVER

Some application programs are particularly sensitive to the specific version of DOS that you are running on your computer. In fact, some programs will not run correctly unless a specific version of DOS is used. To solve this problem and to let you use any application program, DOS versions 5 and later include the SETVER command. It allows you to tell DOS what version it is supposed to act like when running a specific application program. It takes this general form:

SETVER *file-name version*

Here, *file-name* is the name of the program, and *version* is the DOS version number that the specified program requires. For example, if your word processor is called WP.EXE and it requires DOS version 4.00 to run correctly, then specifying this command will allow you to use the word processor with later versions of DOS:

A

```
SETVER WP.EXE 4.00
```

This command will, however, only take effect after you have restarted DOS.

 # SHARE

The external SHARE command is used in networked systems to prepare for file sharing and file locking. Refer to your networking and DOS manuals for complete information.

 # SHIFT

The SHIFT batch command is used to shift the command-line arguments left one position. This allows for more than ten arguments.

 # SORT

The external SORT command sorts text files on a line-by-line basis. It is a filter command that reads standard input and writes to standard output. It takes the general form,

SORT [<*input*] [>*output*] [/R] [/+*num*]

where *input* and *output* are either file names, devices, or pipes. The sorting default is ascending order (A to Z). The /R option causes the file to be sorted in reverse or descending order. The /+*num* option causes the sorting to begin with the *num*th column.

For example, the following command produces a sorted directory listing:

DIR | SORT

SUBST

The external SUBST command allows you to use a different drive specifier to access a drive and directory. That is, you can use SUBST to assign a drive specifier to a drive and directory and refer to that drive and directory by using the drive specifier. In essence the new drive specifier is like a nickname for the other drive. SUBST takes the general form,

SUBST *nickname drive-specifier path*

where *nickname* is the new drive specifier for the indicated drive specifier. The *path* is the path to the desired directory.

To undo a substitution, use this form of the command:

SUBST *nickname* /D

For example, this causes drive A to respond to both A: and E:.

```
SUBST E: A:\
```

SYS

The external SYS command is used to copy the DOS system files to a disk. It has the general form,

SYS *drive-specifier*

where *drive-specifier* indicates the drive that will receive the system files. SYS does not transfer COMMAND.COM, however. SYS must be able to read the system files off the current drive.

For example, the following command puts the system files on the disk in drive B:

```
SYS B:
```

TIME

The internal TIME command is used to set the system time. It takes the general form:

TIME [*hh:mm:ss*]

If you do not enter the time on the command line, you will be prompted for it. TIME expects the numbers 0 through 23 for the hours; that is, it operates on a 24-hour clock. For later versions of DOS, you can enter the time in 12-hour format, but you must specify **a** for a.m. or **p** for p.m. You need not specify the seconds.

For example, the following command sets the time to 12:00 noon:

```
TIME 12:00:00
```

TREE

The external TREE command prints a list of all directories on the specified disk. It has the general form,

TREE *drive-specifier* [/F] [/A]

where *drive-specifier* is the letter of the drive that will be examined. If /F is used, the files in each directory are also displayed. By default, the directory tree is displayed in a graphical form. If your computer cannot display DOS's extended character set, then specify the /A option, which causes the output of TREE to be displayed using normal characters.

For example, the following command displays the directory structure for the disk in A:

```
TREE A:
```

TYPE

The internal TYPE command displays the contents of a file on the screen. It has the general form,

> TYPE *file-name*

where *file-name* is the file to be displayed.

For example, the following command displays a file called TEST:

`TYPE TEST`

UNDELETE

The UNDELETE command lets you unerase a file that you have just erased. For guaranteed results, you must use UNDELETE immediately after an ERASE. If an intervening disk operation has occurred, you might not be able to recover the file. UNDELETE takes this general form,

> UNDELETE *file-name*

where *file-name* is the name of the file.

UNDELETE is part of DOS's error recovery system. (It is available only in versions 5 and later.) Refer to Chapter 12 for complete details and options.

A

UNFORMAT

UNFORMAT is part of DOS's error recovery system. (It is available only in versions 5 and later.) It unformats an accidentally reformatted disk. Refer to Chapter 12 for details on correcting accidents.

VER

The internal VER command displays the DOS version number. It takes no arguments.

VERIFY

The internal VERIFY command turns on or off verification of disk write operations. That is, when turned on, it confirms that the data written to disk is exactly as it should be and that no errors have taken place. It takes the general form,

VERIFY [ON]

or

VERIFY [OFF]

where you specify either on or off.

For example, the following command turns verification off:

```
VERIFY OFF
```

VOL

The internal VOL command displays the volume label of the specified disk. It has the general form,

VOL [*drive-specifier*]

where *drive-specifier* is the name of the drive whose volume label will be displayed. If not specified, the volume label of the current drive is displayed.

For example, the following command displays the volume label of the current drive:

```
VOL
```

VSAFE

The external VSAFE command helps guard your system against a virus infection by monitoring ongoing system activity, looking for suspicious events which might indicate an infection is in progress. This command became available with DOS version 6. It is an installed, window- and menu-based command. Refer to Chapter 14 for details.

XCOPY

The external XCOPY command is a more powerful and flexible version of the COPY command. It takes the general form,

XCOPY *source target* [/A] [/D] [/E] [/M] [/P] [/S] [/V] [/W]

where *source* and *target* are file or path names. The operation of XCOPY is largely determined by the options applied to it. These options are summarized in the following table:

Option	Meaning
A	Copy only those files with the archive attribute turned on; the state of the archive bit is not changed
D:*date*	Copy only those files whose date is equal to or later than the one specified
E	Create all subdirectories, even if empty
M	Copy only those files with the archive attribute turned on; the archive bit is turned off
P	Prompt before copying each file
S	Copy files in subdirectories
V	Verify each write operation
W	Wait until a disk is inserted

For example, the following command copies all files on a disk in A to one in B, including all subdirectories:

```
XCOPY A: B:/S
```

INDEX

D

T